WITHDRAWN

D1563196

WITHDRAWN

ENVIRONMENT, POLITICS AND SOCIETY SERIES
Series Editor: Wolfgang Rüdig,
Department of Government,
University of Strathclyde

PUBLISHED
Andrew Jamison, Ron Eyerman, Jacqueline Cramer
The Making of the New Environmental Consciousness: Environmental
Movements in Sweden, Denmark and the Netherlands

Thomas Poguntke
Alternative Politics:
The German Green Party

Helena Flam
States and Anti-nuclear
Movements

Writing a book is not unlike a long-distance flight...

This book is dedicated to Nicole – for support and company during take-off and flight – and to my parents Heinz and Charlotte and my brothers Gerald and Matthias – for a safe landing.

VILLA JULIE COLLEGE LIBRARY
STEVENSON, MD 21153

Alternative Politics

The German Green Party

THOMAS POGUNTKE

EDINBURGH UNIVERSITY PRESS

JN
3971
.A98
G723618
1993

© Thomas Poguntke, 1993

Edinburgh University Press Limited
22 George Square, Edinburgh

Typeset in Linotron Goudy
by Koinonia Ltd, Bury, and
printed in Great Britain by
The University Press, Cambridge

A CIP record for this book is available
from the British Library

ISBN 0 7486 0393 X

Contents

Foreword

The *Environment, Politics and Society Series* is devoted to the advancement of social science research on the environment. We are currently experiencing a resurgence of public interest in environmental issues. There is no shortage of books describing the seriousness of the environmental problems we face. The contribution of the social sciences has not been as prominent. This series seeks to make a contribution to redress this balance. Environmental problems are not just of a technical nature. The persistence of environmental crises is raising important questions of a social and political kind. Governments increasingly perceive the 'environment' not just as a single issue but as a pervasive concern affecting all aspects of policy making; enviromental pressure groups experience a steady increase in membership, and green parties are establishing themselves all over the world as a permanent feature of political life.

Environmental problems are not likely to disappear overnight. Environmental concern has proved to be enduring, and green issues will continue to play an important role of the politics of the 1990s and the next century. The social sciences are called upon to make a contribution to the analysis of this important field. The challenge to the social sciences presented by the 'environment' is quite substantial. Environmental problems and conflicts transcend national and disciplinary boundaries. More than perhaps any other issue, the 'environment' calls upon the social sciences to develop internationally comparative and interdisciplinary approaches.

This series will bring together a wide range of books addressing the social and political aspects of the environmental crisis. The *Environment, Politics and Society Series* has a strong international and comparative orientation, and also publishes contributions from different academic disciplines.

Without any doubt, the international debate about environmental problems was stimulated to a significant extent by the rise of the German Green Party in the early 1980s. Writing on the day that news of the tragic death of Petra K. Kelly reached the world, it is perhaps fitting to remember the huge international impact of the Greens' entry into the German Federal Parliament in 1983. In those early days there was great excitement about the rise of a new political force which sought to bring a new vision to the world, and expectations were high. Since those heady days, the fortunes of the German Greens appear to have deteriorated markedly. Particularly since the defeat of the West German Greens in the 1990 federal elections, the dominant image in Britain and the USA has been one of decline and failure following unceasing political infighting and personal strife.

Foreword

It is one of the chief virtues of Thomas Poguntke's analysis of the German Greens that it puts such images of inevitable decline into a proper perspective. The German Greens have made an important impact on German politics at various levels, and news of their demise must be considered highly premature. The Greens, as Poguntke concludes, 'are here to stay'. The author presents an empirically rich picture of green politics, looking at green voters and activists, green political programmes and the internal structure of the Party.

This empirical account of the Greens is not only the most comprehensive and up-to-date to be published so far, it is also theoretically informed. Employing the theory of 'New Politics', Poguntke succeeds in integrating theory and empirical inquiry to an unusual degree. The analysis of green parties as a manifestation of the rise of 'New Politics' associated with post-materialist value change has not been without its critics in the past. Poguntke makes a spirited defence of the 'New Politics' approach and maximises its explanatory usefulness by focusing on the totality of German green politics, comprising electoral behaviour, party political activity, political programmes and the internal organisation of the Party. In so doing, he has made a valuable contribution to the theoretical and empirical analysis of German green politics which deserves a wide readership.

Wolfgang Rüdig
October 1992

Preface and Acknowledgements

When I first began to research Green parties in Western democracies it appeared to be less than certain that the object of my academic interest would last sufficiently long. Nevertheless, the 'Green wave' attracted much attention among Western publics, particularly the German example. After all, it was during the heated debate over the deployment of intermediate-range nuclear missiles, and at the peak of extra-parliamentary mobilisation by the peace movement, that the Greens appeared potentially to hold the balance of power, during the 1983 Bundestag election campaign. After more than a decade of parliamentary representation in Land parliaments and participation in several Land governments, the Greens are increasingly perceived as a conventional political party. No doubt this perception was reinforced by some substantial structural reforms following the Greens' unexpected defeat in the 1990 Bundestag elections and the secession of prominent members of the fundamentalist faction. However, the analyses in this book, which cover developments until late 1991, show that the Greens are still characterised by a very distinct social, organisational and programmatic profile – despite some adaptation and moderation. In a nutshell, they are a prototype of a new type of party, the *New Politics party*, which has begun to consolidate its position in Western European party systems.

I would like to express my gratitude for the excellent working conditions I encountered at the European University Institute in Florence and for helpful advice received from many colleagues and friends, most notably, of course, my thesis supervisor Ian Budge, as well as Ferdinand Müller-Rommel, Peter Mair, Martin Greiffenhagen, David Farrell, Paul Webb and Bettina Westle. In addition, I would like to thank Gordon Smith, to whose stimulating teaching and supervision at the London School of Economics I owe much of my further academic progress. I would also like gratefully to acknowledge the valuable support I received from Jürgen Hamberger, Martin Koczor and Julia Urban during data processing and the design of diagrams. Last but not least, I am grateful for the support of Rudolf Wildenmann, Ulrich Widmaier and Max Kaase, who provided me with the necessary institutional infrastructure during completion and revision of the manuscript.

Thomas Poguntke
Mannheim

Part I

Theory

1. Introduction

More than twenty years ago, Seymour Martin Lipset and Stein Rokkan argued that Western European party systems still reflected the major political conflicts of the 1920s. Although there has been considerable de-freezing within political camps – most notably the fragmentation on the Socialist side – their diagnosis held until the late 1970s. Up until then, there was no genuinely new political colour making inroads into Western European party systems, but since, things have changed. So-called 'Green' or 'ecological' parties have had remarkable electoral success in some countries, notably in Germany and Belgium, and more recently in Italy, Switzerland, Finland and Austria.

When the first Green lists were running for Land elections in West Germany in the late 1970s, many political observers took this as yet another example of German exceptionalism. Strange alliances of ecologically-minded farmers of (sometimes, at least) questionable democratic conviction, veterans of the 1968 movement, some of the 'inevitable' figure-heads of radical democratic dissent, and many activists in the anti-nuclear movement of the 1970s began to join forces in order to break the mould of the West German party system, which many political scientists around the globe had become used to regarding as a model of political stability and efficiency. When, in the 1976 Bundestag elections, the three established parties won 99.1 per cent of the popular vote, the 'Modell Deutschland' seemed to have reached perfection.

However, fascination with the smooth functioning of post-war democracy distracted attention from growing unrest outside the established political parties and institutions. Ever since the unexpected confrontation over a projected nuclear power station near the rural village of Wyhl in South Germany, where traditionally conservative wine-growers and progressive ecologists successfully resisted the government in the early 1970s, tens of thousands of people have rallied in mass demonstrations against nuclear power at the sites of Kalkar, Brokdorf, Grohnde and Gorleben. Frequently, these demonstrations have ended in violent clashes with the police – an experience which certainly did not help to increase political trust in established political élites.

The overriding importance of the nuclear issue misled many analysts about the real nature of the nascent Green movement. Virtually from the outset, the majority of activists and voters had much more in mind than just preventing the construction of nuclear power stations or striving for a cleaner environment. Nuclear power had come to symbolise all the detrimental effects of large-scale technology on the environment, and also on the development of a free and democratic society. Not only did it stand for a strategy of further unlimited economic growth with, allegedly, negative effects on the ecological balance; it also epitomised the creation of a 'nuclear state' where the immense potential dangers of handling large amounts of radioactive material would necessitate the perfecting of state surveillance in order to prevent nuclear terrorism. Seen in this perspective, radical democrats were natural partners in the struggle against nuclear power and for ecologically sensible policies.

However, the thematic focus of the Green Party has always been much broader. When, in the late 1970s and early 1980s, squatter movements struggled for a change in inner-city housing policy and developed models of alternative forms of city life, culture and work, and when the peace movement began to mobilise against the deployment of intermediate-range nuclear missiles, all these movements were united by a common set of attitudes and ideals that were neither peculiarly German nor one-sidedly obsessed with environmental protection.

What Ronald Inglehart had called the 'silent revolution' was beginning to make itself heard. Across Europe, Green parties were getting off the ground and established Left Socialist parties were turning green. Activists and voters shared political values and participatory aspirations which were hard to integrate with the mainstream of established political parties and institutions. Conflicts between these adherents of the 'New Politics' and the proponents of 'more of the same' were becoming increasingly important in many advanced Western societies. Already in 1981, Belgian ecologists had been the first to win representation in a national parliament. It was mainly because the German Greens were perceived as potential holders of the balance of power in the Bundestag during a phase of increased international tensions in the wake of the early Reagan years that they attracted such strong attention – which, in turn, distracted many observers from seeing the relative uniformity of these developments across Western Europe.

Obviously, this is not say that the party political effects were equally significant in many European countries. But the underlying *structural* causes of an electoral potential for a New Politics-oriented Green party were relatively uniform across countries. Whether or not these potentials resulted in a successful political party depended on a wide range of *political* and *systemic* factors. These are country-specific and range from the peculiarities of electoral systems to the specific matter of which party, Conservative or Social Democratic, is in power at a particular time. Clearly, opposition parties on the Left will find it easier to adapt to the challenge from the New Politics than left-wing parties in government. From this perspective, Helmut Schmidt's chancellorship has certainly helped the German Greens to get started. The British electoral system, to give another example, pre-empts virtually any attempt to establish a new party in the national party system. The extraordinary performance of the British Greens in the 1989 European election, when they gained 14.9 per cent of the total vote, indicates the size of the New Politics potential in the British electorate.

However, we are not concerned with an analysis of the relative weight of the factors which can explain the success of Green parties. The main focus of this study is on the specific nature of the German Greens as a prototype of a New Politics party – that is to say, as a political party that has been moulded by the specific political orientations and participatory aspirations of the adherents of the New Politics. The central argument is that parties like the German Greens represent a new, distinct type of political party which is clearly related to a new dimension of political conflict structurally anchored in Western societies. Implicitly, this relates to questions about the future of the German Greens after their unexpected defeat in the first all-German elections: if they do belong to this new party family, competing parties will find it difficult to absorb the bulk of the Green electorate without risking the alienation of considerable portions of their traditional clientele, which is concerned with substantially different political goals and feels attracted by a far more conventional political style. Clearly, this does not mean that Green survival is a foregone conclusion. Disastrous political performance is clearly capable of compensating for substantial structural stability. However, predictions about the political skills of future party leadership groups are beyond the scope of academic analysis.

In view of the widespread attention the 'Green wave' – particularly the German phenomenon – has attracted, there are surprisingly few thorough analyses of those parties commonly associated with the surge of the New Politics. Much research, however, has been done on individual-level changes that are seen as the causes for the growing political relevance of the New Politics: literature on shifts in political preferences and behavioural style, as well as on the emergence of new social movements, abounds.

In those studies which concentrate on the effects of the New Politics on Western party systems, the dominant focus is on explaining the emergence and success of parties which were regarded as products of the New Politics (Kitschelt, 1988b; Müller-Rommel, 1982a, 1982b, 1990). Basically, all these studies have used classifications that are based on a single discriminant variable, like the degree of radicalism, characteristics of the electorate, or party origin (Rüdig, 1985b; Müller-Rommel, 1985b). In fact, despite several approaches towards explaining the emergence of this new group of parties, the subject has so far remained largely undefined and unexplored. Attempts to use a comprehensive typological approach on a broadly comparative basis have necessarily been confined to a rather general level of enquiry (Poguntke, 1989b), whereas recent thorough studies of the German and Belgian Greens are mainly limited to aspects of internal processes (Kitschelt, 1989; Kitschelt and Hellemans, 1990). By and large, single-nation studies which relate empirical evidence to a comparative theoretical argument are still missing. This book attempts to fill this gap for the German case by linking the 'Gestalt' of New Politics parties to the characteristics of the New Politics. In order to arrive at a clearer image of the central elements of this phenomenon and its social anchorage, an integration of different approaches to the explanation of the New Politics is suggested. Based on this analysis, an ideal-typical model of a New Politics party is proposed.

The label 'New Politics party' points to a terminological problem: although they are commonly referred to in political debate as 'Green' or 'ecological' parties, the generic term 'New Politics party' should be used for such parties (Flanagan, 1987; Inglehart, 1987; Poguntke, 1987a). This has two advantages: it refers to an established body of theoretical and empirical literature, and it avoids confounding what are really two analytically distinct groups, that is, conservative 'Green' formations and left-wing, emancipatory political parties which are concerned with a broader set of issues than just ecology.[1]

Ideally, such an ideal type, based on a set of cross-nationally valid and empirically-based theories, should be tested on a broadly comparative basis (Lijphart, 1971, p. 692). However, in our context, this would have involved too many sacrifices as regards the depth of the analysis. Furthermore, a single-nation case study can provide many insights in a specific case, although it cannot but produce ambiguous evidence as far as the cross-national validity of the argument is concerned. We have therefore chosen to limit this analysis to the German Greens, particularly since a broadly comparative approach based on the same typological framework has been used elsewhere (Poguntke, 1989b).

METHODOLOGICAL ASPECTS

To a considerable extent, New Politics theories are based on the measurement of individual-level attitudinal changes. Attitudes, however, are only one element in the process which eventually leads to political action or even institutional change. Individuals with comparable attitudinal structures within a given polity will be subject to very different contextual factors. Hence, there will always be more than one possible 'result' of the New Politics. Furthermore, since these contextual factors differ cross-nationally to a certain degree, such results will also differ in outlook across nations. It is therefore obvious that the surge of the New Politics can have a wide range of possible effects on the party system. Our focus on the 'political party' avoids the pitfalls of the attitude-action problematic: one possible aggregate result of shifts towards New Politics will be used as a unit of analysis without our claiming that it is the only possible or likely outcome in a given political system. The advantage is that even if the attitude-action correlation is relatively weak, the used set of theories does not suffer in terms of explanatory capacity. Its predictive power may be apallingly low because of intervening contextual factors, but it is still a useful explanation of a given phenomenon. To put it bluntly: not all postmaterialists vote Green, but the fact that most Green voters are postmaterialists is an important explanation of the specific characteristics of this party.

As indicated already, the analysis in this study will be guided by an ideal-typical model of a New Politics party deduced from the central characteristics of the New Politics. It covers the following dimensions which are conventionally used in party research:

- membership and electorate profiles;
- programmatic orientation;
- party organisation;
- and political style.

This raises the question of the nature and theoretical status of 'ideal types': an ideal type is a utopia, a theoretical construct which is not intended to mirror reality, but to be used as a heuristic tool in order to analyse it (Lenk and Neumann, 1974, p. lxvi). However, for reasons inherent to our topic, our analysis will not attempt to gauge the closeness of our case to the ideal type as suggested by Lenk and Neumann (1974, p. lxvii). Such an approach to measurement can only be used in a meaningful way if the ideal type is built upon categorical variables, which means that it is possible to provide a 'check-list' for the analysis of qualitative characteristics of a given research object: a party, for example, is either based on branches or on cadres; the typology clearly provides a heuristic tool for discrimination.

However, the integration of all important aspects of a political party into an ideal type implies the use of quantitative as well as qualitative dimensions of measurement. To a considerable extent, the analysis will have to be carried out in terms of 'more' or 'less', not 'either' and 'or'. The use of the ideal type as a meaningful point of reference for measurement of quantitative dimensions would necessitate the specification of quantities of changes, for example, what percentage of the party membership should be postmaterialist, in a counter-élite position, or below a certain age. It is obvious that such figures could not be inferred with sufficiently rigorous causal reasoning from such general theories.

In any case, such an approach could not demonstrate the distinctiveness of the new type of party when set against the established parties. In concrete terms, the German Greens may well have a very high percentage of postmaterialists in their ranks, but this does not necessarily imply that their established competitors have not been able to recruit correspondingly high proportions. The crucial criterion for quantitative dimensions is therefore the distance between the established German parties and the Greens.

Hence, we shall use an approach that could be called a 'modified ideal type approach': as far as quantitative aspects are concerned, the ideal type will only specify the direction of change, but not the extent. For these characteristics the model stipulates only a difference in degree, not in principle. Essentially, party change is conceptualised as a movement on a continuum. The ideal type will therefore specify the dimensions on which the new party is different, not the exact outlook of such a party. The leading research question, whether the German Green Party represents a new type of party, will hence be decided on the basis of two criteria:

- the fulfilment of some qualitative criteria and
- sufficient distance from old parties on some quantitative dimensions.

In sum, this book pursues three aims: it attempts to contribute to the understanding of the social changes that have created a potential for a new family of political parties; it links the nature of these changes to the characteristics of the German Green Party, which is probably the most important representative of this new family of New Politics parties; and finally, it discusses the impact of systemic constraints on a newly emerging party like the Greens. More than a decade after their entry into party politics, the Greens are increasingly feeling pressure to adapt to the rules of the game of representative parliamentary democracy. In fact, it can be argued that their failure to cross the West German 5 per cent hurdle in the first all-German elections on 2 December 1990 should be understood as a result of their reluctant adaptation on the federal level (see Chapter 8).[2] However, this study is not concerned with analysing the process that determines the *formation* and *success* of New Politics parties. Clearly, our argument does not imply that the emergence and success of a New Politics party is the necessary result of shifts towards the New Politics in a given polity.

NOTES

1.   The label 'Left-Libertarian party' (Kitschelt, 1988b) suffers from a lack of substantive inclusiveness: it does not include the most important aspects of alternative politics, that is, the peace and ecology questions.
2.   As a result of a decision by the Constitutional Court, the united Germany was divided into two electoral territories with separate 5 per cent hurdles, because a nationwide threshold would have disadvantaged newly formed parties in the former GDR. However, a party which managed to win 5 per cent in one part of the country had all its votes counted. Hence, had the Greens united before the election, the party would have been entitled to seats in West Germany. Their decision to defer unification until the day after the election meant that only two East German Greens were elected to the Bundestag (see Appendix 1)

2. The Characteristics of the New Politics

Before we can approach the competing explanations of the New Politics phenomenon, we need a brief definition and description of what exactly is meant by the label 'New Politics'. As far as the central characteristics of the New Politics are concerned, there is little controversy in the scholarly literature.

Generally, the term is used to refer to a phenomenon that has gained increasing prominence in Western societies over recent years: the interrelated extension of *participatory dispositions and techniques* and the *partial change* of the *political agenda* through the surge of a new set of political demands.

Preparedness to engage in political protest and unconventional political behaviour has become more widespread since the 1960s (Barnes, Kaase *et al.*, 1979, p. 524; Jennings, van Deth *et al.*, 1990; Westle, 1991). Simultaneously, the societal consensus on the hierarchy of political problems that are generally considered to be most important has been eroded. The period of economic reconstruction after the Second World War was dominated by an almost universal desire to find the best path to affluence, political order and physical, particularly military, security. Political conflict centred largely around the antagonism between haves and have-nots (Dalton, 1988, p. 153). This was particularly true for the 1960s and early 1970s after religious and rural-urban conflicts had lost much of their salience in most countries (Budge and Robertson, 1987, p. 396). Whereas the political debate was clearly focused on a common agenda, the 'Old Politics', things have become more complicated since then.

In the 1970s, all advanced industrialised societies have been troubled – to varying degrees – by the growth of groups who have criticised the political goals of the Old Politics. The most visible political expression of these changes was the surge of the 'new social movements'. Activists in the peace and ecology movements no longer approved of political ends like economic growth, attempts to attain military security through strong defence, and the extension of welfare bureaucracies. They began to rank the preservation of nature higher than economic affluence, and to prefer unilateral disarmament over the balance of deterrence, and demanded the extension of individual freedoms and participatory rights (Hildebrandt and Dalton, 1978; Raschke, 1980; Schmidt, 1984, p. 6; Dalton, 1988, p. 134; Baker *et al.*, 1981, pp. 136ff.; Brand *et al.*, 1984; Brand, 1985; Roth and Rucht, 1987).

In the literature, the label 'New Politics' is not only used to refer to the success of a new political paradigm (Raschke, 1980) or the emergence of a new dimension of political conflict (Dalton, 1988, p. 134). Primarily, it refers to the growing importance of a new set of political goals. Correspondingly, items asking for evaluation are generally used to measure the New Politics empirically: respondents are asked whether they approve or disapprove of a specific set of political goals which define the New Politics.[1] It is only as a reaction to these new demands that the established political forces have begun to search for their own answers to the questions posed by the New Politics (Dalton *et al.*, 1984, p. 4). The proposals of established parties for solving the ecological crisis, for example, are clearly inspired by the values and overriding goals of the Old Politics (see Chapter 7). However, the specific topic has been put on the agenda by proponents of the New Politics.

In a nutshell, Old Politics means preoccupation with economic growth, stable prices, a stable economy, strong military defence and conventional political style. Adherents of the New Politics, on the contrary, demand that ecological imperatives guide economic decisions, that rights to participation and the freedom to realise alternative life-styles should be extended, and unilateral disarmament be promoted in order to reduce international tensions. Furthermore, the New Politics is concerned with equal rights for all kinds of social minorities, solidarity with the Third World and a general left-wing orientation. Also, supporters of the New Politics tend to be prepared to engage in unconventional political participation.

The preceding list shows that – apart from the ecological issue and the strong concern with individual self-determination and self-realisation – most goals associated with the New Politics are not recent inventions. It is the specific combination of goals that originate from diverse political camps, as well as their radicalism and the higher salience attributed to them which makes the New Politics a political tendency in its own right. Furthermore, several of these goals have attained a different substantive meaning within the overall framework of the New Politics, that is, in conjunction with other related concerns (see Chapters 4 and 7).

The concept of unconventional participation has two important aspects. On the one hand, it refers to a distinct action repertoire that tends to be used by those with higher education, postmaterialist value orientations and a high level of cognitive skills (Barnes, Kaase *et al.*, 1979, p. 524; Jennings, van Deth *et al.*, 1990). It ranges from relatively 'easy' forms of political involvement like signing a petition to 'difficult', sometimes illegal, activities like blockades and occupations (Barnes, Kaase *et al.*, 1979, p. 81). On the other hand, unconventional action is also characterised by different motivations for participation. Protest techniques are used as means to *challenge the élites* in order to assume *direct* influence over *specific* political decisions. It is important to distinguish this type of political involvement from conventional, *élite-directed* participation, which is characterised by generalised and reactive political behaviour, where the individual simply chooses between alternative political packages that are usually presented by the élites (Barnes, Kaase *et al.*, 1979, p. 208; Kaase, 1982, p. 185f.; Inglehart, 1990a, p. 339).

MAPPING THE POLITICAL SPACE

Clearly, it would be an exaggeration to speak of a complete change in the political paradigm. The old conflict over distribution is by no means resolved. On the contrary, high levels of unemployment have substantially limited the blackmail potential of trade unions: income levels have not increased at the rate of the 1970s. As a result, conflicts over economic issues have maintained their saliency or even gained prominence.

Simultaneously, the New Politics has become important. Advanced societies currently experience an overlap of political agendas and it is unlikely that the New Politics will be able to supersede the Old Politics completely. There are two reasons for this. First, historical analysis shows that the resolution of conflicts rarely means that the underlying causes are eliminated. A *modus vivendi* may be found, but underlying antagonisms remain. The earlier conflicts over political power, for example, have led in many countries to agreements that define the demarcation line between state power and the realm of the church. As a result, such issues have largely disappeared from the political agenda. Nevertheless, they maintain their potential political explosiveness – the French schools conflict and the new German abortion debate of the mid-1980s are but two examples.

Secondly, it is obvious that demands associated with the New Politics are closely related to the sphere of economic production. The repercussions are many and cannot be discussed here in detail. The most straightforward link is between the quest for strict environmental protection and the logic of industrial production under the rules of worldwide competition. Realisation of ecological goals means a redefintion – or extension – of the present concept of affluence and welfare. However, if immaterial goods such as a healthy environment begin to enter this calculation, those who are in lower income brackets are likely to press hard for some material compensation. Arguably, non-growth policies favoured by New Politics proponents revitalise the problem of redistribution of wealth and income. Consistently, New Politics groups are generally situated on the left of the political spectrum (Müller-Rommel, 1984b, p. 540; Inglehart, 1977, p. 60f.; Inglehart 1990b, pp. 54ff.).

The following few examples will further illustrate the most important linkages between the traditional left and the New Politics. Individualism and participatory orientation are highly likely to lead to demands for more 'self-control' and co-determination in the workplace. Openness to change and opposition to hierarchical structures, the need to asssume relatively extensive control over the economy in order to restructure it in an ecologically meaningful way – the motives may differ from those of traditional leftism, but the immediate implications are similar in a number of policy areas.

Manifestly, New Politics goals are not independent of the left–right dimension. Many empirical analyses, however, depict rectangular configurations, that is, two independent dimensions of political conflict. They suggest that a person's position on the Old Politics dimension does not permit a prediction of his evaluation of goals associated with the New Politics. Such studies are based on electors' feeling of closeness to other parties and/or a set of sociopolitical groups (Bürklin, 1981, pp. 365ff.; 1984, p. 219; 1985a, pp. 469ff.; Dalton, 1988, p. 134). It is not surprising, however, that a new political force that challenges the common agenda of all established political parties is met by almost unanimous disapproval of those who continue to believe in the salience of the old political agenda. Programmatic affinities and linkages will only become apparent after a protracted period of political discourse over the new agenda and mass perceptions will follow this process of ideological rearrangement on the level of political élites. For this reason, it is preferable to base the analysis of the dimensionality of political conflict primarily on substantive ideological or attitudinal differences between various political tendencies instead of relying on mass perceptions.[2]

The foregoing discussion has indicated that the New Politics is best understood as a left-wing addition to, and modification of, the traditional left-right dimension (Figure 2.1). Although there may be fierce conflict between the Old Politics Left and the New Politics Left, they are logically and empirically not independent of each other (Budge and Robertson, 1987, p. 395f.; Murphy et al., 1981).

Whether the new agenda which has resulted from the upsurge of New Politics will eventually lead to a 'New Politics Right' that is more than a nineteenth-century version of the present Old Politics Right is rather questionable (Poguntke, 1987a, p. 83f.). Although a moderate right-wing answer to the demands of the New Politics can be envisaged on ideological grounds, there seems to be little electoral potential so far. The growing prominence of ecological themes over recent years may eventually give rise to such developments. Thus far, however, this political space has only been occupied by relatively small groups of die-hard nineteenth-century conservatives who have always suspected that mass industrial society has been a historic error of Western civilisation. Fundamentalist Christian values, concern for the preservation of the environment, and patriarchal or even authoritarian concepts of political rule, build the ideological cornerstones of political groups like the German ÖDP or the former Austrian VGÖ. From this perspective, fundamentalist Green conservatives occupy a place on the brink of system-transcendence.

Spectacular electoral successes gained by populist, xenophobic parties in the late 1980s and early 1990s in several Western European countries may indicate that persistent fragmentation on the Right is under way. This 'New Right', however, can hardly be understood as a right-wing answer to the questions posed by the New Politics. It is primarily nourished by a growing disaffection with the ruling political élites and an increasing fear of social deprivation as a result of economic problems and immigration (Inglehart, 1990a, p. 12). Hence it could tentatively be located near the right-wing pole of the conventional left–right dimension (not shown in Figure 2.1).

In view of the preceding, it is preferable to conceptualise the new 'life-style' dimension as an axis that runs on an acute angle across the old political battle-line dominated by class conflict. Figure 2.1 depicts the configuration of present

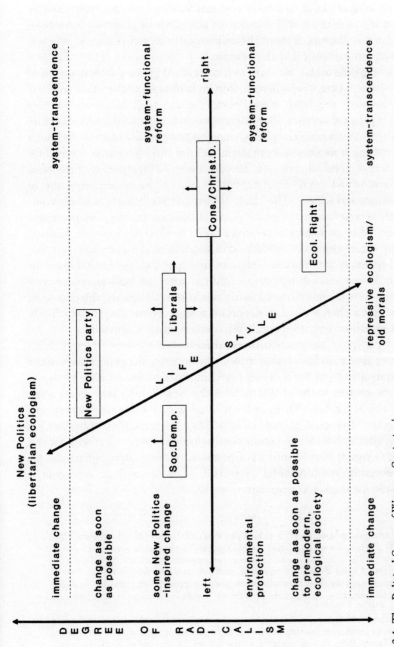

Figure 2.1: The Political Space of Western Societies.[1]

Note:

1. The location of the most common party families in the diagram represents a rough approximation only. As indicated, movement in both directions seems likely for most parties.

lines of political conflict in advanced Western societies. The demands of the
New Politics are also left-wing, but they conflict with positions on the traditional
Left. For the sake of clarity and cross-national validity, religious, territorial or
linguistic conflicts that are still relevant in a number of countries have been
disregarded in this diagram. It should be understood as an analytical and heuristic
tool for shaping the empirical analysis below.

The left-wing pole of the 'life-style' axis is occupied by the political utopias of
the New Politics, whereas repressive ecologism is situated at the other end.[3] As
already mentioned, the label 'New Politics' is also used frequently for this
dimension of political conflict. Our diagram suggests an analytical dividing line
between system-conforming and system-transcending political utopias. Although
almost everything is negotiable in practical politics this distinction is useful for
the evaluation of political concepts. Beyond doubt, full realisation of the New
Politics utopia would entail a substantial change in the present structure of
Western politics and society. The ideals of direct democracy are not fully compatible with representative forms of political decision-making; an economic
system subjected to ecological imperatives would need to rely (also) on steering
mechanisms other than the market; unilateralism and neutralism call the
established system of international relations into question; the radical quest for
personal autonomy and self-realisation conflicts with the built-in tendency of
modern states to regulate individual living conditions. Obviously, the time-span
that is allowed for change plays an important role in determining on which side
of the conceptualised systemic boundaries a certain group is situated.

There is plenty of variation between these poles. Moderate New Politics
strategies may aim at gradual change without endangering the performance of the
industrial system and without seriously stretching systemic boundaries. Moderate
Conservative answers to the challenge from the New Politics may revive some
ideas from Social Catholicism in order to cope with the growing depersonal-
isation of society: In a sense, it could be argued that the principle of subsidiarity is
akin to the alternative idea of autonomous self-help groups – but without the
egalitarian, emancipatory thrust. Furthermore, Conservative proposals for
system-conforming environmental protection – as opposed to ecologism –
attempt to use the market as a regulative device.[4]

NOTES

1.   Hildebrandt and Dalton, 1978, p. 77; Baker *et al.*, 1981, pp. 142ff.; H. Schmitt, 1987,
     p. 81. For his pilot study, Schmitt has used 'neutral' items, that is, items which do not
     convey a normative judgement, in order to measure only the agenda. A brief glance at
     the list of items shows, however, that emphasis on a specific political problem is
     frequently not separable from substantive goals: a respondent who considers 'environ-
     mental protection' an important problem will hardly be in favour of more pollution
     (pp. 73ff.).
2.   On the level of party politics, the German example supports this argument: starting
     from an indifferent position on the left–right dimension soon after its foundation,
     the Green Party moved gradually to the left in the perception of the electorate
     (Chap- ter 5).
3.   In a recent work, Dalton uses different terminology. The proponents of New Politics

goals are subsumed under the label 'New Left' and their opponents are called 'New Right', whereas the concept 'New Politics' is used for the dimension of political conflict involved (1988, p. 134). This solution suffers from the disadvantage that the term 'New Left' is still associated with the post-1968 resurgence of Marxist thought.

4. For they sake of brevity, these few examples may suffice at this point. For a more detailed analysis of the political implications of the New Politics see Chapter 4.

3. The New Politics: A New Political Paradigm or Just a Fad of the Young?

In principle, three important elements of the New Politics which served in most countries as mobilising issues are by no means new. Nuclear energy production, the policies of growth and the strategy of nuclear deterrence had been relatively uncontroversial for many years. Although nuclear armament was a contentious issue in some countries before the mid 1960s, particularly in Great Britain and West Germany, the respective movements did not reach levels of mobilisation comparable to those of the 1980s. It may be objected that the NATO twin-track decision created a new strategic situation for the Western European countries and hence intensified East–West tensions. But it is doubtful whether it were such strategic intricacies that primarily motivated the peace protest. It was probably the symbolic acceleration of the nuclear arms race that sparked off the peace campaign of the 1980s.

The observation that policies which had been consensual for decades suddenly sparked off intense political conflict suggests that the basic political orientations of parts of society must have undergone significant changes. There are several competing explanations for these changes, which will be presented in detail below. However, all these approaches link their arguments to a number of aggregate changes which are common to all advanced industrialised societies.

These changes are generally subsumed under labels such as 'modernisation', 'post-industrial society' or 'affluent society'. Economic success after the Second World War and the peaceful development of the Western hemisphere have prepared the ground for these developments. Primarily, they consist of the growth of the new middle class, a vast expansion of higher education, and dramatic advances in mass communications. They are the results of long-sustained post-war trends which have brought about similar effects in all Western societies, though not always on the same scale.[1]

Figure 3.1 depicts in a simplified form the most important factors in the process of political innovation. For the sake of clarity, a unidirectional model has been selected, and so a wide range of possible feedback effects have not been included in this illustration. The outer left column of this figure is generally accepted by all theorists as providing important clues for understanding the processes which have led to the emergence of the New Politics. However, some authors argue that the political preferences of New Politics proponents should be understood as the immediate result of the interaction of aggregate changes with macro-political factors; these interconnections are depicted below the dotted

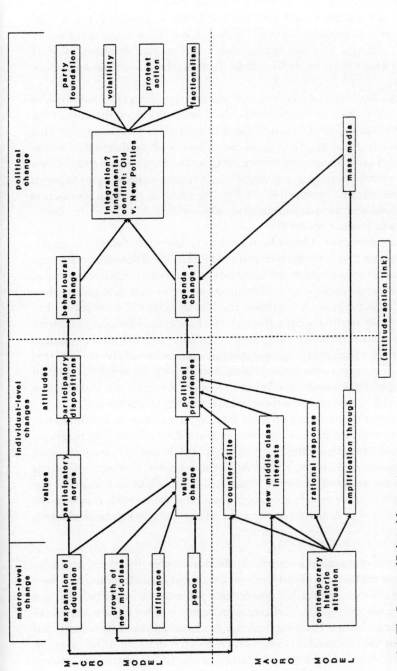

Figure 3.1: The Process of Political Innovation.
Note:
1. Agenda change means that individual attitudes have attained political relevance, either through media attention or through opinion polls, through media attention or through some kind of political action.

line in Figure 3.1. Others take a 'detour' via individual-level norms and value orientations in order to explain why certain age cohorts and social categories tend to favour the goals of the New Politics and the concomitant political style. They focus primarily on the micro-model, which is laid out in the upper half of Figure 3.1, although they use macro-level factors to explain individual-level changes. In what follows we shall examine the strengths and weaknesses of these approaches.

Undoubtedly, the immediate and most visible expression of the New Politics are the so-called new social movements. Party formation along the lines of the new conflict usually occurs at later stages of political development.[2] For this reason, theories explaining the success and failure of all kinds of social movements have inspired approaches relating specifically to the phenomenon of new social movements. Without going into the complexities of the attempt to assign rival theories to neat boxes, it is useful to be aware of the basic distinction between *breakdown* and *structural change* approaches (Kitschelt, 1988b, pp. 196ff.; Markovits and Meyer, 1985, p. 6).

From the perspective of breakdown models, mobilisation ought to be understood as response to relative deprivations produced by the failure of the system to provide outputs which match the expectations and norms that are generated through the system itself. Whereas functionalists expect protest to recede when system performance begins to improve, the Marxist school is more inclined to think in terms of inevitable demise of systems (Kitschelt, 1988b, p. 225). Structural change theorists, on the other hand, argue that societies tend to produce new aspirations which they are structurally ill-equipped to satisfy. In this view, social change arises from the tension between such new goals and the capacity of the existing system to adapt. In relation to new social movements and the New Politics, not all variants of these theories have attained prominence.

For our purposes, what is important is to focus our attention on the distinction between explanations which interpret the surge of the New Politics as a temporary irritation and those which argue that the new agenda and the unconventional political style are here to stay.[3] The subsequent discussion is primarily aimed at identifying the principal chains of arguments. The authors mentioned in the respective contexts are not always umambiguous proponents of this approach. On the contrary, most of them refer to a mix of explanations with various emphases.

SYSTEM PERFORMANCE EXPLANATIONS

In the context of macro-level-centred breakdown models, Jens Alber attributes the success of the German Green Party – a prominent example for the relevance of the New Politics – primarily to inadequate performance by the political and economic system (Alber, 1985). A central explanatory factor is the emergence of an academic proletariat resulting from the combined effects of the educational expansion in the 1960s and the economic crisis of the 1980s. In Alber's view, an economically deprived academic proletariat has chosen a 'counter-élite' strategy in order to find redress for its grievances. The argument is founded on empirical analyses of the social bases of Green politics which do indeed seem to support its thrust. A closer look, however, shows that not only unemployed but also academics in secure and well-paid jobs tend to vote Green (Kitschelt, 1986, p. 18). The finding that 47 per cent of unemployed academics and grammar-school graduates (Abiturienten) vote Green does not necessarily imply that their party preference is induced by their frustrating job situation. On the contrary, some of them may find their situation quite compatible with their preference for alternative life-styles, while others may be waiting for a place at university or they may be in the process of applying for adequate employment. Furthermore, this group does not dominate the Green vote. Nevertheless, the empirical questions will be addressed in detail in Chapters 5 and 6.

Apart from the unsatisfactory empirical foundation of the argument, however, Alber fails to explain why an economically deprived group should struggle for fundamental political change associated with zero growth and material self-limitation. It would be more understandable in terms of their social group interest were they to agitate for unrestrained growth in order to enhance the chances of their own personal success.

Whereas Alber's approach is, in principle, applicable to other advanced societies, Bürklin's argument draws on conditions that are specific to a few advanced democracies. In his view, the life-cycle of party systems means that the third generation after the establishment of a new regime suffers from a lack of attachment to the established party system (Bürklin, 1984, p. 43). The intensity of party loyalties, so his argument goes, is bound to erode with growing distance from the last period of mobilisation (Bürklin, 1984, p. 41; 1985a, p. 477f.). Whereas the second generation is still subjected to relatively intense socialising influences on the part of parents (the 'realignment generation'), the third generation grows up under conditions of political normality. Such periods of political acquiescence are not likely to make for strong socialising effects. Hence the vulnerability of the 'third generation' to new ideologies and new parties.

Additionally, the third generation regularly finds that most élite positions are still occupied by the preceding generations which came to power in the wake of the establishment of a new political regime (Bürklin, 1984, p. 46). Naturally, such lack of systemic integration furthers sympathy for political ideologies that can be instrumentalised to challenge the incumbents of élite positions. In the early 1980s, this 'inevitable' lack of adequate career prospects has been supplemented by the combined effects of structural saturation of the labour market and the exigencies of the economic crisis (Bürklin, 1985a, p. 446; 1985c, p. 209f.).

In order to cope with the problem of explaining the contents of counter-élite politics, Bürklin refers to specifically German traditions of political thought and 'idealistic' protest that go back to the late eighteenth and early nineteenth century. Relevant, and specifically German, also is the separation of politics and morals and the corresponding distinction between the ethics of conviction and of responsibility (Gesinnungsethik v. Verantwortungsethik) (Bürklin, 1984, pp. 91ff., 151; 1985c, p. 188).

Since idealism has always been the preserve of intellectuals, so the argument goes, it is consistent for a German counter-élite to instrumentalise idealism for the pursuit of its interests (Bürklin, 1984, p. 100). In addition, the general idealism of youth amplifies this effect – this will become weaker once the third generation 'grows up' (Bürklin, 1984, p. 39f.).

Although the suggestion of a third, idealistic generation is appealing from a German perspective and experience, it conflicts with many results gained from electoral research. After a system change and a reconstruction of a national party system, we should expect party loyalties to be unstable and relatively unstructured to begin with. Consistently, the electoral history of the West German party system shows a clear movement from fragmentation and volatility in the 1950s to increasing consolidation and stability in the 1960s and 1970s. It is hard to see why – all other things being equal – a sudden collapse of the transmission of party loyalties from one generation to the next should occur after the second generation.[4] There are, however, substantial changes which can account for the decline of party loyalties: the weakening of class and religious ties, the dissolution of traditional socio-political milieux and the growing individualisation of society can explain why the present young generation is more receptive to new parties than its predecessors (Raschke, 1985, p. 33; Flanagan and Dalton, 1984; Dalton *et al.* 1984, pp. 8ff.). Furthermore, this approach implies that the New Politics should be confined primarily to countries which underwent a dramatic system change after World War II. New social movements, however, are also part of the Scandinavian, Belgian, Dutch and British political scene.

Despite the relatively pronounced social location of the New Politics in the highly educated strata of society, it is questionable to consider people who have gone through modern higher education as intellectuals in the nineteenth century meaning of this term – which is implied by the argument. Furthermore, the élite-centred explanation (Bürklin, 1984, p. 46) ignores a constituent characteristic of new social movements: typically, these orginate from the grass roots and are decidedly anti-élitist mass movements. Finally, the concept of idealism is an 'empty box'. It is not clear why an alienated third generation should favour emancipatory idealistic goals and not, say, the grandeur of the nation or the resurrection of a religiously dominated society –as do a considerable proportion of Islamic intellectuals.

Although Bürklin's approach contains elements of structural change theories (Kitschelt, 1988b, p. 226; Bürklin, 1984, pp. 192ff.), the main thrust of the argument suggests that adequate élite action or a partial economic – not ideological – success on the part of Green activists will lead to a decline in the Green challenge. Consequently, in later writings Bürklin predicts the inevitable decline of the Green Party (Bürklin, 1987).

STRUCTURAL CHANGE AND COGNITIVE MOBILISATION

Another line of argument, inspired by structural change approaches, predicts a brighter future for alternative politics. It draws on both, micro- and macro-level factors. In this view, it is not the deficient performance of modern societies but, on the contrary, their very success that generates political strain and protest. Affluence, the spread of higher education, social mobility and the individualisation of the occupational life have generated new preferences that cannot be satisfied by existing institutions (Kitschelt, 1988b, p. 196; Schmidt, 1984, p. 12). The spread of markets and bureaucracies has led people to react against restraints on autonomy and the decline of democratic control of social change (Kitschelt, 1985, p. 3; 1988b, p. 204). The origin of these movements also explains their preferred organisational model: owing their existence to a considerable extent to the reaction against bureaucracies and anonymous structures, they strongly prefer decentralised organisation (Kitschelt, 1985a, p. 5).

An important effect of the modern welfare state is the expansion of sectors of employment that depend on transfer payments from public budgets or collective social security systems. This allows certain occupational groups to retain their alternative utopias unscathed by the harsh realities of market-place competition (Schmidt, 1984, p. 11; Baker et al., 1981, pp. 152ff.). In addition, the diminishing marginal utility of further economic growth, particularly for those in higher income brackets, is especially relevant for employees in non-market sectors (Raschke, 1985, p. 23; Fuchs, 1983, p. 130; Baker et al., 1981, p. 152f.).

Besides these structural changes which generate and facilitate the New Politics protest, the vast expansion of education since the 1960s is considered to be a crucial micro-level variable in accounting for the emergence of protest movements. It has provided considerable numbers of the younger generation with adequate intellectual skills and resources effectively to challenge established élites and their politics (Kitschelt, 1985a, p. 3, 1988b, p. 196; Dalton, 1984, p. 273; Dalton et al., 1984, p. 18f.)

The spread of the mass media attains particular importance in the context of this approach. Intellectual resources without adequate opportunities to use them outside conventional channels of participation would not have effects comparable to those of the surge of the New Politics. At most, they would result in increased intra-organisational factionalism. Skilful instrumentalisation of the electronic media, however, can serve as a superior functional equivalent for intra-organisational struggle in the pursuit of specific goals: the occupation of a building site, factory chimney, or vessel heading for a chemical waste dumping area in the North Sea can have far more profound effects on public opinion and the course of public events than a speech in a party sub-committee. More generally, the increased importance of mass media communication has reduced the organisational requirements for effective political action. These changes have worked in favour of spontaneous, loose organisation (Barnes, Kaase et al., 1979, p. 39; Kaase, 1984, p. 17).

VALUE CHANGE

Whereas system performance explanations cannot explain the New Politics leanings of the well-paid and more secure, structural change approaches fail to account for the tremendous age differences between supporters and opponents of alternative politics – even after controlling for education, social class, and employment sector. Apparently, the direct – if not mechanistic – explanation of present political behaviour through contemporary individual conditions of life is not entirely satisfactory.

Another school of social scientists is, therefore, more concerned with individual value orientations. In its view, the clue for adult political behaviour can be found in processes of childhood and, less prominently, adolescent and adult socialisation. Values, being distinct from social norms, are not expectations directed towards the individual from outside. On the contrary, they constitute an 'ego-central self-constituent concept of order' (Kmieciak, 1976, pp. 136ff., 150ff.). 'To say a person has a value is to say that he has an enduring prescriptive or proscriptive belief that a specific mode of behaviour or end-state of existence is to be preferred to an opposite mode of behaviour or end-state. This belief transcends attitudes towards objects and towards situations, it is a standard that guides and determines action, attitudes toward objects and situations, ideology, presentations of self to others, evaluations, judgements, justifications, comparisons of self with others, and attempts to influence others' (Rokeach, 1973, p. 25). In sum, values have two important functions: they determine a wider range of situation-specific attitudes (Kmieciak, 1976, p. 188) and they regulate behaviour (ibid., p. 150).

Epistemologically, the value concept is a hypothetical construct, that is to say, a theoretical concept with 'surplus meaning' which cannot be reduced to the language of observation. Values are measured through questionnaires which require choices of certain options. Their 'real nature' is then extrapolated from such responses to 'symbolic desiderata' (Kmieciak, 1976, pp. 150ff.). In our context this means that Inglehart's items for the measurement of postmaterialist value orientations cannot be taken 'literally'. Instead, the symbolic underlying meaning of a given pattern of response is of substantive interest.

In the context of New Politics theories, Inglehart's theory of postmaterialist value change and the related – albeit not conforming – explanations of unconventional political participation are of central importance. The core of Inglehart's widely debated argument is well known and therefore needs only brief mention here. [5] Drawing on Maslow's theory of a natural hierarchy of needs, Inglehart argues with his 'scarcity hypothesis' that individuals place 'the greatest subjective value on those things which are in relatively short supply' (Inglehart, 1981, p. 881). According to the hierarchy of needs, peaceful and affluent societies should experience increasing relevance of 'higher-order' (non-material) goals such as belonging, esteem and the satisfaction of intellectual or aesthetic needs (Inglehart, 1977, p. 22). It ought to be kept in mind, however, that postmaterial- ism theory is about changes in maginitude and emphasis, not about the emergence of completely new political value orientations (Inglehart, 1977, p. 13). The concept – and its misleading label – do not imply that economic aspects become unimportant to postmaterialists. Other authors have made this point even more strongly by suggesting that, rather than representing the devaluation of materialist goals, postmaterialism means an increasing emphasis on non-materialist concerns (Hondrich and Vollmer, 1983, p. 90).[6]

Only in combination with socialisation theory can this 'scarcity hypothesis' account for the substantial inter-generational differences in political value orientations and behavioural style. In this perspective, people 'tend to retain a given set of value priorities throughout adult life, once it has been established in their formative years'. (Inglehart, 1977, p. 23) This does not exclude the possibility of changes in basic values during adult life. It means, however, 'that the probability of such change diminishes substantially after one reaches adulthood'. (Inglehart, 1977, p. 23).[7] Consequently, there should be a substantial time-lag between cause and effect. More specifically, a generation that has been reared under conditions of physical security and affluence may continue to strive for postmaterialist goals even in periods of substantial economic recession. Consistently, the younger generations are more postmaterialist than their elders (Inglehart, 1977, p. 32; 1980, p. 152; 1981, p. 885; 1990a, p. 94).

Obviously, there are enormous individual differences in living conditions within the same age cohort. A middle-class family background and higher education are conducive to the development of postmaterialist orientations – both variables indicate a comparatively comfortable and secure environment during childhood and adolescence (Inglehart, 1977, p. 93). However, the exclusive emphasis on the socio-economic pre-adult environment as the explanation for the rise of postmaterialism has been widely criticised. Other, more specific socialising influences such as the dominant norms coveyed through education, apparently have an independent effect on the formation of political values (Lafferty, 1975; Flanagan, 1979, 1982a). This does not mean that long-term, persistent change is less likely. On the contrary, prevailing educational and societal norms are less subject to short-term fluctuation than is economic development.

Alternative interpretations of Inglehart's findings have suggested that the figures primarily mirror the combined results of life-cycle and period effects. In this view, the usual tendency of young people to be less concerned with material goals – not least because they have not yet experienced the need to care for themselves – has been amplified through the effects of affluence in Western societies (Böltken and Jagodzinski, 1985, pp. 479ff.; van Deth, 1983, p. 69). Meanwhile, longitudinal data has provided further evidence that postmaterialism has continued to persist through periods of prolonged economic downturn and high unemployment. And, more importantly, the value profiles of the respective generations are well in tune with modern economic history (Inglehart, 1981, p. 889; 1983a, pp. 84ff.). However, Inglehart's theory explicitly allows for period effects and does not rule out a modest impact of the life-cycle on value orientations (Inglehart, 1977, pp. 23ff., 87ff.; 1981, pp. 881ff.; 1983a, p. 82; 1990a, p. 82f.; cf. Dalton, 1986, p. 436). Contrary to other authors Inglehart has nevertheless maintained that the data reflect a substantial element of long-term generational change which already has visible effects on the dominant lines of political conflict in advanced industrial societies (Inglehart, 1979, 1983b; 1984; 1987).

Despite well-founded doubts concerning not only the conceptualisation but also the operationalisation of postmaterialism theory,[8] Inglehart's measure remains an important tool for identifying the New Politics-prone section in society (cf. H. Schmitt, 1987, pp. 24ff.). This is particularly true for the behavioural dimension. Although unconventional political participation cannot be explained solely through value orientations, postmaterialism is strongly associated with the propensity to become involved in protest action: postmaterialists with a high level of ideological conceptualisation (which is strongly related to education) score highest on the protest potential scale (Barnes, Kaase *et al.*, 1979, p. 267). Strictly speaking, these findings report not action but attitudes about one's own likely behaviour. Meanwhile, other studies have clearly demonstrated the link between postmaterialism and engagement in new social movements (Müller-Rommel, 1984a, 1984b, p. 447f.).

As already mentioned, the value change approach can explain generational differences in the popularity of the New Politics and – equally important – its actual content (Hildebrandt and Dalton, 1978, p. 78). The substantive aspects of the New Politics are, of course, the subject of contending evaluations. Whereas Inglehart is talking about 'change', others, who share his diagnosis of generational change, worry about the (possible) decay of traditional values (Noelle-Neumann, 1978; Klages and Herbert, 1983).

Implicitly, aspects of social class position are contained in Inglehart's theory: allowing for period effects means that a change in contemporary conditions will affect – or even override – deeply-rooted value orientations that have been moulded during a person's formative years. It is essential to be aware of the nature of human values: they are conceptualised as being stable and persistent, but they are not regarded as being completely *invariable*!

Consistently, Inglehart predicts that an economic crisis will slow down or even reverse the trend towards postmaterialism (Inglehart, 1981, pp. 888ff.). However, he does not elaborate on the effect different individual adult living conditions may have on persons who enter post-adolescence with exactly the same value profile. Clearly, someone who spends his adult life in comfortable and secure settings is more likely to retain his postmaterialist convictions than his former college fellow who happens to be unemployed. Obviously, contemporary individual living conditions like social class and sector of employment (see section above) need to be integrated in an explanation of the causes of individual political convictions (Cotgrove and Duff, 1981).

The Link Between Attitudes and Action

Even if contextual factors are integrated into an explanation of individual value orientations, there remains the complex problem of the attitude–action link. The central underlying assumption is that value priorities influence (via attitudes) individual behaviour: shifts in individual political orientations will have more or less direct effects on the the political behaviour of the populus and – consequently – on the nature of the political institutions and organisations of a given society. However, there are numerous publications which report staggeringly weak relationships between verbally expressed attitudes and actually performed behaviour (Marsh, 1971, p. 462). Frequently, this is taken as evidence for the suggestion that values are not stable and persistent (Bürklin, 1984, p. 38).

Values may well be relatively stable and persistent, however, and it is only a large number of contextual factors that frequently inhibit their translation into congruent action. This is particularly true for protest action, because it is largely unstructured and hence less 'familiar' to individuals than conventional modes of participation. Consequently, attitude–action correlations are never particularly strong (Rootes, 1981, p. 424). Also, the fact is often disregarded that many different attitudes (or values) may be associated with the same action. Attitudes which are not tested by the interviewer may in fact be placed higher in the individual's order of rank and hence may have the determining impact on ensuing behaviour.

Frequently, the questions posed in this debate are erroneous, supposing a direct causal link between attitude and action. 'Attitude', however, is only one of the conditions which structure human behaviour. *Incongruence* between standards (values, norms, targets) and cognitions (knowledge, skills, expectations) leads to the *choice* of an adequate path of action. This choice is also influenced by abilities, means, resources and other situational factors (Kmieciak, 1976, pp. 204ff.; Barnes, Kaase *et al.*, 1979, p. 46; Münch, 1972, p. 91). Hence, cognitions themselves have a decisive influence whether or not an individual experiences incongruence. The academic observer may often interpret a situation quite differently from the observed individual and may therefore expect the test-person to take a certain action. To give an example in the context of this book: in the public debate, nuclear power generation is widely associated with detrimental environmental effects and a substantial inherent risk. The informed observer would therefore expect postmaterialists, who rank environmental protection higher than economic growth, to be opposed to nuclear energy production. Some postmaterialists may simply be unaware of the detrimental environmental consequences of nuclear power and hence not be opposed to it. Or they may simply find that it represents a lesser evil compared to other methods of power generation.

The foregoing example makes clear that – apart from standards and cognitions – many other intervening variables influence the actual choice of action. Anticipation of repression is certainly part of the cognitive process which precedes behaviour. With regard to unconventional protest, however, the legitimacy of a certain kind of action will be just as important. Usually, activists regard themselves as acting on behalf of a wider constituency. Consistently, their action will be guided by a 'utility calculation' that seeks to strike a balance between effective action and the securing of relatively strong public support (Marsh, 1974, p. 108). As a consequence, this means that the trend toward protest behaviour may

accelerate once such forms of action have attained a first level of public acceptance.[9]

Additionally, resources such as money, time, necessary social contacts, sheer
physical ability, and opportunity to pursue the preferred path of action also play
an important role. Familiarity with a certain kind of action and the existence of
structures for channelling these activities therefore strengthen attitude–action
relationships (voting!), whereas highly unstructured and rare actions are even
more dependent on intervening variables (Rootes, 1981, p. 424). The results of
empirical investigations of attitude–action consistency are further put into perspective by the ever-present problem of 'stimulus similarity' (Marsh, 1971, p.
462).

The preceding arguments imply that attitudes and values cannot be used to
establish simple cause–effect linkages. That is to say, they have a very limited
predictive capacity as such. However, in comparable political situations, the
attitudinal structure of given populations may well provide us with important
clues about the future course of events (Klages and Herbert, 1983, p. 29).

Value and attitude research is useful to identify *potentials* which *could* be the
basis of a new party or a new form of political movement in a given political
setting. Clearly, not all potential supporters will participate in the end. On the
contrary, the identified potential represents an upper limit that is only theoretically available.

Catalytic issues are particularly important factors in the process that leads to
the eventual mobilisation of such potential. A highly polarising issue is likely to
cause such strong incongruence between standards and cognitions that
situational obstacles may be overcome. Correspondingly, disputes over nuclear
power or nuclear missiles have had a higher mobilising effect than other problems: a larger proportion of potential actors act according to their attitudes in
such situations. The example shows that weak correlations between attitudes and
actions may in some cases merely stem from the absence of such issues at the time
of testing.

HISTORICAL SITUATION AND RATIONAL RESPONSE

The importance of catalytic issues for the translation of attitudes into behaviour
suggests that the overall historical situation has also an important independent
effect on the growing relevance of New Politics issues. By 'historical situation' we
mean that specific periods of the political history of Western nations are always
characterised by a set of political problems with high 'objective salience'. To give
an obvious example: the dramatic events leading up to German unification
clearly dominated the German political agenda during this period (Kaase and
Gibowski, 1990, p. 19). The linkage can be conceptualised as follows: *agenda
change* emerges out of the interaction of attitudes with concrete problems. In a
way, the historical situation provides a 'stock' of politically relevant issues. The
selection process that determines which of them actually gain public salience and
mould the agenda of political discourse depends not only on the distribution of

interests and political attitudes in society but also on the inherent relevance of these issues.

The interdependency is obvious: attitudes and interests geared to the ideals of New Politics would not be politically conflictual in a perfect New Politics world. On the other hand, several problems that have gained political prominence recently are by no means new. Nuclear energy production, nuclear deterrence, environmental hazards and Third World famine are not, as mentioned above, recent inventions. This indicates that their political salience is partly the result of societal changes that have led to a spread of attitudes and interests among Western publics that make people more sensitive to such problems. At the same time, the scope and extent of these problems have reached new and arguably unprecedented levels in recent years. This fact is frequently disregarded in the debate on the causes of New Politics. As mentioned above, the set of relevant problems ('Problemhaushalt') of a society constitutes an important explanatory factor for political innovation. The following succinct examples will provide some evidence for the suggestion that not only attitudes and interests but also the real problems have changed.

Although the first nuclear power stations were constructed in several advanced industrialised nations in the 1950s, they became a target of protest only in the 1970s (Poguntke, 1988). Clearly, the risk associated with nuclear energy production did not change fundamentally in the course of two decades. However, anti-nuclear protest was never as single-issue-minded as it appeared to be at first sight. On the contrary, it was always strongly motivated by a quest for a comprehensive revision of the dominant logic of economic growth policy. Nuclear power stations had come to symbolise all detrimental effects of big technology and unlimited growth on the environment and civil liberties (Nelkin and Pollack, 1980, p. 129). Bearing in mind this symbolic function of nuclear power, the timing of protest becomes understandable: the growth of individual-level sensitivity to environmental problems coincided with dramatic ecological deterioration since the early 1970s (Global 2000, 1981; Meadows et al., 1972). Pollution is now seriously threatening the natural bases for human life.

Similarly, the threat of nuclear war gained additional imminence in the 1980s, particularly in the wake of the heated debate on the deployment of medium-range nuclear missiles in Western Europe. The progress of nuclear arms technology has led to extremely short pre-warning time and immense target accuracy. As a consequence, considerations of 'winnable nuclear war' shocked Western publics who suddenly realised that the unthinkable had become a possible option in military sand-table exercises.

Finally, the growth of welfare bureaucracies and the 'spread' of the state has led to a growing external determination (that is, heteronomy) of individual life in all Western societies. Over-regulation by the state is increasingly impinging on individual autonomy and self-determination. Simultaneously, technological progress has already created the infrastructure for encompassing state surveillance of individual life: modern computer networks make vast amounts of – sometimes very personal – data available to bureaucracies and/or police and secret services. Recent inventions such as machine-readable passports and identity cards have certainly not reduced worries about civil liberties.[10] These developments have coincided – and collided – with a growing quest for self-determination and the realisation of alternative life-styles in advanced societies.

The preceding examples show that the coincidence of a certain set of real problems (the historical situation) with a 'corresponding' attitudinal reservoir in society explains the surge of the New Politics. So far, the formation of New Politics-oriented attitudes has been explained in terms of underlying value orientations and/or interests that emerge from class position, employment sector or career prospects. However, the historical situation can also have a direct impact on attitudes. Conditions may be perceived as being so serious that people are led to think and act in ways quite contrary to those in which their value and interest structure would normally guide them: this effect could be called '*rational response*' (see Figure 3.2).

A prominent example is the regular increase of the environmental vote in the neighbourhoods of projected nuclear power stations or similar large-scale projects. It would be unreasonable to attribute this to a skewed distribution of postmaterialists or employees in the higher echelons of the service sector. Also, the risk of nuclear contamination is not significantly higher in the immediate environment of a nuclear power station: an interest-centred explanation fails to explain why those living close to such a plant should have a greater interest in obstructing the contruction compared with those who live fifty miles from the building site. It is more cogent to attribute the different attitudes towards nuclear power to the different levels of information that are the result of the debate regularly being more intensive in the close neighbourhood of any large-scale project (Mez, 1983).

It could be objected that the historical situation, that is, a new set of political problems, is sufficient to explain the emergence of the New Politics. Approval of the goals and the ideals of the New Politics, however, is so heavily concentrated in specific segments of Western societies that additional explanatory factors like attitudinal profiles and specific interest structures of these groups need to be integrated into a satisfatory explanation of the processes that have led to the growing salience of the New Politics agenda (see Chapters 5 and 6 for empirical evidence).

VALUES, INTERESTS, PROBLEMS: COMBINED EFFECTS

The preceding discussion of competing explanations of the New Politics demonstrates that these approaches are – on the whole – complementary and not mutually exclusive (Chandler and Siaroff, 1986, p. 303). Consequently, a convincing explanation of the New Politics needs to integrate elements from all approaches. The subsequent recapitulation exemplifies this argument: postmaterialism can explain why certain groups feel more attracted by the New Politics than others. However, value change theory does not specify conditions under which such propensities lead to actual behaviour. Structural change and system performance approaches, on the other hand, concentrate on contemporary social and economic factors that may lead a person to think and behave in a certain way.[11] They cannnot explain, however, why people in comparable situations frequently behave in very different ways. The same shortcoming applies to the focus on the historical situation, which emphasises the effect of the inherent relevance of political problems on the political agenda and on political action.

Consistently, the political action study that is concerned with participatory change as an important element of the New Politics shows that the propensity to get involved in unconventional political action is related not only to postmaterialism but also to age and levels of education (Barnes, Kaase *et al.*, 1979, p. 377).[12]

There are basically three factors which influence support for the New Politics. Their interaction can be conceptualised in the following model, which represents a synthesis of the preceding discussion (see Figure 3.2):

• *Values* (postmaterialism)
These are the most basic determinants of behaviour. Past and present socio-economic status (SES) and past and present historical situation have an important impact on their formation.

• *Present Socio-economic Status* (job security, service sector or civil service employment, new middle class)
Present socio-economic status enters the process leading to behaviour at several points. First, it has an impact on individual value orientations even after an individual has moved beyond its formative years. Second, it influences a person's interests and can thereby have a direct impact on attitudes. Third, it determines a person's situational context to a large extent – which is an important factor in the attitude–action link. This means that SES is a synonym for certain skills and conditions of life which are identifiable through generalised variables, which may lead to the choice of different paths of action by people with identical individual attitudes.

• *Historical situation* (ecological crisis, bureaucratisation, threat of nuclear war)
The historical situation has two effects: It 'provides' issues that motivate action according to pre-existing preferences.[13] And it can induce 'rational response'.

These factors provide the most important cues for the formation of attitudes and behavioural dispositions – which directly guide individual behaviour. They are strongly influenced by value orientations but also by the direct impact of socio-economic status. Under certain conditions, these factors will be overridden by rational response.

Consistently, the following – admittedly simplifying – model depicts these factors on the same level (see Figure 3.2). It identifies the principal linkages on

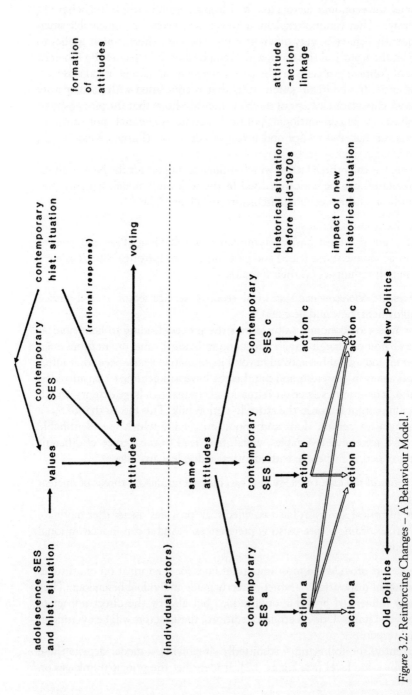

Figure 3.2: Reinforcing Changes – A Behaviour Model.[1]

Note:

1. This schematic depiction does not represent a hierarchy of strength of single predictors. SES may be a better predictor *per se* than values. Also, the strength of the individual links will vary according to individual factors and the given political and historical situation.

two levels. The upper part of the diagram depicts the formation of attitudes, which are then treated as given in the lower part, which is concerned with the translation of attitudes into behaviour. The dotted line symbolises the impact of a multitude of individual-specific situational factors that intervene in the process leading to behaviour. However, they are not measurable through generalised aggregate variables.[14]

The model shows that the same value type can be associated with different types of attitudes. A postmaterialist worker is more likely to be sceptical about New Politics demands than a postmaterialist student who is very remote from the sphere of economic production. On the other hand, he will be more sympathetic to such concerns than his materialist colleague who is not 'cross-pressured'. The same argument applies to the role of socio-economic status. Not all teachers, for example, are proponents of the New Politics although their class position and their sector of employment provide parallel stimuli favouring such propensities. Their view of the world is also affected independently by their value orientations. Finally, the 'objective' salience of particular problems may lead people to take attitudinal positions quite independent of their own value orientations and/or socio-economic interests.

As far as voting for a New Politics party is concerned, a relatively strong correlation between New Politics preferences and corresponding voting decisions can be expected. Other, more 'difficult' types of action, however, are more dependent on intervening variables. If we control for all individual-specific factors that are symbolised by the dotted line, there remain two important factors which can be discussed in general terms: the present socio-economic status of a person and the overall historic situation. Not only are they relevant for the *formation* of attitudes, they also influence the *translation* of attitudes into political behaviour.

The most eye-catching message that emerges – in conjunction with the above – from the diagram is that we are confronted with reinforcing societal changes that work in favour of New Politics: an affluent (new) middle class upbringing favours the formation of postmaterialist value orientations. Also, it makes it very likely that such a person goes through higher education and enters a middle class position. This, in turn, amplifies postmaterialist dispositions that have been moulded during childhood and adolescence. At the same time, a high degree of education and a secure and affluent social position make a New Politics orientation more 'affordable' and active engagement easier, because such a person will normally have the necessary skills and resources. Finally, highly educated persons, regardless of their value orientations, are the most likely group to base political evaluations on a high level of information and knowledge – the 'rational response effect'.

FASHION OR PERSISTENT CHANGE?

All factors leading to a New Politics orientation tend to be correlated and therefore have a mutually reinforcing effect on individual political preferences.

Nevertheless, those with New Politics potential are far from representing a homogeneous social group. Many of those who favour alternative politics will be led by the reinforcing effects of socio-economic status and value orientations. However, others may be primarily motivated by intellectual reasoning. Their personal life-style may be very un-alternative and they may not feel at all emotionally attracted by the style of the New Politics. Finally, there is a societal segment which is concerned with protest as such, almost irrespective of the substantive issues involved. Its preference for 'expressive political style' serves as a major motivation for political involvement (Barnes, Kaase *et al.*, 1979, p. 527).

Basically, all major factors that explain the surge of the New Politics are related to long-term, persistent changes: socio-structural change, the expansion of higher education, and the living conditions of affluent Western societies represent stable hallmarks of advanced industrialised countries. Furthermore, there are good grounds to attribute a substantial degree of permanence to shifts towards postmaterialist value orientations. Finally, the problems addressed by the New Politics are highly unlikely to be solved in the near future. It follows from this that the New Politics phenomenon represents not just a short-term irritation of Western societies that is mainly caused by a temporary failure of the political and economic system to provide appealing career prospects for an academic 'counter-élite'. On the contrary, it follows from the theoretical discussion that the growth of the New Politics ought to be understood primarily as the result of long-term changes.

In addition to this anchorage in individual-level and aggregate changes, New Politics movements have already created a vigorous subculture that ranges from biological food production, Third World shops and rural co-operatives to financial networks and international co-operation. In the Federal Republic an alternative bank, the 'Ökobank', has been founded, and 'alternative' Nobel prizes are awarded in Stockholm for outstanding activities in the struggle for an ecological and peaceful world that respects individual autonomy and civil rights. These societal structures exist relatively independently from 'hot' issues like the peace issue. Their unspectacular functioning has two important effects. They provide an infrastructure for mobilisation as soon as a relevant focus for protest emerges, and they work in a very concrete way on the grass roots towards the spreading of alternative ideas – in fact they are a part of the complex process that determines the formation of societal and individual values; the alternative subculture is an independent source of political socialisation and education and hence capable, to a degree, of creating its own support. Obviously, this argument is even more relevant in cases where the New Politics has led to the emergence of a genuine New Politics party.

In many ways, this subculture is comparable to the Socialist, Communist and Catholic milieux that dominated socio-political life in the first half of the twentieth century. However, there are important differences: whereas the old subcultures were largely dominated and controlled by their respective political parties, the alternative subculture has far more autonomy. It provides an 'attitudinal reservoir' for specific political ideals, and it is left to one or several political parties to mobilise its support. Also, these new 'value milieux' are less dependent on organisational reinforcement, because modern media communication serves as a partial substitute for traditional organisational networks.

NOTES

1. The existence of these trends is not seriously disputed, therefore no further discussion is necessary in the given context. For further references see Barnes, Kaase *et al.*, 1979, pp.: 28, 50; Baker *et al.*, 1981, p. 82; Inglehart, 1977, pp. 7ff.; Lane and Ersson, 1987, pp. 46ff.; Müller, 1987).
2. See below for a detailed account of the possible effect of the New Politics on the political level.
3. Although the categorisation of approaches according to two or three headings may do violence to some nuances, it is nevertheless useful to be aware of the principal lines of argument.
4. Admittedly, the history of electoral research is far too short to decide this question conclusively on the basis of sound empirical observation.
5. It is not possible – and not necessary in this context – to do justice to the large body of literature which is concerned with the debate on Inglehart's theory and measurement of postmaterialism. See among others van Deth, 1983; Lehner 1979; Böltken and Jagodzinski, 1985; Flanagan, 1979, 1982a, 1982b; Inglehart, 1971, 1983a, 1985a, 1985b; Lafferty, 1975; Lafferty and Knutsen, 1985; Mastekaasa, 1983; Müller-Rommel, 1983; Oberndörfer *et al.*, 1985; Gabriel, 1986.
6. This interpretation is supported by analyses which show that the voting behaviour of postmaterialists is stronly influenced by the evaluation of the economic competence of the government (Küchler, 1984b, pp. 14ff.).
7. Socialisation theory is a strongly contested battleground, but its pitfalls are not of primary importance in the context of value change theory. Socio-economic change is normally a long-term process. Although there may be dramatic events like the 'black Friday of 1929', the population rarely is exposed to sudden change. Economic history therefore provides only a rough categorisation of socialisation generations, which renders disputes about the relative importance of childhood and adolescence socialisation less important. Even such historic watersheds as the end of World War II in Germany have no unambiguous implications for value change theory: It is difficult to decide whether the bombing in 1944 or the 'hunger winter' after the war was the more dramatic – and hence formative – experience.
8. See Müller-Rommel (1983) for a good overview; see also note 5 for references.
9. Obviously, this is not an inevitable process. As the discussion has shown, the attitude–action link is far more complex. Of course, such a process might be stopped by state repression. However, it is worthwhile being aware of the inherent dynamics of changing behavioural styles.
10. Clearly, these developments play an important role in the context of structural change approaches: the use of computer technology by the state provokes reactions from citizens that are concerned with the protection of their individual sphere of life. On the other hand, cheap and powerful personal computer networks provide an important resource for mobilising against state action.
11. Although both approaches concentrate on contemporary living conditions, they disagree about the probability that persistent change is occurring (see relevant sections above).
12. In engagement in protest action, age plays an important role because it indicates sheer physical ability to participate in demonstrations or blockades.
13. 'Pre-existing' means that these preferences have been generated independently from the historical situation.
14. For the sake of clarity, the model disregards several relevant factors. As mentioned above, the repression potential and the media structure of a given society also influence behaviour.

4. The New Politics Party: A New Type of Party

In many ways, Old and New Politics goals are mutually exclusive. The ideals of the New Politics involve political utopias that are perceived to be diametrically opposed to the objectives of the Old Politics which are favoured by the majority of the population (Kmieciak, 1976, p. 225; Inglehart, 1977, p. 365; Dalton *et al.*; 1990, p. 5).

The concern of the New Politics with substantive democratic values, like direct participation, has left-wing, even system-transcending implications (Barnes, Kaase *et al.*, 1979, p. 525f.; Fuchs, 1983, p. 130). Giving first priority to ecological imperatives conflicts with the dominant values of industrial societies which have become used to the idea of persistent economic growth. Pacifist and neutralist leanings question an integral part of the basic framework of politics in most countries: the dogma of (nuclear) deterrence and membership in NATO. Finally, emphasis on self-determined work entails a challenge to the concentration of private ownership of the means of production in few hands. Although several elements of the New Politics agenda are also supported by traditional, mainly left-wing parties, this specific set of political demands, in conjunction with the central idea of an ecological society, aims at a different social, political and economic arrangement (Poguntke, 1987a, p. 78f.). Furthermore, the use of unconventional forms of political action in pursuit of these goals is met with disapproval by *status quo*-oriented societal majorities (Barnes, Kaase *et al.*, 1979, p. 207).

Obviously, this does not mean that most political conflicts related to the New Politics could not be resolved through negotiated compromise. When practical solutions have to be found as regards how given situations or policies can be corrected or changed, compromise can in most cases be reached through deals over the time-span involved. However, such opposing world views are hard to reconcile within the same political party because there is no direct external compulsion to reach compromise, such as the need to keep a coalition going or to retain international competitiveness. Additionally, the *problem of integration* posed by the New Politics involves an important behavioural dimension. It follows from this that any genuine attempt to adapt to this challenge involves fundamental programmatic, behavioural and, as a corollary, organisational changes that are tainted with the risk of antagonising a substantial part of the traditional core support of such a party.

Manifestly, the fundamental contrast between the priorities of Old and New Politics means that a considerable and resourceful minority could not adequately be represented by the established political forces. However, since the discontented groups are highly participatory and effective, they are themselves capable of gaining access to the political process.

In principle, there are five possible effects of the emergence of the New Politics conflict; they depend largely on the responsiveness of the party system to new demands and the nature of thresholds against the entry of new political forces into parliament:

• the formation of various new social movements that are concerned with New Politics demands: the peace movement, the ecology movement, the anti-nuclear movement, as well as others expressing minority concerns.

• the takeover of a small party by New Politics proponents and its transformation into a New Politics party. Due to the fact that the New Politics is situated on the left of the traditional left–right continuum, this absorption is only possible in the case of small left-wing parties.

• the splitting of a larger left-wing party into a traditional left-wing party and a postmaterialist left group. Alternatively, internal factionalism may result.

• alienation of the New Politics-oriented segments of society and their withdrawal of support for the political system. This alienation is a likely result in the case of unsuccessful new social movements and/or their supression by the political authorities.

• the foundation of a new political party, mainly by forces that have been active in the social movements.

Clearly, a combination of these effects can occur, depending on a multitude of systemic and political factors that cannot be discussed exhaustively in the present context. Party foundation or transformation – and to a certain extent also factionalism – means that individual-level changes become institutionalised in a twofold way:

• *organisational*, because the participatory norms and aspirations of New Politics groups will be reflected in the organisational structure in the party.

• *ideological*, by the formulation of ideological positions generic and particular to this organisation.

The latter point refers to the fact that organisation precedes the formulation of a coherent ideology in many cases. Whereas a relatively diffuse agreement on a set of core issues can be sufficient to lead to organisation, theory-building becomes a necessity when day-to-day politics requires coherent political positions on all political problems.

Although factionalism and new social movements do not exist without organisation, the Green Party, representing the institutionalised result of the surge of New Politics in Germany, will be the exclusive focus of the empirical analysis, which will be guided by the methodological instrument of an ideal type.

THE MODEL CONSTRUCTED

Any party necessarily reflects the attitudinal, behavioural and social composition of its social bases. Of course, this correspondence does not mean a straightforward translation of individual preferences into the design of a collective body. The 'sum' is clearly more than its component parts.

Constitutional and legal factors, the format of party competition, political culture and the general political situation of the country have an independent influence in moulding a party. Nevertheless, most external factors have a parallel impact on all parties. They can be conceptualised as systemic boundaries that determine the maximum variation in the outlook of various parties in one polity. Within these boundaries, however, New Politics parties should be clearly identifiable as a product of conflict over the dominant political paradigm and political style.

The very nature of an ideal type, however, means that such external factors are not integrated in the model. It is exclusively based on the central characteristics of the New Politics. Hence, an 'ideal' New Politics party would be characterised by the following four features: *New Politics ideology; participatory party organisation; unconventional political style; membership and electorate profiles dominated by New Politics groups*.

Thus far, the central characteristics of the New Politics have been described in rather general terms. Clearly, the argument that New Politics parties represent a new and distinct party family needs to be based on a more detailed description of the substantive elements of this ideal type and its relation to the underlying New Politics phenomenon. Hence, the following pages will be concerned with a detailed description of the four elements of the ideal type. It should be kept in mind, however, that using an ideal type as a theoretical construct also means referring to an 'ideal' New Politics phenomenon.

NEW POLITICS IDEOLOGY

Ecology

Concern with ecological politics is one of the most prominent themes of the New Politics. The link with the underlying causes of the New Politics is quite evident. First, an intact environment caters for aesthetic needs. Second, persons who are less concerned about the functioning of the economy are likely to shift their attention to non-material problems like the protection of nature. In political terms, this implies that the imperatives of the ecological system assume priority over conventional economic rationality out of principled considerations. First and foremost, this leads to the rejection of unlimited and unregulated economic growth, which is seen to pose a fundamental threat to the ecological balance. It involves opposition to large-scale projects in general and often concentrates on resistance against nuclear power stations, which have come to symbolise all the detrimental impacts of big technology on the environment and on liberal freedoms (Nelkin and Pollack, 1980, p. 129). Instead, small-scale, environmentally adapted and resource-conscious production is demanded.

Mere opposition to nuclear power stations, however, may be combined with endorsement of conventional economic strategies – which does not represent an 'ecological' political orientation. Ecologism, on the other hand, cannot embody acceptance of, or even support for, nuclear power generation.

Individualism

Emphasis on individuality is a necessary element of self- actualisation (Inglehart, 1990a, p. 134) and as such an integral part of the New Politics. This area covers concern with individual self-determination in the widest sense: it includes all classical Liberal freedoms, but transcends this tradition by emphasising more strongly the individual components and aspects of these rights. Loosely formulated, it extends Liberalism in the direction of anarchism. To clarify: if we conceptualise a continuum 'state/patrimonial power' – 'individual freedom', Social Democracy and Conservatism would be positioned on one side, and Liberalism closer to the other end, with anarchism occupying the extreme 'freedom' position.

Hence, in the context of New Politics, emphasis on individual liberties is not so much about areas protected from too much state interference as about 'state-free zones'. Individualism embodies both traditional Liberal concerns, including liberalised abortion and divorce, and respect for minorities and demands for a minimum of state interference with individual life. The latter amounts to a quest for a maximum of tolerance for 'alternative' life-styles. Finally, feminism can be understood as a separate, albeit related, phenomenon because it represents a specific expression of individual self-actualisation and self-determination.

Participatory Democracy/Direct Democracy

For many adherents of New Politics, the strong emphasis on individualistic, self-determined participation describes both a normative goal and their actual mode of behaviour. This is also reflected in the parties' unconventional outlook, and will be discussed below.

On the ideological level, it gives rise to the concept of participatory democracy as the main principle of political and social organisation. The essence of it is direct participation in decision-making on specific issues as opposed to the usual choice between political programmes which are then specified and realised by professional politicians (Kaase, 1982, p. 185f). It means that the lower units of any societal organisation ought to have extensive decision-making powers, which implies decentralised structures. Ideally, the lowest unit has most resources and competences, and the higher-level bodies only take over tasks which the basic unit is structurally incapable of mastering. Access to decentralised bodies facilitates direct and concrete influence on decisions that affect daily life – unlike the present organisation of democracy, which functions in a much more abstract and mediated way (Wiesendahl, 1991).

Thus, decentralisation is not, as in conservative strategies, intended to shield 'big politics' from the participatory demands of the populace. On the contrary, it is seen as the essential precondition for meaningful participatory opportunity on all levels, because it distributes power to more units and makes politics more transparent and hence intelligible. As already indicated, this principle of organisation should extend to all spheres of society, which means in concrete terms that participatory opportunities should be vastly expanded.

Leftism

Empirical research on the ideological orientations of postmaterialists and new social movement activists has indicated that the New Politics is not independent from the traditional left–right dimension (Inglehart,1977, pp. 60ff.; Budge *et al.*, 1987; Müller-Rommel, 1984b, pp. 450ff.). To a degree, this is a result of the inherent capacity of the left–right dimension to incorporate new issues. Due to its social-psychological function as a culturally anchored convenient 'shorthand' means of political orientation, newly emerging political issues tend to get evaluated according to their relation to this dominant dimension of political conflict (Dalton, 1985, p. 293; 1986, p. 444; Inglehart and Klingemann, 1976).

In addition, there are unambiguous inherent logical links between the political goals of the New Politics and the perennial normative content of the left–right dimension (Cotgrove and Duff, 1980, pp. 344ff.). Essentially, the terms 'left' and 'right' are defined in relation to their meaning for the pursuit of greater political, economic and social equality (Lipset *et al.*, 1954; Inglehart, 1977, p. 212; Klingemann, 1982, p. 217; Bürklin, 1980, p. 227).

A few remarks may suffice to indicate the principal logical links between the New Politics and central aspects of traditional left-wing policies. As already mentioned in Chapter 2, the quest for autonomy and more participation have repercussions for the preferred organisation of industrial production, business life and democratic governance. Furthermore, ecologically-adapted industrial production cannot be enforced without a substantial degree of political control over the economy. Furthermore, a certain level of relative material scarcity as a result of non-growth policies necessitates egalitarian measures for legitimation: if the cake is not to be ever-growing, so that everybody has the reasonable expectation of getting somewhat more every year, redistributive policies are likely to become more salient. The alternative strategy, which is to resort to more repression in order to cope with the erosion of legitimacy, is impossible due to the inherent anti-authoritarianism of the New Politics. Consistently, the links between the New Politics and traditional left-wing concerns have led to a partial change in the public understanding of the substantive meaning of the left–right dimension (Dalton, 1988, p. 121).

Third World

Persons who care less about their own material well-being are obviously more likely to be prepared to make true sacrifices in order to enhance living conditions in the Third World. Such attitudes also tap the postmaterial value of belonging in the widest, that is to say global, sense (Baker *et al.*, 1981, p. 141; Inglehart, 1977, p. 384). Consistently, adherents of the New Politics tend to be strongly concerned with Third World problems and favour redistribution from North to South.

Unilateral disarmament

Postmaterialists emphasise security less than materialists but are more concerned with values like 'belonging' and 'reconciliation'. Therefore, they can be expected to be more sceptical towards the dominant logic of international relations based on security. People with a high degree of education may take a corresponding position as a result of an intellectual judgement made in the course of the missile debate of the early 1980s, which led to a substantial increase in public awareness of, and information on, the problematic of nuclear strategy. These groups are prepared to take decisive unilateral steps in disarmament policy in order to approach a situation based on mutual trust instead of deterrence.

PARTICIPATORY PARTY ORGANISATION

The 'ideal' organisational structure of a New Politics party follows from the normative positions of New Politics proponents as well as from their behavioural dispositions. Obviously, normative ends are easiest to realise within one's own party. On the other hand, direct translation of individual behavioural norms and practices into party structures cannot be assumed, because external, environmental factors have a strong impact. An extreme example is the German party law (Parteiengesetz) which lays down the internal structure of political parties to a substantial extent (Poguntke, 1987c).

Nevertheless, we can crudely conceptualise organisational structures as 'frozen' processes which are determined by individual attitudes, behavioural styles and environmental factors. Hence, if an organisation comprises members with overwhelmingly participatory leanings, a 'push' will exist for organisational structures to become more open to participatory aspirations. With the necessary qualifications, the organisational properties of a New Politics party can therefore be deduced from the characteristics of the individuals who are likely to get involved in such a party.

Consequently, we can expect a New Politics party to be decidedly participatory in its outlook. Furthermore, any tendency towards oligarchisation and hierarchisation within such a party would not only meet ideological resistance but also élite-challenging participatory action by the party's rank and file (Barnes, Kaase et al., 1979, p. 208; Kaase, 1982, p. 185f.; Inglehart, 1990a, p. 339).

Such a party's organisational structure is likely to be characterised by anti-hierarchy measures like involvement of the rank and file in specific policy decisions, open access to party meetings on all levels, provisions for a strong control of elected office holders, or limited permitted periods in elected offices. Obviously, such a list can never be exhaustive – the potential variations of such provisions are almost unlimited and to a certain extent country-specific. This means that the analysis of a specific party organisation can only be guided by the preceding aspects but needs to be based on a qualitative judgement of the overall character of a given party organisation.

UNCONVENTIONAL POLITICAL STYLE

The disposition of a large part of a New Politics party's potential supporters towards unconventional political action should also be detectable in the way the party acts as a collectivity. Due to the participatory composition of such a party, a strong impetus should exist for the party as a whole to engage in extra-parliamentary, unconventional forms of political action, such as demonstrations, boycotts, strikes and the like. However, only a small fraction of those potentially in sympathy with a political party actually join the party. In the case of a New Politics party, this portion may even be smaller because of the predominance of unconventional participatory dispositions within this social group (Poguntke, 1992c). Consequently, a considerable share of these political energies will normally be invested in the 'milieu' of such a party, that is, in citizen initiatives and extra-parliamentary movements. Therefore, a New Politics party will rarely be the most numerous force in unconventional political actions and will be often confined to a participant rather than a dominant role.

MEMBERSHIP AND ELECTORATE PROFILES

As discussed earlier, the social potential for a New Politics party consists of individuals who are concerned with New Politics issues out of their postmaterial value orientations and/or because of their specific social position, which makes such issues appear to correspond particularly to their interests. An independent or reinforcing factor can be the appeal the unconventional political style of such a party exerts on protest-inclined persons.

These groups can be defined by the empirical categories that we shall use for measurement. However, situation-specific factors like neighbourhood opposition to environmentally detrimental projects may independently compel significant numbers of electors to vote for a New Politics party and hence dilute the picture considerably. This explains why the electoral profile of such parties is normally less distinct than one would otherwise expect.

Keeping this caveat in mind, voters for New Politics parties should tend to be *postmaterialists, young, highly educated, new middle class.* In most countries, individuals with such a social profile tend to live in *urban* areas. We have already discussed the links between the New Politics and a general left-wing orientation. Consistently, we can expect a majority of voters of a New Politics party to place themselves on the *left* of the political spectrum.

ON MEASUREMENT

Epistemologically speaking, the ideal type consists of a set of theoretically deduced expectations about the characteristics of a party that is based on the New Politics. These dimensions of measurement cover all important aspects of a political party. Primarily, the ideal type is therefore a *classificatory* device, which will be the guiding line for the subsequent anaylsis of the German Green Party.

Setting an ideal type Old Politics party against the New Politics party would mean stretching the typological approach too far. Clearly, this would do violence to the variety of different parties that are nevertheless all rooted in the Old Politics paradigm. However, from the perspective of the conflict between Old and New Politics, the typical outlook of Old Politics parties is the negative mirror image of a New Politics party. Irrespective of the immense diversity on the Old Politics side of this conflict all these parties are characterised by the fact that they have no similarity with the model developed above. Or, to phrase it more explicitly, they tend to be not concerned with, or even opposed to, the goals of the New Politics; they are socially anchored in the Old Politics segments of society; their party organisation does not cater for participatory aspirations of the grass roots; and they are likely to be opposed to unconventional forms of political behaviour.

It is clear, however, that the above statement defines the opposite end of an underlying continuum, an ideal-typical Old Politics party. As already mentioned, most things in politics are negotiable, and parties of the traditional Left are particularly likely to adapt to some extent to the challenge of the New Politics. Therefore we need to conceptualise party change in terms of an underlying continuum whose endpoints are defined by ideal-typical Old and New Politics parties.

Methodologically, the research questions posed through the ideal type model involve two different kinds of dimensions: whereas programmatic, behavioural and organisational characteristics represent qualitative differences to Old Politics parties, membership and electorate profiles refer to quantitative diversities.

Therefore, an empirical analysis based on our ideal type necessarily needs two reference points: comparison of a hypothesised New Politics party, that is, the Greens, with adjacent parties is needed in order to demonstrate sufficient distance on quantitative aspects. For qualitative characteristics, conformity with the ideal type is, in principle, sufficient as major focus. However, it could still be objected that – contrary to the theoretical argument – an established party may have transformed into a New Politics party. In our case, use of the ideal type as sole yardstick for analysis would only demonstrate that the Green Party conforms to the ideal type. Strictly speaking, however, there would be no empirical evidence that the remaining German parties have not also moved towards the New Politics end of the underlying continuum. Consequently, the analysis of the German Greens extends to all established German parties, illustrating contrasts and – fewer – similarities and signs of adaptation.

Part II

The German Green Party

5. The Electorate of the Green Party

In our theoretical introduction we have discussed why certain groups among the population are more likely to be attracted by the New Politics than others. The multi-stage model explains the interaction of certain value orientations, behavioural dispositions, a particular socio-economic status, and specific historic conditions. Apart from the last aspect, all these explanatory factors can be explored by survey data analysis. Hence, before we turn to a systematic analysis of the social and ideological composition of the Green electorate, it is necessary to give a brief account of the political context which has had an independent impact on the development of the electoral fortunes of the Greens in the Federal Republic.

POLITICAL SEASONS AND THE SUCCESS OF THE GREEN PARTY

In the second half of the 1970s, the West German party system seemed to have reached unprecendented levels of consolidation and stability. In the 1976 Bundestag elections, the three established parties won 99.1 per cent of the vote, seemingly leaving radical opposition parties without the slightest hope of ever surmounting the 5 per cent hurdle required by West German electoral law in order for a party to win seats in the federal parliament. However, culmination already bore the seeds of decay. Nuclear sites such as Brokdorf, Grohnde, Gorleben and Wyhl became the symbols of enormous mass mobilisation against the nuclear energy policy supported by all established parties (Roth, 1985, p. 51). As a result, the governing Social Democratic Party was deeply split over the issue of nuclear energy production (Häusler, 1988, p.121f.). However, the authority of Chancellor Helmut Schmidt and the constraints of coalition politics prevented a breakthrough by the Social Democratic anti-nuclear wing until the SPD lost governmental power in 1982.

As a result of the inability of the established party system to respond to growing anti-nuclear sentiments, alternative anti-nuclear groups began to realise that extra-parliamentary protest would not lead to a fundamental policy change (Klotzsch and Stöss, 1984; Müller-Rommel and Poguntke, 1990b). Consequently, they formed electoral lists for Land elections. In summer 1978, the combined results of three ecological and alternative lists came close to the 5 per cent hurdle in the Hamburg Land elections. One month earlier, a 'Green List for Environmental Protection' had won 3.9 per cent in the Land election of Lower Saxony (see Table 5.1). This was a clear indication that the established party system was in danger of breaking up for the first time since the right-wing

Table 5.1: Green Party – Results in Land Elections.

Date of Election	Land	Percentage	Difference from Previous Elec.
04.06.1978	Hamburg	4.6[1]	
04.06.1978	Lower Saxony	3.9[2]	
18.03.1979	Berlin	3.7[3]	
18.03.1979	Rhineland-Palat.	no participation	
29.04.1979	Schleswig-Holstein	2.4[4]	
07.10.1979	Bremen	5.1[5]	
16.03.1980	Baden-Württemberg	5.3	
27.04.1980	Saarland	2.9	
11.05.1980	North Rhine-Westph.	3.0	
10.05.1981	Berlin	7.2	+3.5
21.03.1982	Lower Saxony	6.5	+2.6
06.06.1982	Hamburg	7.7[6]	+3.1
26.09.1982	Hesse	8.0	
10.10.1982	Bavaria	4.6	
19.12.1982	Hamburg	6.8	– 0.9
06.03.1983	Rhineland-Palat.	4.5	
13.03.1983	Schleswig-Holstein	3.6	+1.2
25.09.1983	Bremen	7.8[7]	+2.7
25.09.1983	Hesse	5.9	−2.1
25.03.1984	Baden-Württemberg	8.0	+2.7
10.03.1985	Saarland	2.5	– 0.4
10.03.1985	Berlin	10.6	+3.4
12.05.1985	North Rhine-Westph.	4.6	+1.6
15.06.1986	Lower Saxony	7.1	+0.6
12.10.1986	Bavaria	7.5	+2.9
09.11.1986	Hamburg	10.4	+3.6
05.04.1987	Hesse	9.4	+3.5
17.05.1987	Rhineland-Palat.	5.9	+1.4
17.05.1987	Hamburg	7.0	−3.4
13.09.1987	Bremen	10.2	+2.4
13.09.1987	Schleswig-Holstein	3.9	+0.3
20.03.1988	Baden-Württemberg	7.9	– 0.1
08.05.1988	Schleswig-Holstein	2.9	−1.0
29.01.1989	Berlin	11.8	+1.2
28.01.1990	Saarland	2.6	+0.1
13.05.1990	Lower Saxony	5.5	−1.6
13.05.1990	North Rhine-Westph.	5.0	+0.4
14.10.1990	Bavaria	6.4	−1.1
20.01.1991	Hesse	8.8	– 0.6
21.04.1991	Rhineland-Palat.	6.5	+0.6
02.06.1991	Hamburg	7.2	+0.2
29.09. 1991	Bremen	11.4	+1.2

Notes:
1. In 1978, three green-alternative groups ran for the Land election (GLU: Grüne Liste Umweltschutz; AUD: Aktionsgemeinschaft Unabhängiger Deutscher; BWL: Bunte Liste – Wehrt Euch). These groups preceded the foundation of the Green-Alternative List of Hamburg, which acts as the Green Land party.
2. In 1978, the Grüne Liste Umweltschutz (GLU) participated in the Land elections. It was an organsational forerunner of the Greens in Lower Saxony.
3. In Berlin, the Alternative List acts as a Green Land party. The 1990 all-Berlin election is not shown in the table, because the results are not comparable to previous West Berlin elections.
4. In 1979, the Grüne Liste Schleswig-Holstein (GLSH) ran in the elections.
5. Bremer Grüne Liste (BGL).
6. Grün-Alternative Liste (GAL).
7. In 1979, the Green List of Bremen won four seats in the state legislature. Before the 1983 election, the Bremen Greens split and a Green Land party was founded which won 5.4 per cent of the vote and five seats. The Green List of Bremen gained only 2.4 per cent and won no seat. For the analysis of the electoral developments, the results of both groups are collapsed.

Sources: Statistisches Bundesamt, 1989; Forschungsgruppe Wahlen, 1991.

National Democrats (NPD) had won representation in several Land legislatures at the end of the 1960s.

Little more than a year later the Bremen Greens were the first in the Federal Republic to win seats in a Land parliament, and when the Greens of Baden-Württemberg demonstrated in March 1980 that it was also possible to win seats in a state without the conducive concentration of an alternative subculture typical of the city states of Bremen, Hamburg and Berlin, expectations and hopes for the 1980 Bundestag elections grew. It can be argued that it was not least the candidacy of the controversial CSU leader Franz-Josef Strauß which kept the Greens out of the Bundestag: Many SPD supporters with green sympathies decided to vote for Helmut Schmidt in order to prevent the success of Franz-Josef Strauß whose democratic credentials were viewed with considerable scepticism by the German Left (Papadakis, 1984; Gatter, 1987; Cornelsen, 1986; Langguth, 1984).

As was to be expected, the disappointing 1.5 per cent at the 1980 Bundestag elections proved to be only a temporary set-back, and by the next Bundestag election, in 1983, Green parliamentarians had already taken seats in five Land legislatures. The Green success on the federal level met with enormous international interest. However, interpretations which saw the 'green wave' as yet another example of German exceptionalism characterised by political romanticism or democratic immaturity were proven wrong by the spread of the 'green disease' to other West European party systems. Throughout the 1980s, green and alternative lists in most West European countries won seats in parliaments (Müller-Rommel, 1989, p. 15; Müller-Rommel and Poguntke, 1989, pp. 12 ff.), and it was somewhat ironic that the most successful Green Party could not keep up with its sister parties in the 1989 European elections: together with their Dutch allies, the German Greens were the only Green Party in the EC which could not improve its vote significantly (Niedermayer, 1989a).

In order to interpret the Green electoral development in a meaningful way, we need briefly to recall the most important *political factors* which have influenced the performance of the Green Party at the polls. As already mentioned above, the foundation of green and alternative lists was sparked off by the inability of all established parties to respond to the growing anti-nuclear protest of the late 1970s. The alienation of parts of the young and highly educated generation from the established party system gained substantial momentum as a result of the decision by the governing Social-Liberal coalition in December 1979 to deploy intermediate-range nuclear missles should the then Soviet Union not be willing to withdraw similar weapons from Eastern European countries. In the early 1980s, the Greens were swept into several Land parliaments by the combined thrust of the peace and anti-nuclear movements which reached unprecedented levels of extra-parliamentary mobilisation in the Federal Republic (Küchler, 1984a; Schmitt, 1990, p. 14f.; Müller-Rommel and Poguntke, 1990b; Müller-Rommel, 1985b; Papadakis, 1984; Roth, 1985; Roth and Rucht, 1987).

There were, however, two other important factors which created a conducive climate for the Greens at the time of the 1983 Bundestag elections. The most severe financial scandal in the history of the Federal Republic, the so-called Flick affair, added much to the growing alienation from the established political classes. It became apparent that all Bundestag parties had been involved in illegal financial transactions in order to secure tax-free party funding through German industry, and that many senior politicians had personally received large donations for their party. Although no politician has been convicted of corruption so far, the impression remained that a strong company could influence political decisions through its financial power. Secondly, the heated debated over the forest disease ('Waldsterben'), which culminated around the time of the 1983 Bundestag elections, made the severe and far-reaching consequences of the ecological crisis visible even to those parts of the population which had thus far tended to dismiss green concerns as immature obsessions of young intellectuals or drop-outs.

Consequently, the Greens managed to win 5.6 per cent of the total vote and 27 seats in the Bundetag, breaking the mould of the 'two-and-a-half party system' for the first time since 1957 on the federal level. However, the mechanics of the party system began to work against the Greens as soon as the Social Democrats had lost governmental incumbency in Bonn. The New Politics-oriented wing of the SPD gained influence in the party and as a first spectacular result of its beginning ideological reorientation the SPD voted in November 1983 against the NATO twin-track decision which had been initiated by its own chancellor Helmut Schmidt four years earlier (Leif, 1990, p. 2; Schmitt, 1990, p. 139f.; Obermeyer, 1985). The next major policy change came in the wake of the Chernobyl shock, when the SPD called, in 1986, for a phasing out of nuclear energy production in the Federal Republic over the next decade (SPD, 1986b). These highly visible and – not least – symbolic decisions were substantiated by the drafting of a new basic party programme which took account of the whole range of New Politics concerns, such as the ecological limitations to economic development, the growing quest for direct political involvement, women's rights, disarmament, and solidarity with the Third World (SPD, 1986a, 1989a; Poguntke and Schmitt, 1990). The ongoing debate over the basic programme was accompanied by calls for an 'ecological restructuring of industrial society' – a phrase which had been coined by the Greens some years earlier (Die Grünen, 1986; SPD, 1989b, 1989c).

Obviously, a party's image cannot be changed overnight. Programmatic change needs considerable time for internal debate and decision-making. And it probably takes even more time to convince the public that change is not meant to be merely tactical. In this light, the candidacy of Johannes Rau for the 1987 Bundestag election symbolised the ambivalence of the SPD at that time. By categorically ruling out any prospect of a red-green coalition, Rau appeared to be a symbol of the old traditional SPD at a time when the programme commission under the influence of Willy Brandt, Erhard Eppler and Oskar Lafontaine was already shifting the emphasis towards New Politics concerns.

Hence, it is not surprising that Green Land parties continued to participate successfully in the Land elections following the 1983 Bundestag contest. However, with the fascination of novelty wearing off and the increasing credibility of the Social Democrats as an alternative for moderate New Politics voters, political seasons began to change. The Greens could not continue to increase their electoral fortunes at the same pace in the last third of the 1980s. Although the impression may seem somewhat ambiguous at first sight, there is a clear pattern which becomes apparent if we disregard the electoral setbacks of Green Land parties in the elections of Hesse (1983) and Hamburg (1982, 1987). In those cases, the respective Land parties were penalised for their unwillingness to form governments with the Social Democrats – an option which has always been strongly supported by the Green electorate ever since the Greens entered the electoral arena (Forschungsgruppe Wahlen, 1983, 1987a; Müller-Rommel and Poguntke, 1990b, p. 278f.).

More important is the fact that, during the last years of the 1980s, the Greens could neither significantly improve their position in Länder where they had been weak nor could they always hold on to their strongholds. In Saarland and Schleswig-Holstein, they have repeatedly failed to cross the 5 per cent hurdle, in North Rhine-Westphalia they just made it by the absolute minimum of 5 per cent in 1990, and in Baden-Württemberg (1988) and Lower Saxony (1990), where they had been strong traditionally, they even lost votes.[1] It may be objected that in the cases of Schleswig-Holstein and Saarland, attractive, New Politics-oriented SPD candidates (Oskar Lafontaine and Björn Engholm) made it particularly difficult for the Greens to appeal to marginal voters. However, things were quite different in Baden-Württemberg, where a weak Social Democratic

Party should have left ample space for Green success, and in North Rhine-Westphalia, where a long-standing Social Democratic one-party government should have offered even more space for Green gains. Also, the clear preference of the Social Democratic candidate in Lower Saxony, Gerhard Schröder, for a red-green coalition should not have damaged Green electoral fortunes – rational voters willing to secure a stable majority against the governing Christian–Liberal coalition should have kept faith with the Greens in order to keep them safely above the 5 per cent barrier.

However, the favourable electoral climate for the Greens was not only eroded by the reorientation of West German Social Democracy. The Soviet leader Michael Gorbachev has damaged the electoral prospects of the Greens probably more than any West German politician. By agreeing to withdraw all intermediate-range nuclear missiles from Eastern Europe, he has removed the peace issue, which has worked in favour of Green electoral fortunes, from the political agenda. And the problems posed by the fall of the Berlin Wall – a direct result of Gorbachev's *perestroika* – have overshadowed all other political problems in the Federal Republic (Kaase and Gibowski, 1990). It was particularly detrimental in this situation that the Greens, as a result of continuous factional fighting, took a long time to formulate their position on German unification. At a time when political developments had created a situation that had made German unification unavoidable, the Greens were still reluctant to accept this *fait accompli* – at a time when more than 60 per cent of Green supporters and more than 80 per cent of the total population expected German unification to happen (Poguntke, 1990a; Forschungsgruppe Wahlen, 1990b). Arguably, there are three factors which account for the surprising failure of the Greens to overcome the 5 per cent hurdle on 2 December 1990 in the Western part of the country: the party's inability to respond coherently to the rapidly changing political context before the first all-German election, an unfavourable political agenda and the conspicuous lack of engagement throughout the campaign (Poguntke, 1992b; Boll and Poguntke, 1992). Let us now turn to the underlying *structural* factors which explain the emergence and success of the German Greens.

THE FOCUS OF ANALYSIS

We have argued in Chapter 2 that postmaterialists, and particularly those in new middle class positions, are likely to form the core electorate of a New Politics party. In addition, special historic circumstances such as the environmental crisis and, particularly in the early 1980s, the problem of the arms race may have induced so-called 'rational responders' to support a New Politics party. It is obvious that the latter supporters will tend to be highly educated and in a social position that is comfortable enough to permit engagement with 'luxury concerns'. Finally, mobilisation for New Politics goals may stem from the attraction of alternative-style politics. Again, the adherents of unconventional political action can often be found in the better educated sections of society.

We have seen that the underlying motivations for the engagement of these groups with New Politics may differ, although they share several socio-structural characteristics: they tend to be young, urban, and new middle class. However, when we move from electoral potential – that is, New Politics orientations – to actual party preference, a number of intervening *political* factors come into play. Party preference is not only based on ideological affinity but also on candidate orientations and the format of party competition at a given point in time, which means there is always a considerable element of tactical voting involved.

Furthermore, dealing with electoral data confronts us with the problem that a considerable portion of voters do not behave according to the theories political scientists like to develop. This means that some individuals will always base their voting decisions on factors which are not covered by any of the theories on electoral behaviour. Hence, a certain degree of 'dilution' appears in any party's electoral profile. The argument can be stretched further: some Communist parties have considerable numbers of middle-class voters. However, they are normally regarded as working class parties. This goes to show that electorates ought not be considered as the single most important criterion of typological distinctiveness.

A substantial number of electoral analyses of the German Greens have been published. Going back as far as the early 1980s, they generally corroborate our argument.[2] It has to be kept in mind, however, that any newly emerging party has the capacity – particularly in its early stage of development – to attract protest votes from quite diverse sections of society (Veen 1984, p. 7). This means that the electoral profile of a new party may not be as pronounced as its ideological profile might lead us to expect. On the other hand, once such a party has become more established it may be able to attract increasing numbers of 'rational' voters who may again blur its sharp electoral profile.

The essence of our theoretical argument, however, extends beyond the proposition that the electorate of a genuine New Politics party is characterised by a typical New Politics profile and corresponding attitudinal orientations. In order to provide evidence for the argument that we are indeed confronted with a distinctly new type of political party we need to demonstrate that it is clearly far removed from all other relevant parties in a given system on all relevant dimensions of the ideal type.

The subsequent analysis pursues both aims. First, we will analyse the social structure of German party support. Then, we take a close look at the belief system of Green voters. Finally, the problem of distinctiveness is addressed.

Before the various facets of the social structure of German party support are discussed, it appears necessary to consider the nature of sociological categories. Usually they are designed to measure just one specific aspect of an individual's social existence or his or her specific living conditions. Such a specific property may be shared by many others who are antithetical on almost all other aspects. Hence, we need a multitude of measures that inform us about a whole range of socio-structural variables in order to be able to say something meaningful about a person's likely political outlook or a political party's specific electoral profile.

In addition, many categories are far from being 'in tune' with the theoretical debate and the social reality. The category 'white collar worker' (Angestellter), for example, comprises all shades of white collar workers from those with relatively low qualifications up to those in managerial positions. It does not differentiate between positions that require extensive qualifications and, to use an extreme example, an employee in a supermarket. However, the exigencies of survey research often do not permit a large number of categories when interrelations between variables are analysed, because cell entries would become too small in many cases.

The way out of this dilemma is to combine different variables in order to obtain a more realistic image of social reality. Social class alone does not give us much information about a party's electorate. However, if we can demonstrate that a certain group tends to be white collar, young and highly educated, we have already excluded many people who would still be in the category of white collar. Obviously, this means that we cannot expect very pronounced differences between the parties for all variables. On the contrary, it is only the specific combination of a number of variables that can demonstrate a party's position in the party system.

A straightforward method of combination is the construction of additive indices. Hence, the last section of this chapter will present such an index that combines a large number of relevant variables into one concise multivariate measure. Although six Allbus surveys (1980, 1982, 1984, 1986, 1988, 1990) and the Eurobarometers 21, 25 and 31a (1984, 1986, 1989) have been analysed, the presentation will be limited primarily to the most recent results. The remarkable stability of the underlying patterns makes a more comprehensive presentation of the empirical results largely superfluous. Furthermore, our primary focus is on the composition of the parties' electorates, which means that fluctuations in party strength, caused by the actual timing of the surveys, are not important. Of course, this argument is based on the (reasonable) assumption that a party's electoral appeal will normally vary fairly evenly across different segments of the population. Finally, a comprehensive presentation of longitudinal data would jeopardise the readability of this chapter. Hence, only in cases of significant change over time will such data be presented. Furthermore, the almost complete absence of any substantial change in the Green electoral profile will be demonstrated through a number of diagrams and the results of the electorate index, which summarises the most important aspects of the Green electoral profile. It needs to be emphasised that analyses of the 1990 Bundestag elections have not found important structural explanations for the failure of the West German Greens to overcome the 5 per cent hurdle. On the contrary, whereas the profile of the West German Green electorate has remained stable, the overall electoral appeal of the party had declined as a result of a combination of those political factors which have been addressed above (Schultze, 1991; Gibowski and Kaase, 1991).

There is only one factor which undermines the stability of the underlying patterns – the FPD. Having played the classic role of a pivotal party almost since the foundation of the Federal Republic, the Liberals underwent an unavoidable

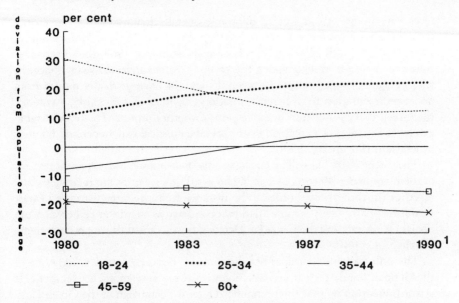

Figure 5.1: Green Voters – Overrepresentation of Age Cohorts (postal ballot and West
   Berlin not included).
Note: 1. West Germany only.
Source: Representative Electoral Statistics.

process of electoral change after they left the social-liberal coalition and joined
forces with the Christian Democrats. This means that – in general – the Liberal
electorate was closer to the SPD support in 1980 and 1982 than afterwards.

A PARTY OF THE EDUCATED CLASS?: THE SOCIAL STRUCTURE OF GERMAN PARTY SUPPORT

The following pages are concerned with an analysis of the social profiles of
German party support. According to the ideal type developed in the previous
chapter, the analysis will be guided by the question to what extent Green support
is concentrated in a young, urban, highly educated, new middle class electorate.

   Youth is probably the single most pronounced characteristic of Green voters.
The importance of the age factor is beyond academic debate, although the actual
causal function of age for the emergence of the New Politics is still controversial:
some authors argue that we are essentially confronted with a generational conflict that is likely to recede once the core groups get older and more mature.
Alternatively, others adhere to the socialisation thesis and maintain that the
younger generations are injecting fundamentally new values and behavioural
styles into the fabric of society. In this view, a New Politics adherent will keep
faith with a New Politics party even when he or she moves into a higher age
category. Analyses of the 1987 and 1990 Bundestag elections support the latter
argument: the Green Party scored its best results among those 25 to 34 years old.
The youngest cohort, which has been socialised under conditions of economic

recession, though still in very comfortable overall circumstances – came only second (Forschungsgruppe Wahlen, 1987b, p. 261; Jesse, 1987, p. 238f.; Schultze, 1987, p. 12, Schultze, 1991, p. 79). Four years earlier, in 1983, the Greens had achieved their best results among the group of voters under 25 years of age. In addition, middle-aged people between 35 and 44 have gradually moved from under-representation to over-representation (Figure 5.1). Obviously, a vote for the Green Party is not just an expression of youthful unrest. To a considerable extent, it can also be explained by the specific political experiences of different generations (Poguntke, 1990b).

The Green Party has still by far the youngest electorate. More than two-thirds of them are under 36 years of age. Whereas all other parties are relatively close together (in the expected order!), the distance from the Greens to the nearest established party (SPD) is more than twice as large as the distance between the Social Democrats and the Christian Democrats, who are at the opposite extreme (Table 5.2).

The only variable that does not discriminate between parties is *sex*: none of the German Bundestag parties has a noteworthy sex bias among its electorate. It is worth mentioning that the pronounced feminist campaign of the Green Party has not had the effect of improving significantly the party's electoral attraction for women. Whether it has served to prevent the defection of radical feminist Green voters is a question which can hardly be answered empirically. However, there are indications that the Greens have become somewhat more attractive for women under 35 in recent years (Kolinsky, 1988; Forschungsgruppe Wahlen, 1990a).

Social class is certainly one of the most important factors that determine individual behaviour and hence voting preferences. It is not only that social class is still hereditary to a considerable extent, telling us much about the probable living conditions of an individual during the formative years of political socialisation. Social class also gives us important information about present living conditions, the 'situational factors' that influence political action.

Table 5.3 gives a complete account of the social situation of German party supporters. The measure is based on the individual, not on the occupation of the head of household. The Green Party can count on its strongest support in those quarters of society that are particularly open to ideas associated with the New Politics: students, people in white collar positions, and civil servants, who enjoy absolute job security in Germany.

However, compared to the data from 1984, the social profile of the Greens has lost some of its distinctiveness. The proportions of civil servants and white collar workers have declined somewhat. Given the exceptional political developments of the year 1990 and the fact that the 1988 Allbus data still show the familiar over-representation of these social categories, it can be assumed that this does not yet signify a stable trend.

It has been suggested that the electoral success of the Greens can primarily be explained by the specific situation of the members of a counter-élite who see

Table 5.2: The Age Composition of Party Support (%).[1]

	CDU/ CSU	SPD	FDP	Greens	Potential Voters
Under 36	21.7	36.1	25.3	67.9	33.6
36 – 55	35.2	34.6	44.4	26.1	34.9
Over 55	43.1	29.3	30.3	6.0	31.5
Total per cent	35.1	42.2	9.7	10.8	
N	870	1047	241	268	2482

Missing cases: 569
Average age: CDU/CSU 51.7; SPD 45.2; FDP 47.3; Greens 32.8; population mean 46.3.
Note:
1. See Appendix for detailed information on the database of this chapter. Unless specified otherwise, all contingency tables presented in this chapter are significant on the
0.001-level (chi-square test). All tables are based on the 'potential voters', which
means that only the categories 'don't know', 'would not vote' and 'no answer' were
coded missing. Although they have been omitted from the tables, totals include minor
parties, because the profile of all potential voters is a more meaningful point of
reference for comparison than the profile of only those who intend to vote for one of
the relevant parties, i.e. CDU/CSU, FDP, SPD, and Greens.
Source: Allbus, 1990.

Table 5.3: The Social Composition of Party Support (%).

	CDU/ CSU	SPD	FDP	Greens	Potential Voters
Self-employed	6.3	3.4	9.3	4.2	5.1
Civil servants[1]	5.7	6.0	7.6	4.6	5.8
White collar[2]	21.4	25.1	29.5	25.6	24.3
Workers	10.6	14.3	7.6	10.7	12.2
Students[3]	4.5	9.0	6.7	25.2	9.0
Housewives/men	17.4	17.4	14.8	14.9	16.9
Unemployed	1.3	1.6	1.3	3.8	1.8
Retired	29.1	20.7	20.3	3.4	21.6
Other[4]	3.5	2.4	3.0	7.6	3.4
Column total	100.0	100.0	100.0	100.0	100.0
Total per cent	35.0	42.3	9.7	10.7	
N	885	1035	237	262	2445

Missing cases: 606
Notes:
1. 'Beamte'; includes professional soldiers.
2. 'Angestellte'.
3. Includes the category 'in education' (1.5 per cent).
4. Includes farmers, family members of self-employed ('mithelfende Familienangehörige'),
other non-employed persons and men doing their military or social service.
Source: Allbus, 1990.

their 'legitimate' career expectations frustrated by the structural saturation of the respective segments of the labour market: state bureaucracies, the educational sector, but also many other academic professions (Bürklin, 1984, pp. 45ff., 201f.; 1985a; 1985b). Even more pronouncedly, Alber (1985, p. 220) identifies the typical Green voter as young, highly educated, but unemployed or outside the labour market.

While it is true that a disproportionately high number of Green supporters are still in education, the largest portion of the Green electorate is in a new middle class – and hence relatively secure – position. Consequently, we have to explain the phenomenon that people whose personal economic expectations are almost diametrically opposite vote for the same party.

This – at first sight – incoherent or even contradictory impression is amplified if we take a look at the income distribution of German party supporters (Table 5.4). A large number of Green voters are in low income brackets. Clearly, this is largely a function of the age structure of Green Party support: many Green voters are still in education or at the beginning of their professional careers necessarily earning comparatively small incomes. Although this can hardly be interpreted as an indicator of economic deprivation, it is certainly true that these individuals are not in a comfortable and secure economic situation. On the other hand, there is also a substantial proportion of Green voters in the higher income brackets.[3]

Apparently, both economic security and insecure career prospects allow for Green voting. (Czada, 1990, p. 150). One explanation is that the career prospects of school leavers and university graduates are better than some analysts make them out to be. A high level of education is still the most important precondition for getting a well-paid and relatively secure job in Germany. In addition, it seems plausible that the specific conditions of university life make students quite indifferent to economic hazards or to the problems of the labour market (Cotgrove and Duff, 1980, pp. 340ff.). After all, they are the electoral group that is most detached from the production process. Hence, it could be argued that it is not economic deprivation (Bürklin, 1984, p. 47) but the distance from the production process which makes students susceptible to ideas associated with the New Politics. It is certainly not accidental that this distance to the production process is also typical for civil servants and many members of the new middle class.

According to the deprivation thesis, the unemployed should be particularly attracted by the Green Party.[4] While they are over-represented among Green voters (Table 5.3), they do not make up a dominant portion of the Green electorate. Also, the large number of young Green supporters has to be taken into account. The Greens, more than other parties, will have a certain number of supporters who have just left school, university or the army and are in the process of looking for a job, applying for a job, or waiting for a place at university.In sum, when all these aspects are taken into consideration, the data do not support the argument that a substantial portion of Green voters belong to an 'academic proletariat'.

There are a number of reasons why New Politics supporters should be highly

Table 5.4: The Income Structure of Party Support: Monthly Net Income Per Capita in German Marks (%).

	CDU/ CSU	SPD	FDP	Greens	Potential Voters
No Income	15.7	15.9	11.3	18.2	15.6
Under 1,000	14.0	16.3	14.4	31.3	17.0
Under 2,000	26.8	32.0	23.1	23.8	31.9
Under 3,000	23.8	22.7	22.6	16.4	28.5
Over 3,000	19.6	13.1	28.7	10.3	16.5
Total per cent	34.3	43.1	9.7	10.6	
N	693	869	195	214	2,018

Missing cases: 1,033
Source: Allbus, 1990.

Table 5.5: Levels of Education and Party Support: Highest-Level Final Exam (%).

	CDU/ CSU	SPD	FDP	Greens	Potential Voters
Hauptschule[1]	52.4	53.3	31.4	26.0	47.9
Mittlere Reife	24.7	22.1	29.3	24.0	24.1
Abitur[2]	20.0	23.0	38.9	49.6	26.1
Total per cent[3]	35.1	42.1	9.8	10.7	
N	858	1,028	239	262	2,443

Missing cases: 608
Notes:
1. Unlike in most other Western countries the German education system is rigidly structured and distinguishes between three levels of school achievement: 'secondary modern school' (Hauptschule, 9 years); 'O levels' (Mittlere Reife, 10 years); 'A levels' (Abitur, 13 years).
2. Includes Fachhochschulreife, which is awarded after the successful completion of the 12th year at Gymnasium (grammar school) or after the final year of a special 'Fachoberschule'.
3. Columns do not add up to totals because the category 'no final exam passed' (1.9 %) has been excluded.
Source: Allbus, 1990.

educated (see Chapter 3). In general, they belong to the politically active and participatory part of the population – characteristics which are furthered by a high level of education. Also, education is the most important indicator of formative affluence (Inglehart, 1977, p. 73), which is the central precondition for the formation of postmaterialist value orientations.

Again, our expectations are met convincingly (Table 5.5). People with medium and high levels of education have a disproportionately large share of the

Table 5.6: German Party Support: Size of Community (%).

	CDU/ CSU	SPD	FDP	Greens	Potential Voters
Under 20,000[1]	44.8	35.1	30.3	29.9	37.7
Under 100,000	24.6	22.5	24.9	20.9	23.2
Over 100,000	30.7	42.3	44.8	49.3	39.1
Total per cent	35.0	42.3	9.7	10.8	
N	871	1,051	241	268	2,487

Missing cases: 718
Note:
1. In the wake of the administrative reform of the 1970s, small villages have been combined to towns. Hence, communities with fewer than 20,000 inhabitants are frequently made up of even smaller, more parochial entities.
Source: Allbus, 1990.

Table 5.7: Value Orientations of German Party Support (%)[1].

	CDU/ CSU	SPD	FDP	Greens	Potential Voters
Postmaterialist	15.2	37.1	31.9	70.2	32.1
Mixed	64.2	50.1	58.7	25.7	53.5
Materialist	20.7	12.8	9.4	4.2	14.3
Total per cent	35.0	42.3	9.6	10.8	
N	857	1,035	235	265	2,446
Postmaterialists minus materialists	−5.5	24.3	22.5	66.0	17.8

Missing cases: 605
Notes:
1. The original four-item measure of Inglehart was used (Inglehart, 1977, p. 28). The wording of the question has been modified over time, whereas the actual items remained unchanged. The Allbus, 1990 wording reads as follows: 'In politics, one cannot have everything at the same time. You will find some goals on this list that can be pursued in politics. If you had to choose between these goals, which one is most important to you *personally*? And which one comes second?: maintaining order in the nation?; giving people more say in important political decisions?; fighting rising prices?; protecting freedom of speech?' (For a detailed discussion of postmaterialism theory, see chapter 3.)
Source: Allbus, 1990.

Green electorate. Furthermore, it has to be taken into account that the figures underestimate the true level of education of Green voters: the Green Party has a large number of young supporters who may be in their final year before the Abitur. However, they fall into the medium category despite their being relatively close to achieving the highest level of school education.

It is not surprising that the Green electorate is concentrated in urban environments (Table 5.6). Service sector employment and universities, the electoral strongholds of the Green Party, tend to be situated in large cities. Furthermore, urban areas usually have a high density of alternative subcultures which provide the necessary network of communication for the recruitment of new supporters and voters (Müller-Rommel and Poguntke, 1990a; Poguntke, 1992a; Veen, 1988).

As far as the purely descriptive part of this analysis is concerned, our theoretical expectations have been met convincingly. Green Party support is indeed young, urban, highly educated and new middle class. Our data do not support the idea that Green voters belong predominantely to an 'academic proletariat' (i.e. unemployed academics) who seek compensation for frustrating career prospects through political activism that attempts to question the overall societal *status quo* – because that academic proletariat holds the *status quo* responsible for its own situation. In addition, a brief glance at the Tables shows that the parties are aligned on an extended left–right continuum on which the CDU is always placed on the right-wing side whereas the Greens occupy the opposite end of this dimension. Furthermore, SPD and FDP are usually closer to the Christian Democrats than to the Greens. The problem of party system configuration, however, will be addressed in detail in a separate section below.

THE BELIEF SYSTEM OF GREEN VOTERS

a) Value Orientations

Postmaterialist Value Orientations

Postmaterialist value orientation is the single most important explanatory factor for the emergence of the New Politics and – as a consequence – the Green Party vote (see Chapter 3). For this reason, postmaterialists have more than a two-thirds majority among Green supporters (Table 5.7). However, this does not mean that having post materialist value orientations is almost synonymous with having a preference for the Green Party: only 23.7 per cent of German postmaterialists cast their vote for the Greens – which corroborates our suggestion of a multi-stage process that leads to a Green vote (see Chapter 3). It is therefore not surprising, that – in absolute numbers – more postmaterialists (48.9 per cent) vote SPD: other factors may override their postmaterialist orientation, or they may be satisfied with the gradual and selective Social Democratic adaptation to the New Politics.

Whereas all established parties are relatively similar with regard to the value composition of their electorates, the Greens are very different: if we look at the percentage difference between postmaterialists and materialists, they have a 41.7 per cent lead over the neighbouring established party, the SPD. The range between the established parties, on the other hand, is considerably smaller.

A longitudinal analysis since the foundation of the Green Party in 1980 leads

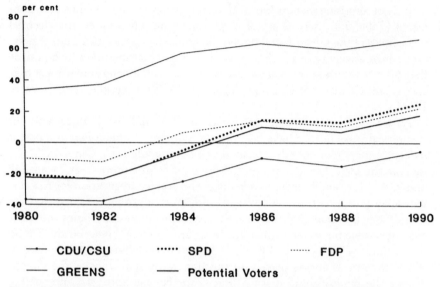

Figure 5.2: Value Orientations over Time – Postmaterialists minus Materialists.
Source: Allbus.

to two important findings: whereas there is a stable increase of postmaterialism in West German society (Inglehart, 1990a, p. 93), the relative positions of the political parties have remained remarkably stable (Figure 5.2). It is noteworthy that the SPD and FDP have swapped positions between 1984 and 1986. This was mainly due to a faster increase in the Social Democratic share of postmaterialists, which suggests that the SPD's strategy of programmatic adaptation to the challenge of the New Politics leaves an imprint on the composition of the party's electorate. In any case, the high proportion of postmaterialist FDP voters is remarkable, because it indicates a gap between electorate and party élites. After the change of coalition partners, the party leadership steered an unambiguous Old Politics course. Despite this fact, party loyalties proved to be strong enough to ensure enduring support from voters whose political preferences were in many respects not very close to FDP party policies. On the other hand, we must not forget that we are presently discussing value orientations which are only indirectly relevant for political preferences and voting behaviour. Many electoral studies show that economic policies still play the dominant role. And the composition of the electorate is just one part of the rather complex picture that makes up a political party.

Religious Orientations

Religious orientations are at least as central to individual personality as political values; and they are politically highly relevant (Smith, 1980, pp. 17ff.). Knowledge of the value profile of German party support makes the prediction of the religious outlook of the German electorate easier: empirically, frequent church attendance is conducive to materialist value orientations (Inglehart, 1977, p. 89)

Table 5.8: Church Affiliation by Party Support: Church Membership and Church Attendance Combined (%).[1]

	CDU/ CSU	SPD	FDP	Greens	Potential Voters
Protestant[2]	34.4	40.5	48.9	33.0	38.1
Catholic	51.0	30.2	27.1	23.0	36.8
No church affiliation	14.6	29.3	24.0	44.1	25.1
Total per cent	35.5	41.8	9.5	10.8	
N	855	1,007	229	261	2,407

Missing cases: 644[3]

Notes:
1. In the Federal Republic, church membership is acquired through one's being baptized as a child. Many retain their church membership out of habit despite their indifference towards religion. Therefore, all formal church members who never attend religious services were coded 'no church affiliation'.
2. Includes Protestant Free Churches.
3. The categories 'Other Christian Churches' (1.0 per cent) and 'Other Religious Communities' (0.3 per cent) have been defined as missing.

Source: Allbus, 1990.

and therefore not likely to be positively related to voting for a New Politics party.

At first sight this may be surprising, since religion could be considered as a classic case of non-materialist orientation. The confusion is caused partly by the unfortunate labelling of Ingelhart's value types, which emphasises the economic aspects of value change. However, postmaterialism does not only mean the downgrading of economic goals. Equally importantly, it is about the pursuit of individual autonomy, self-realisation and self-determination (see Chapter 3). The conflict with the relatively rigid authority structures of organised religion is evident. But also the intrinsic logic of religion is hard to reconcile with these emancipatory goals. After all, religiousness entails in most cases acceptance of a set of clearly defined, frequently moral, rules. Even if the individual is no longer under external, institutional control, the conduct of personal life is, to an extent, subjected to normative control through a set of standards that are not self-determined in the first place. It goes without saying that different denominations vary in this respect, and there is one current of progressive Protestantism that emphasises personal responsibility for the conduct of individual life very strongly.

It is not surprising, from this perspective, that the Greens are by far the most secularised party (Table 5.8). The established parties are situated at the expected locations: the Christian Democrats have the smallest number of voters who claim never to cross the doorstep of a church in order to attend a religious service. Again, the Social Democrats have moved closer to the Greens. Whereas in 1984 the range between SPD and CDU was only half as big as the distance to the Greens, the Social Democrats have now a location equidistant from both parties.

The widespread religious indifference among Green voters is remarkable

62

considering the important role progressive factions of the Protestant churches have played in various social movements – notably the peace movement – which have been constitutive for the success of the Green Party. The Protestant Church Convention (Kirchentag) in Hamburg that was held in June 1981 was one of the decisive milestones for the peace movement on its way to mass mobilisation (Brand *et al.*, 1984, pp. 216ff.; R. Schmitt, 1987, p. 19). However, it could be hypothesised that for these church-affiliated groups also intrinsic religious motivation plays a more important role than formalised participation in the religious life (R. Schmitt, 1987, p. 23). This would be consistent with their participation in the Church Convention, which is very much a non-formalised, participatory event.

If this were the case, we should obtain different results when asking for religious feelings instead of church attendance. Asked in 1986 to place them-selves on a 10-point scale ranging from 'completely religious' to 'not at all religious', only 17.1 per cent of Green supporters chose the four categories closest to the religious pole (Appendix 3). This result indicates that the overwhelming majority of Green voters are indeed not only distant from institutionalised religion but also quite indifferent to religious feelings as such. Authors who argue that the Green Party represents a new kind of spiritual or even religious movement seem to be misled by a relatively small core of religiously motivated activists (Hesse and Wiebe, 1988). They may attract a larger number of participants whose primary motivation is not religious but political. The church provides them with the necessary infrastructure for the pursuit of specific political goals, for example through provision of meeting rooms, links to like-minded initiatives, and the like.[5] There are two reasons why the churches are particularly attractive as 'organisational crutches' for new social movements. They are independent from political parties, and they have an excellent infrastructure of parish houses. Neither West German political parties nor trade unions are similarly well housed.

b) The Attitudinal Profile of German Party Support

Issue Positions

The first part of this chapter was concerned with the analysis of social character-istics which are known to mould value orientations of individuals. We then looked at two kinds of value orientations: directly political value preferences (materialism v. postmaterialism), and religious values that are only indirectly relevant for political attitudes.

Both influences – together with situational factors – shape political attitudes, that is, political orientations which relate directly to the realm of politics. This section is concerned with the exploration of the attitudinal profile of the German electorate. The bitter internal conflicts in the Green Party (see Chapter 7) would lead us to expect a relatively fissured attitudinal landscape. Earlier analyses, however, have identified a 'largely coherent political-ideological profile' of Green voters (Veen, 1984, p. 15). The search for consensual and contentious policy areas among the Green electorate in comparison with the established

Table 5.9: Left–Right Self-Placement (%)[1].

	CDU/CSU	SPD	FDP	Greens	Potential Voters
Extreme Left	0.6	7.6	0.4	14.9	5.2
Left	6.7	42.9	15.0	48.9	27.6
Centre	42.3	39.2	62.9	25.2	41.0
Right	36.9	8.0	20.8	9.5	20.2
Extreme Right	13.5	2.3	0.8	1.5	6.1
Total per cent	35.0	42.4	9.7	10.6	
N	861	1044	240	262	2,463
Mean score	6.69	4.56	5.70	4.20	5.40

Missing cases: 588
Note:
1. A 10-point scale was recoded into five categories.
Source: Allbus, 1990.

parties is the leading theme of the following pages. Since we want to remain within the framework of our argument, we will concentrate mainly on areas that are relevant from a New Politics perspective. There are a number of aspects that are relevant in our context: the mean position of the parties' electorates on the left-right continuum, their attitudes towards environmental problems and social justice and, finally, behavioural dispositions.

The *left–right continuum* is a conventionally-used summary measure of an individual's overall political orientation (Inglehart and Klingemann, 1976; Klingemann, 1972, 1982; Sartori, 1976). Knowledge of a person's position on the left–right continuum allows us to predict his or her political preferences for a whole range of more specific issues with a relatively low risk of error.

The inherent political quality of the New Politics suggests that the Green electorate should be clearly positioned to the left of the political centre. This expectation is borne out by the figures of Table 5.9. The Green electorate has the highest portion of respondents who place themselves in the left or extreme left categories. It is no surprise, however, that Social Democrats and Greens are relatively close to each other on the left–right continuum, because this measure does not distinguish between the Old Politics-oriented Left and left-wing positions inspired by the New Politics.

The data demonstrate that – as far as the electorate is concerned – the Green Party has now consolidated itself in a pronounced left-wing position. At the very beginning of the party's electoral career, things were more ambiguous. Spatial analyses of the electorate placed the party relatively close to the centre on the left–right dimension (Bürklin, 1981, p. 367). This indifference, however, was short-lived. When the conservative environmentalists who felt attached to Herbert Gruhl's vision of a right-wing ecological project left the party in 1980 and 1981, it soon became apparent that the Green Party's political aims necessarily implied a general left-wing orientation. As a result, the party occupied a firm

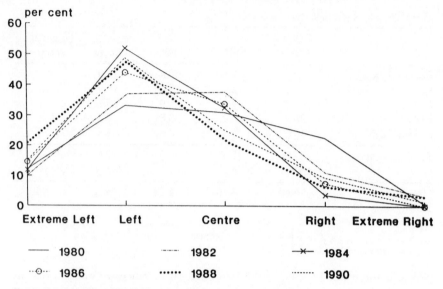

Figure 5.3: Ideological Profile of Green Electorate, 1980–90.
Source: Allbus, Eurobarometer 21, 1984.

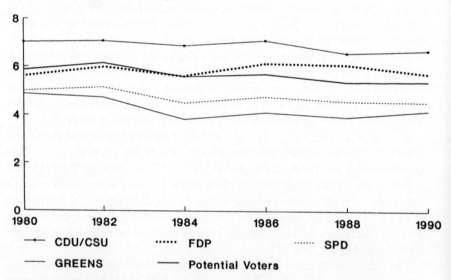

Figure 5.4: Ideological Profile of German Parties, 1980–90 (means of a 10-point scale).
Source: Allbus, Eurobarometer 21, 1984.

place on the political left from the early 1980s onwards (Veen, 1984, p. 4; Dalton
& Baker, 1985, p. 36; Forschungsgruppe Wahlen, 1983, p. 41; Roth, 1987, p. 8;
Fogt and Uttitz, 1984, p. 221). Figure 5.3 shows that this process of ideological
consolidation was more or less completed by 1984. At the same time, however,
Figure 5.4, which is based on the mean scores of the respective parties' elector-

Table 5.10: Social Justice and Environment: Personal Opinion / Environment: Personal Relevance.[1]

Index Means[2]	Social Justice (1984)	Environment: Opinion (1988)	Environment: Relevance (1988)
CDU/CSU	0.63	0.72	0.38
FDP	0.62	0.76	0.43
SPD	0.42	0.77	0.44
Greens	0.32	0.90	0.62
Mean (p.v.)[3]	0.50	0.76	0.43
N (p.v.)	1,984	1,914	1,939

Notes:
1. See appendix 2 for details of index construction. A high score signifies satisfaction with the social system, perception of a high degree of environmental pollution, and high personal relevance of pollution. The indices are standardised by the number of variables, range 0–1.
2. For strenth of parties see table 1, appendix.
3. p.v.: potential voters.
Source: Allbus, 1984/1988.

ates, demonstrates that the overall pattern has been remarkably stable since the foundation of the Green Party.

Any discussion of the parties' positions on the left–right dimension would be meaningless, however, if different sections of the electorate understood this concept in fundamentally different ways. The first index in Table 5.10 combines several questions that refer to the respondent's perception and evaluation of social justice in the Federal Republic. The result shows convincingly that the Green electorate is by no means indifferent towards certain traditional Old Politics concerns with the distribution of wealth, income and opportunities. Green voters also conceptualise their own position on the left–right continuum in economic terms. As was to be expected, they are most sceptical about the fairness and justness of German society. Also, it is no surprise that the Social Democrats are relatively close to the Greens in this specific policy arena. Although the data are from 1984, there is no reason to suggest that this should have changed substantially over the course of six years – particularly since virtually all other patterns have remained very stable. This proposition is corroborated by a result from the 1990 Allbus survey, where 71.7 per cent of potential Green voters regarded the class conflict in West Germany as 'strong' or 'very strong' (SPD: 65.2 per cent).[6]

Concern with the state of the *environment* was the dominating motivational force for the formation of the Green Party in its early stages of development. Consequently, Green voters should be more attentive to environmental problems than supporters of other parties. Two dimensions of environmental concern were tested. The index 'Environment: Opinion' (Table 5.10) measures the respondent's evaluation of the magnitude of environmental hazards, whereas the third column ('Environment: Relevance') gives us the extent to which someone feels personally affected and troubled by environmental damage.

The mere awareness of a certain problem does not automatically have an impact on an individual's behaviour. Only if someone feels strongly about a certain grievance is this likely to induce behaviour aimed at reducing the dissonance between norms and reality. It is therefore reasonable to expect Green voters to feel more personally involved with regard to the state of the environment than their fellow citizens with other party preferences. The argument is borne out by the empirical results: the distance between Greens and established parties is even larger when supporters are asked about their personal concern.

The exceptionally high degree of consonance between Green policies and the political preferences of Green voters is also highlighted if we look at the evaluation of various *social movements* which figure prominently in the party's self-declared political role as a mouthpiece for social protest (Table 5.11). The almost complete approval of sos Nature movements across all parties reflects the traditionally established, bourgeois character and the consensual approach of organizations like BUND[7] or the German section of the WWF. They are not social movements and are included here merely for comparative reasons.[8] Approval of the ecology movement, on the other hand, is clearly related to the respective party's position in the ecological debate. This indicates that the population does identify sos Nature movements only with demands for –widely consensual – environmental protection, not with the goals of an ecological politics. Manifestly, the distinction between environmental protection and ecological politics is not just an academic one (see Chapter 7). It is clearly anchored in the political consciousness of the populace (Hofrichter and Schmitt, 1991, p. 473).

Sympathy for genuine (R. Roth, 1985) new social movements – the peace, ecology and anti-nuclear movements – is distributed according to party preferences, although there have been significant changes in the late 1980s. In 1986, the electorates of all established parties were to a greater or lesser extent split over the assessment of these movements. Green supporters, on the other hand, agreed almost unanimously with their political goals. Compared with the findings from 1986, two important changes are noticeable. First, the overall level of approval of new social movements has risen. This is particularly true for the anti-nuclear movement, where the data clearly show a lasting 'Chernobyl effect'. Second, the electorate of the FDP is far more positive about the peace movement. However, it needs to be pointed out that by 1989, the peace movement had lost most of its polarising capacity, since the INF treaty had already been signed and the end of the Cold War signalled a historic turning-point in defence policies.

Since these three movements stand for the three central political themes of the Green Party, the data indicate a high degree of ideological consonance between the party and its support. However, it is important to draw attention to the fact that the Greens do not live up to their self-proclaimed role of the parliamentary arm of the new social movements. Particularly if we look at the data on potential movement activists, that is, those who would be willing to join a movement or who are already active (Table 5.12), it becomes clear that Green

Table 5.11: Social Movements and German Party Support: Positive Evaluation (%).[1]

	CDU/ CSU	SPD	FDP	Greens	Potential Voters
SOS Nature Movement	93.6	96.2	100.0	98.4	95.2
Ecology Movement	46.5	74.6	58.7	100.0	64.8
Anti-Nuclear Movement	41.1	71.6	40.5	91.4	59.7
Peace Movement	51.8	85.1	80.1	93.9	71.9
Total per cent[2]	36.3	42.3	3.5	8.0	
N	346	403	34	76	953

Missing cases: 249
Notes:
1. Original four-point scale was dichotomized. See appendix for details.
2. Due to different numbers of missing cases, totals vary slightly for each question. Totals given are those for 'SOS Nature Movement'.
Source: Eurobarometer 31a, June 1989.

Table 5.12: Social Movements and German Party Support: Possible Membership.[1]

	CDU/ CSU	SPD	FDP	Greens	Potential Voters
SOS Nature Movement	80.4	84.9	92.8	98.8	83.5
Ecology Movement	30.5	65.1	44.6	97.4	52.3
Anti-Nuclear Movement	26.3	58.1	39.2	91.0	47.2
Peace Movement	39.5	72.6	77.5	96.0	61.0
Total per cent[2]	34.9	43.6	3.8	8.0	
N	265	331	29	61	759

Missing cases: 443
Notes:
1. The categories 'is a member' and 'might join' were combined, because the first category had an irrelevant N (1.5. – 3.5 per cent of the total). See appendix 3.10 for details.
2. Due to different numbers of missing cases, totals vary slightly for each question. Totals given are those for 'SOS Nature Movement'.
Source: Eurobarometer 31a, June 1989.

supporters are not the most numerous force inside many movements (Pappi, 1989; Schmitt, 1990; Rucht, 1987; von Beyme, 1986).

Most of the data in Table 5.12 refer not to behaviour but to attitudes of the respondent about his or her own likely action – under circumstances that are left unspecified by the survey questions. The concept of behavioural disposition has been introduced in order to grasp this 'intermediate' social phenomenon which is clearly closer to action than an attitudinal statement (Barnes, Kaase et al., 1979, pp. 59, 79). Although it is not entirely uncontroversial to discuss behavioural dispositions under the general heading of attitudes, it would be just as question-able to introduce this aspect under a separate headline. In any case, the link

Table 5.13: Minority Rights and Party Support.

	Mean[1] N
CDU/CSU	4.08
SPD	3.51
FDP	3.18
Greens	2.34
Mean (p.v.)	3.57
N[2]	1,196

Notes:
1. Additive index of four questions. Mean of a seven-point scale. A high score indicates approval of the repatriation of guest workers in times of economic crisis and little tolerance of alien life-styles. See appendix 3 for wording of questions and strength of parties.
2. Only half of the sample were asked this set of questions.
Source: Allbus, 1990.

between the evaluation of these movements (Table 5.11) and the unspecified openness to potential membership is evident. As in Table 5.11, SOS Nature movements are completely uncontroversial and respected. More than 80 per cent of the electorate are prepared to consider membership in such an organisation. By contrast, the remaining new social movements can count on far fewer potential activists among the German electorate. Supporters of the CDU/CSU are particularly sceptical about possible membership in the anti-nuclear and ecology movements, whereas the peace movement is broader based among the German public.

The most conspicuous finding from the data on potential movement activism is the extraordinary homogeneity of the Green electorate. Obviously, Green voters agree almost unanimously with the strong emphasis of the party on unconventional political action which is a central characteristic of the political style of new social movements. Clearly, all other parties have much less homogeneous followers from this perspective. However, the gap between the Greens and the established parties has become smaller over the years and this means that the Greens will find it even harder in the future to have a decisive impact on movement politics.

Besides commitment to ecology and peace, striving for individual liberties, minority rights and libertarian ideals is a central element of the Green political agenda. The data in Table 5.13 show that Green voters agree with their party even on a political issue where the opposite position is apparently more popular. They strongly support the right of immigrant workers to remain in Germany including in times of high unemployment and they take a very tolerant stance regarding their way of life. This is one of the policy areas where the Liberals are relatively close to the Green Party, since it relates to classic Liberal freedoms. The attitudinal profile of the Social Democratic electorate, on the other hand, is influenced by the high proportion of manual workers, who tend to be more directly threatened by unemployment.

Table 5.14: Functioning of Political System (%).[1]

	CDU/ CSU	SPD	FDP	Greens	Potential Voters
Well	32.6	14.3	16.2	6.3	20.2
Fairly well	60.9	70.5	66.2	52.6	64.8
Needs much reform	6.1	14.2	17.6	38.9	14.0
Needs total change[2]	0.1	1.0	0.0	2.1	0.9
Total per cent	36.8	45.3	6.9	9.3	
	755	930	142	190	2052

Missing cases: 1,000

Notes:

1. See appendix 3 for full question.
2. The number of cases in this category is insignificant. Strictly speaking, no percentages should have been calculated. However, they are included here for the sake of completeness.

Source: Allbus, 1988.

So far, this analysis has portrayed the Green Party as a political force that is blessed with an attitudinally very homogeneous electorate that agrees to an exceptionally high degree with the party's political goals, which are unambiguously moulded by the ideals of the New Politics. A series of items from the Eurobarometer 21 (1984) and the Allbus 1990 supports this impression. In order to single out the most important 'identities' of the Green belief system, issues where more than 80 per cent of the Green sympathisers took the same position are listed below. The percentages of the closest party – in every case but one the SPD – is given in brackets. Green supporters do not agree:[9]

- that some books should be censored: 81.5 per cent (54.2 per cent)
- that students are social parasites: 86.2 per cent (66.0 per cent)
- that nuclear power should be developed further: 80.3 per cent (62.7 per cent)
- that immigration of people asking for political asylum should be stopped completely (neighbouring party FDP): 90.9 per cent (80.3 per cent)

and they agree:

- that homosexuals are just like others: 91.1 per cent (62.9 per cent)
- that military expenditure should be cut: 93.8 per cent (76.1 per cent)

Percentages close to the 100 per cent margin are very rare in survey research, especially for a large number of items. None of the established parties scored similarly high on any of these items. The only exception was the assessment of SOS Nature movements, which are completely uncontroversial in German society. The image of overwhelming consensus gets some scratches, however, if we focus on Green orientations towards the political system.

Table 5.15: Satisfaction with Democracy (%).[1]

	CDU/ CSU	SPD	FDP	Greens	Potential Voters
Satisfied	93.7	84.9	90.8	67.5	86.5
Not satisfied	6.3	15.1	9.2	32.5	13.5
Total per cent	36.9	45.3	6.8	9.3	
	761	934	141	191	2,061

Missing cases: 991
Note:
1. Dichotomised 6-point scale; see Appendix 3 for full question.
Source: Allbus, 1988.

Orientation towards Polity

Particularly in their early years, the democratic credentials of the Greens were less than uncontroversial. Frequently, they were alleged to express the tradition of anti-democratic political thought in Germany (Schmidt, 1986, Müller, 1984; Gotto and Veen, 1984). Their attitudes towards the functioning of the political system (Table 5.14) contradict such suspicions – at least with regard to subjective intentions of the Green electorate. Although there is a substantial minority which argues for far-reaching reform, there is virtually nobody who believes in a complete change in the political system of the Federal Republic. The figures clearly demonstrate that the Green electorate strongly favours reform – but within the basic boundaries of the present political system.

Whereas this question seems to refer to a general evaluation of separate objects of political support (Easton, 1975), that is, the constitutional fabric, its realisation and the political actors within the system, a question intended to measure satisfaction with the object 'democracy' in a purely general sense yields corresponding results (Table 5.15). There is a solid two-thirds majority among Green voters which is satisfied with West German democracy. Nevertheless, the proportion of dissatisfied is much higher than among the electorates of the established parties.

This substantial degree of discontent with the functioning of the German democratic system must not be confused with a general rejection of the constitutional fabric of the Federal Republic. Both questions also measure output orientations by referring to the 'functioning of the political system' or 'satisfaction with the regime'. Hence, they tap the juncture between diffuse and specific support for West German democracy (Westle, 1989). Since there is virtually nobody who supports fundamental change, these figures cannot be understood as an indication of a general rejection of democracy by Green voters. In fact, it has been shown elsewhere that the levels of diffuse support of democracy do not differ significantly between potential Green voters and the electorates of the established German parties (Westle, 1990, p. 275).

The less than enthusiastic evaluation of the performance of West German

Table 5.16: Trust in the Bundestag.

	CDU/ CSU	SPD	FDP	Greens	Potential Voters
No trust[1]	12.2	29.1	22.3	52.6	24.0
Neutral	20.8	24.7	32.1	26.8	23.5
Trust	67.0	46.2	45.6	20.6	52.5
Total per cent	43.8	39.9	4.9	10.8	
N	996	906	112	246	2,272

Missing cases: 732
Note:
1. A 7-point scale (see Appendix 3) was recoded into three categories: the mid-point was used as a separate category and the extreme values on either side were collapsed into one category.
Source: Allbus, 1984.

democracy is also reflected in Green attitudes towards the Bundestag. Asked about their level of trust in the German Bundestag, which refers to more specific evaluations of political actors within a central institution of democracy, Green voters are substantially more sceptical than supporters of other parties (Table 5.16). Despite the presence of Green MPs in the Bonn parliament there is a confidence gap between the established institutions and the anti-establishment voters. This is also true for the third power, the judiciary. More than a third of the Green electorate have no trust in law courts, whereas a similar proportion take the opposite view, leaving little less than a third in a neutral position (Eurobarometer 21, 1984).

The foregoing tables have shown that the dominant orientation of Green sympathisers towards the political system is best characterised by a deeply-rooted scepticism about the way institutions function (Veen, 1984, p. 8). It needs to be kept in mind, however, that political trust and the acceptance of political institutions is strongly influenced by the evaluation of incumbents and their policies. Hence, such distrust indicates dissatisfaction with the criteria that are relevant for the decision-making process rather than a rejection of the process itself (Bürklin, 1984, p. 178; Döring, 1990). Therefore, these attitudes should not be confused with undemocratic or even anti-democratic orientations. On the contrary, the acceptance of the rules of the democratic game among Green voters is slightly above the population average (Bürklin, 1984, p. 178). But some alienation from the political system exists, if every third Green voter feels unfree in Germany, compared with only 7 per cent of the total population.[10] Their alienation may be understood as a result of very high participatory and democratic standards which are permanently confronted with an unsatisfactory reality.[11]

The findings of this section are also relevant from a somewhat different perspective. Interestingly enough, the established parties, who are characterised by a high degree of internal diversity concerning political issues, reach relatively high levels of consensus when orientation toward the political regime is explored (Table 5.15). The Green support, on the other hand, is considerably less united when we ask about general satisfaction with the performance of the democratic regime. Questions about trust in central institutions of the polity yield similar results. Such lack of homogeneity is a familiar pattern for the established parties. Due to their 'catch-all' appeal, they necessarily attract voters with relatively diverse attitudinal structures. In the light of the extremely high consensus among Green voters on concrete political goals, however, this diversity needs explanation.

It could be argued that the orientations of the Green electorate mirror the central strategic conflict in the Green Party between the so-called 'Realists' and the 'Fundamentalists' as it has dominated the internal debate in the party for most of the 1980s.[12] On the élite level, there has also been little dissent about political goals, but bitter conflict over suitable ways and strategies to realise them. It seems reasonable to suggest that these strategic antagonisms are at least partially caused by different evaluations of the German political system: clearly, someone who is not convinced of the responsiveness and democratic quality of the system is likely to be less open to a strategy of reformist adaptation. In particular, such people should be extremely sceptical about their own participation within such institutions, particulary in governmental responsibility. They should be attracted by the fundamentalist strategy of working for a sweeping change of mass political consciousness in order to effect fundamental political change. Alternatively, so our potential argument goes, those who think more positively about the performance of democratic institutions should argue for a reformist strategy in order to change things through the given institutions – the classic 'Realo'-strategy of seeking coalitions with the SPD.

Empirical findings, however, do not support this line of argument. Overwhelming majorities of the Green electorate have nevertheless been in favour of red–green coalitions – despite the substantial degree of alienation from the established political process that is shown by the figures presented above. Before the 1983 Bundestag election, 94 per cent of Green supporters declared that they would be in favour of a coalition with the SPD if the election results facilitated such an arrangement (Forschungsgruppe Wahlen, 1983, p. 28). Despite exacerbating internal strategic conflicts in the following years, almost the same proportion supported the Realist position before the 1987 election (85 per cent) (Forschungsgruppe Wahlen, 1987a, p. 60). These results corroborate our argument that a significant minority of Green voters is primarily dissatisfied with the way democracy functions in the Federal Republic, not with the institutional arrangements as such. They may be less enthusiastic about reformism than those who think more positively about West German democracy. However, they are obviously more pragmatic than fundamentalist Green politicians who have always resisted the temptations of political power.

THE CONFIGURATION OF THE GERMAN PARTY SYSTEM FROM A NEW POLITICS PERSPECTIVE

As mentioned earlier, the attempt to demonstrate that the Green Party represents a new type of political party involves – for all relevant dimensions – two separate steps. We need to show that the Green Party comes close to our hypothetical model, and we need to provide evidence that all other parties are sufficiently distant from it.

The foregoing sections have focused primarily on the first step – the social and attitudinal characteristics of Green Party support compared to that of the established German parties. Frequently, but in a rather cursory way, we have referred to the underlying pattern that has emerged across all Tables. This problematic will now be discussed in detail. Whereas the relative positions of German parties have been analysed for separate variables so far, they will now be combined into several multivariate measures in order to obtain a clearer image of the overall format of the West German party system. Relevant criteria for the analysis of party system format are the relative positions of the parties according to the principal dimension(s) and the distances between parties. These can be measured multidimensionally – in terms of the political or social cleavages which are relevant for the electoral preferences of the population (Lipset and Rokkan, 1967; Zuckerman, 1982). Since we have concentrated on central and politically relevant social and attitudinal properties of the German parties, we can expect a clear structure to emerge.

We have argued that, theoretically, the New Politics dimension should be conceptualised as an addition to the left–right continuum that runs at an acute angle across it (Figure 2.1). So far the results have corroborated the expectation that the left–right-conflict is capable of 'assimilating' cross-cutting conflicts (Dalton, 1986, p. 444; Budge and Robertson, 1987, pp. 394ff.). Despite the injection of a whole set of new political issues through the emergence of the New Politics, the left–right continuum has remained the dominant dimension of the West German party system: those who show a high interest in the goals of the New Politics place themselves to the left of the political centre, and they accord with central themes of traditional left-wing politics, namely the problem of equality (Tables 12.9 and 12.10). Comparative research has shown, however, that there is a 'muted' left–right continuum in West Germany, which can be explained by the economically moderate stance of the SPD and the high relevance of East–West relations (Budge and Robertson, 1987, p. 394; Klingemann, 1987). The subsequent discussion will show whether the pattern holds if we focus on a wide range of issues and social characteristics.

The analysis of the relative positions of the German parties and the distance between them involves quantitative dimensions. This confronts us with a number of specific complications that are absent in the case of qualitative differences: in most cases it is not possible to define 'critical' values on sound theoretical grounds. A method which might intuitively be considered is the application of a 50 per cent or 75 per cent rule. However, what about two cases just above and just below this cut-off point? Furthermore, this method can work well only with dichotomised variables.

Additionally, any secondary analysis is plagued by the lack of survey questions which correspond to specific research interests. In our case, virtually none of the questions is suited to tap the difference between 'system-conforming' and 'system-transcending' New Politics issues. To give an example: many SPD-voters may well reject the statement that 'nuclear power should be developed further' but much fewer would approve of halting all nuclear power stations within the lifetime of a parliament. Hence, the measured quantitative difference between the various parties might often be less pronounced than the real ones.

Also, positions on specific issues are influenced by political events and hence susceptible to short-term fluctuations. This means that, whereas differences between parties might be more stable, absolute levels of responses may well vary considerably. Publication of the latest figures about the forest disease, that is, the decay of forests due to air pollution, is likely to inflate the overall awareness of environmental problems in the population, whereas the differential sensitivity of various parties' electorates will remain largely unaltered. Finally, it is highly unlikely that a party system consists only of parties relatively close to ideal types. Hence mixed types will occur, which means that quantifiable distances may not always be very impressive.

When all these problems are taken into consideration, it appears reasonable to adopt a pragmatic approach with respect to the measurement of quantitative properties. Survey data might not measure exact ideological or behavioural distances between parties' electorates, but it is perfectly capable of reflecting relative positions. Hence we should require two properties from our empirical results:

1. The relative positions of the parties should be consistent with theoretical expectations across all variables, and the Greens should be situated near the New Politics pole of an underlying continuum.
2. There should be clear quantitative distances between the parties.

Quantitative distances are measured by differences of means and percentage differences. For categorical variables, the calculation of percentage differences is the most straightforward and easily interpretable method, because they are comparable across variables and tables. Furthermore, this measure of association is insensitive to highly skewed marginals, which regularly occur, because the Greens are electorally much weaker than the large German parties (Reynolds, 1977, pp. 19ff. and 48f.; Blalock, 1981, p. 224).

Since we are dealing with survey data, we need to make sure that the differences between parties that will be presented in the following tables have not just been obtained due to statistical chance. T-Tests were used for interval-level data and chi-square tests for categorical data. In the latter case, contingency tables were always based on pairs of parties as independent variables.

Table 5.17: The New Politics Element in German Party Support: A New Politics Electorate Index.

a) Means	1980	1982	1984	1986	1988	1990
CDU/CSU[1]	0.19	0.20	0.21	0.22	0.19	0.29
SPD	0.26	0.24	0.26	0.28	0.30	0.34
FDP	0.29	0.30	0.33	0.29	0.35	0.36
Greens	0.44	0.50	0.53	0.53	0.57	0.53
Mean (p.v.)	0.25	0.25	0.27	0.28	0.28	0.32
N (p.v.)	2,319	2,305	2,231	2,125	2,030	2,358

Range: 0–1

Difference of Means[2]	CDU/CSU	SPD	FDP	Greens
1980		0.07	(0.03)[3]	0.15
1982		0.04	0.06	0.20
1984		0.05	0.07*	0.20
1986		0.06	(0.01)	0.24
1988		0.11	0.05*	0.22
1990		0.05	(0.02)	0.17

Notes:
1. For strength of parties see Table A 1.1, Appendix 1.
2. The index represents an interval scale which permits difference of means tests (see Appendix 1 for details).
3. Values that are statistically not significant on the 0.001 level are in brackets. Starred values (*) are significant only on the 0.05 level. However, it should be kept in mind that significance tests are sensitive to small numbers of cases. It is therefore not entirely surprising that some distances involving the FDP are not significant, because of the combined effects of a small N and a small distance of the FDP to its established neighbouring parties (Blalock, 1981, pp. 161ff.; Norusis, 1982, p. 47).

Source: Allbus, 1980–90.

a) Electoral Profile

All important social characteristics of German party support have been presented in the tables above. In all cases, the theoretical expectations were met convincingly. Such presentation, however, is plagued by the disadvantage that it does not provide us with a concise summary measure of the extent to which a party's electoral profile comes close to our expectation of an ideal New Politics electorate. All the variables analysed thus far can only give us parts of the puzzle. In order to come closer to a complete picture, we have combined the following variables that make up the core of the New Politics phenomenon: occupation, place of residence, age, education and value orientations.[13]

It may be objected against the inclusion of postmaterialism that we are combining essentially different categories of properties into one single index:

sociological characteristics and value orientations. Indeed, postmaterialism is strongly correlated with the remaining variables. From this point of view, it could be regarded as a shorthand measure for these variables. However, there is no specific theoretical significance attached to this index. We are just looking for a convenient summary of the most important factors that favour a New Politics orientation. All these variables have already been presented in separate tables above. A high score just means that an individual resembles our ideal type New Politics voter.[14]

The calculation of this index yields two important results. First, there is a remarkably stable tendency on the part of the Green electorate to become more pronouncedly New Politics-like (Table 5.17; see also Figure 5.5). The slight decline in 1990, which was, due to German unification, a very exceptional year, should not be regarded as the starting-point of a new trend. In the light of early Green history, the development is hardly surprising. In their founding phase, the Greens attempted to forge a very wide 'rainbow' coalition comprising conservative conservationists as well as 'greenish' Marxists. At that time, the party claimed to be 'neither left nor right, but in the front'. After a brief period, however, most conservatives left the party, which became an unambiguously left-wing political force (Table 5.9 and Chapter 7). After this conservative exodus from the party, right-wing, traditionally-oriented conservationists withdrew their electoral support for the Green Party. Some of them were attracted by the right-wing ÖDP (Ecological-Democratic Party) of Herbert Gruhl, who was one of the leading 'founding fathers' of the Green Party.

The results clearly show that early irritations about the political orientation of the Green Party have lost their impact on the party's electoral appeal. The Greens have succeeded in building stable and clearly identifiable electoral support. Analyses of the 1987 general election indicate that this process has continued and that the identification of Green voters with their party has grown continuously – in extent as well as in intensity (Forschungsgruppe Wahlen, 1987a, p. 9). Second, according with our theoretical argument, there is an impressive distance between the Greens and the remaining German parties, which are relatively similar from a New Politics perspective. Furthermore, the relative positions of all parties have remained very stable over the course of one decade.

It is noteworthy, however, that the electorate of FDP is – on average – closer to the profile of the Greens than the Social Democrats. This did not even change when the Liberals left the coalition with the SPD and joined forces with the Christian Democrats in Autumn 1982, although their move led to a considerable turnover in the electoral support of the FDP. At that time, many 'Left-Liberals' defected to the SPD and were replaced by more right-wing-oriented voters (Forschungsgruppe Wahlen, 1983, p. 37).

This highlights the fact that the New Politics is also a bourgeois, middle class phenomenon. Since our measure does not differentiate between old and young members of the new middle class, the FDP gets a score for its middle class character, which tends to correlate with another New Politics factor, that is, a

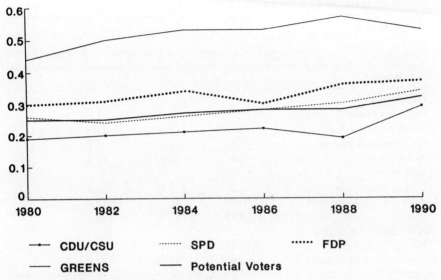

Figure 5.5: New Politics Electorate Index, 1980–90.
Source: Allbus

high degree of education. In the case of the Social Democratic Party, the considerable New Politics element (see Tables 5.2 – 5.7) is balanced out by very strong anti-New Politics forces: The old traditional working class stands against the young new middle class faction of the party.

b) Values and Attitudes

Whereas the foregoing section has been devoted to the electoral profiles of the German parties, we shall concentrate now on the attitudinal space between party electorates. The following table depicts the space between the parties, which are aligned according to the rank orders that emerged from Tables 5.7–5.16.

The first condition stipulated above is met convincingly: The Green electorate is always clearly situated near the New Politics pole of the underlying continuum. Furthermore, the gap is widest for all but six – theoretically intelligible – exceptions between the Greens and the neighbouring established party: it is no surprise that the Green electorate is relatively similar to Social Democratic voters when it comes to questions which refer to the traditional left–right dimension (Table 5.18). Opposition to nuclear power is another issue where Social Democratic and Green positions are, unlike in the early 1980s, relatively similar – which is reflected in a high level of sympathy for the anti-nuclear movement among SPD supporters. Finally, as mentioned above, the end of the Cold War has largely deprived the peace movement of its polarising nature.

Apart from the FDP, all German parties have extremely stable relative positions: the order CDU – SPD – Greens is never disturbed (condition 2). This is also true for time-series data. The fact that the FDP changes places with the SPD for

Table 5.18: Space Between Parties.[1]

a) Sequence 1

Variable[2]	CDU/ CSU	FDP	SPD	Greens
% Difference				
Postmaterialists				
minus materialists[3]	28.0	1.8*	41.7	
Democracy: Satisfaction	(2.9)	(5.9)	17.4	
Functioning of System[4]	16.4	(1.9)	8.0	
Not religious	9.4	(5.3)	14.8	
Evaluation:				
Ecology Movement	(12.2)	(15.9)	25.4	
Anti-Nuclear Movement	(-0.6)[5]	31.1	19.8	
Peace Movement	28.3*	(5.0)	(8.8)	
Membership disposition:				
Ecology Movement	(14.1)	(20.5)	32.3	
Anti-Nuclear Movement	(12.9)	(18.9)	32.9	
Difference of Means				
Index: Environment opinion	(0.04)	(0.01)	0.13	
Index: Environment relevance	(0.05)	(0.01)	0.18	
Left-right dimension	0.99	1.14	0.36	
Index: Social justice	(0.01)	0.20	0.10	

b) Sequence 2

Variable	CDU/ CSU	SPD	FDP	Greens
% Difference				
Bundestag: Trust[6]	20.8	(0.6)	25.0	
Membership disposition:				
Peace Movement	33.1	(4.9)	18.5*	
Difference of Means				
Minority rights	0.57	0.33*	0.84	

Notes:
1. Values that are statistically not significant on the 0.001 level are in brackets. Starred values (*) are significant only on the 0.05 level.
2. For details see relevant tables above.
3. Only amount is given, without signs.
4. Category 'functions well' was used for party the calculation of party distances.
5. This was the only occasion where the FDP was more to the 'right' than the Christian Democrats.
6. Category 'trust' was used for the calculation of party space.

some variables is consistent with theoretical expectations: the liberal electorate is often not significantly distant from one of the larger parties' voters. Although statistical insignificance may result from the low frequencies for the Liberals, it would be erroneous to disregard this phenomenon entirely. It may in fact be indicative of the role the FDP plays in the West German party system. As a pivotal party, the Liberals are bound to be relatively close to both established parties in mutually exclusive policy areas in order to be able to bring about a 'change of power' (Soe, 1985, pp. 118ff.).

It is hard to imagine that it is entirely due to chance that the Liberals are closer to the Greens on items that refer to classic Liberal concerns, that is, the question of toleration of minorities and the orientation towards a central institution of the state. The analysis of programmatic differences shows that the Green concept of the role of the state has strong roots in classic Liberal thought (see Chapter 7). In fact, it has been argued that the different views of the role of the state represent a secondary dimension in the West German party system (Pappi, 1984). The minor importance of this dimension becomes evident when we re-call the various coalition governments, which have – with the single exception of the Grand Coalition – followed the left–right pattern. Also, the coalition preferences of the German electorate accord with the left–right continuum (Forschungsgruppe Wahlen, 1983, p. 28; 1987a, p. 9).

To summarise, both conditions formulated above have been clearly met by the empirical analysis: the profile of the Green electorate corresponds to theoretical expectations (i.e. about the electoral profile of the ideal type), and it is sufficiently distant from all other parties. As far as the electorate is concerned, the Green Party represents a distinctly new type of political party. The results from time-series data have demonstrated that the specific characteristics of the Green electorate have become even more pronounced: at the end of the 1980s, Green voters are more New Politics-oriented, more left-wing, and more postmaterialist than in the early 1980s – although the 1990 data may indicate movement in the opposite direction.

Green supporters tend to accord with the political goals of their party. New Politics themes particularly are almost universally accepted by potential Green voters. For the established parties, on the contrary, the emergence of the New Politics means that their electorates are split to varying degrees over goals relating to important policy areas. Whereas the CDU/CSU still goes relatively unaffected, the SPD is facing troubled waters in its attempt to satisfy an electorate with a wide range of almost mutually exclusive preferences.

NOTES

1. The actual extent of the electoral set-back of the Baden-Württemberg Greens in the 1988 elections is difficult to assess because in 1984 the Land party failed to nominate candidates for three constituencies. Since voters have only one vote in Baden-Württemberg Land elections, the Greens could not get any votes from these constituencies in 1984.

2. Most studies cover only some of the aspects that will be discussed in the subsequent sections. See, for example, Berger *et al.*, 1985; Dalton *et al.*, 1985; Bürklin, 1985b,

1985c; Feist and Krieger, 1985, 1987; Fogt and Uttitz, 1984; Forschungsgruppe Wahlen, 1983, 1987a, 1987b, 1990c; Mez, 1983; Jesse, 1987; Schultze, 1987; Veen, 1984, 1985.

3. The outstandingly high proportion of FDP voters in the highest income category once again highlights the party's function as an old middle-class-based party.

4. The survey underestimates the true unemployment figures. In 1990, the official rate was 7.2 per cent.

5. This argument is corroborated by the results from a survey of Green Party delegates; see Chapter 6.

6. See Appendix 3 for exact wording of question.

7. By the mid-1980s, however, the 'Bund für Umwelt- und Naturschutz' embarked on a more aggressive and protest-oriented course, particularly when the project of a nuclear reprocessing plant near the Bavarian village of Wackersdorf led to a mobilisation of rural protest in a traditionally conservative area.

8. The wording of these questions is not entirely unproblematic. See Hofrichter and Schmitt (1991) for a detailed discussion.

9. All questions except those on nuclear power and political asylum, which are from Allbus 1990, are from Eurobarometer 21, 1984.

10. Results from a representative population survey commissioned by the Konrad-Adenauer-Stiftung in March 1984 (N = 3000) (Veen, 1985, p. 360f.; see also Fogt and Uttitz, 1984, p. 224).

11. Set against idealised norms, however, reality is inevitably unsatisfactory! Whether such radical democratic norms are likely to – unintendedly – erode the present reasonable functioning of democracy, because they are a challenge to its organisational structures, is of course another question.

12. See Chapter 7 for a detailed account of Green factionalism.

13. An additive index (Friedrichs, 1973, pp. 165ff.) was constructed. Each person was given one score for each of the following properties: postmaterialism, civil servant ('Beamter') or professional soldier or white collar worker ('Angestellter'), residence in cities with more than 100,000 inhabitants, Abitur or Fachhochschulreife, and age under 36. All cases were deleted if one or more missing variables occurred.

14. A similar approach was used by Manfred G. Schmidt, who found that 60 per cent of all young, highly educated, left-wing postmaterialists have a preference for the Green Party (Schmidt, 1984, p. 9).

6. The Green Party Activists

The significance of the exact social composition of a party's membership is debatable. Social class does not always give us unambiguous information about a person's likely political outlook. The Left Socialist parties in Scandinavia and France are prominent examples of Socialist parties which are not working class (von Beyme, 1982, p. 262; Cerny, 1977), and which therefore throw doubt on the extent to which sociological factors can explain the intricate linkages between social position, attitudinal orientations and political activity. Furthermore, the social gap between the electorate and those active inside parties usually widens as we go up the party hierarchy.

From the perspective of the New Politics, the social profile of the Green membership is therefore not over-significant in itself. What we are concerned with is detecting any significant differences between the party's electorate – which has been identified as being typically New Politics – and Green members and/or activists. For a better understanding of the ideological debates and the internal dynamics of the party we need to explore the social and political background of those who are active or at least members of the party. We will also take a close look at the belief systems of Green activists.

Data on party membership is generally rare and not very reliable (von Beyme, 1982, pp. 262ff.). In the case of the Green Party, the situation is even worse: apart from the bare numbers, no other information on party membership is available. Green preoccupation with data protection has served to inhibit any systematic membership statistics on the federal level. There was therefore no alternative in terms of this research to conducting a survey of party delegates at the national party conference in Offenburg, December 1985. In the light of what we know about the organisational structure of the Green Party, it seems reasonable to assume that party delegates – or so-called 'middle-level élites' – are a relatively representative cross-section of the party membership.[1] A very high membership–delegate ratio (approximately 1:40) supports this argument (comparable figures for the other parties are: CDU 1:865; CSU 1:146; SPD 1: 2494; FDP 1:197).[2]

The absence of an integrated database prevents any systematic comparison between activists of different parties comparable to that carried through for the electorates. But the data on Green Party delegates makes it possible to use results from the middle-level élite project (H. Schmitt, 1987), which covers all established German parties, as a point of reference throughout the discussion.

THE MEMBERSHIP OF THE ESTABLISHED PARTIES

a) Social Background

One of the most noticeable developments in the evolution of the West German party system is the trend exhibited by the Bundestag parties of becoming ever more similar socially. Although it would be an exaggeration to speak of an 'Einparteienstaat' (Narr, 1977) from a sociological perspective, all established German parties have been heavily based on the white collar segments of society since the early 1970s. As far as the Liberal party is concerned, things have not changed dramatically; the FDP has always been the classic bourgeois party. This influx from the middle classes did not bring about fundamental change for the CDU and CSU, which have always been able to rely on two social pillars, the Catholics and the middle classes. But the Social Democratic Party underwent a dramatic change that fundamentally altered the social identity of the party. The share of newly recruited members from working class homes decreased steeply, especially among the young generation (Feist *et al.*, 1978, p. 180). Whereas 55 per cent of new party members were manual workers in 1958, their share has gone down to 21.5 per cent in 1982. 'By 1982 barely one-fifth of new recruits were manual workers. White collar workers now formed the largest single group of new party members' (Padgett and Burkett, 1986, p. 73).

From a party unambiguously moulded and dominated by the working class the SPD evolved into a modern 'catch-all' party (Kirchheimer, 1969). Although the Social Democrats have still by far the largest portion of working class members, the SPD is no longer a working class party: Members with a middle class background are the single largest group within the party (Table 6.1).

Among those who hold party offices the social balance has changed even more. The SPD was literally 'taken over' by well educated white collar activists (Feist *et al.*, 1978, p. 180). Even in North Rhine-Westphalia, a state that is dominated by heavy industries, working class members were in a minority position as early as 1974: 50 per cent where white collar or self-employed compared with 44 per cent working class. Apart from the – politically irrelevant – precinct cashiers, working class members were under-represented to varying degrees among all other party functionaries (Feist *et al.*, 1978, p. 183). This marks a substantial change since the 1950s, when manual workers were adequately represented in local parliaments and up to middle-level party élites. The higher echelons of political power, however, even under Weimar, were already dominated by 'workers' functionaries', that is employees of the labour movement who normally came from a working class background (Heimann, 1984, p. 2,184). Correspondingly, the working class share of the party membership was estimated at 21 per cent in 1981 (Becker and Hombach, 1983, p. 59).

However, there have been insurmountable limits to wider recruitment on the side of all parties. The traditional – albeit shrinking – subcultural strongholds remained out of reach for the other side, that is active Catholics for the SPD and unionised Protestant workers for the CDU. As far as membership is concerned, the

Table 6.1: The Social Structure of Party Membership(%).[1]

	CDU (1978)	CSU (1978)	SPD (1980)	FDP[2] (1977)
Self-employed	25.4	33.3	4.7	19.0
New middle class[3]	39.7	34.5	35.5	44.0
(Civil servants[4]	12.3	13.2	10.7	14.0)
(White collar[5]	27.4	21.3	24.8	30.0)
Worker	10.7	14.9	28.1	5.0
Pensioner	5.2	6.8	8.7	12.0
Housewife	10.4	4.7	11.5	11.0
Student	6.6	4.1	6.7	9.0
Other	2.0			

Notes:
1. Although these figures are somewhat old, they can be assumed to be still relatively accurate, since membership fluctuation in German parties is traditionally low.
2. In the late 1970s the FDP was a typical new middle class party of Left-Liberalism. The internal balance of power has certainly shifted since the 'Wende' toward the self-employed middle class and economic Liberalism (Soe, 1985, p. 172).
3. Includes the following categories (Civil servant, White collar), which are given in brackets.
4. 'Beamte.'
5. 'Angestellte'.
Source: von Beyme, 1982, pp. 266ff.

Table 6.2: Party Conference Delegates–Subjective Class (1979) (%).

	CDU	CSU	SPD[1]	FDP
Worker	5	7	28[2]	2
Middle class	48	61	46	40
Upper middle class	39	28	23	53
Upper class	5	4	4	5

Notes:
1. The data were collected in 1978/79.
2. Normally, this includes many full-time trade union functionaries.
Source: H. Schmitt, 1987, p. 132.

established German parties did not lose their hold on their traditional clienteles, but they ceased to be dominated by these subcultures.

The middle class bias of all established German parties is even more pronounced if we look at the social composition of delegates to national party conferences. Although the 'middle-level élite' project[3] has used subjective social stratification, which is not directly comparable to the data in Table 6.1, the figures in Table 6.2 give a vivid impression of the social similarity of those active in party politics.

The most noticeable exception is the SPD, which has a substantial number of working class delegates, although it seems reasonable to suspect that some full-time union functionaries are 'hidden' in this category. Generally speaking, political activity in Germany seems to be the preserve of the middle classes. For a traditional middle class party like the FDP this does not cause problems. But the large German parties are far from being socially representative of their electoral support.

b) New Politics in Old Parties?

Despite the social similarity, there is still political conflict in German politics: it is a commonplace that social background does not lead automatically to corresponding political attitudes. In order to explore the different attitudinal profiles of party delegates, the 'middle-level élite' project commissioned a battery of survey questions that were designed to tap the contrast between the Old and New Politics. Party delegates were asked how they ranked a number of political problems in order of importane. A substantial weakness of the study, however, is the almost complete lack of questions referring to peace and disarmament (cf. H. Schmitt, 1987, p. 86).

In 1979, the middle-level élites of the established parties were still largely indifferent to the New Politics agenda. This indicates that the certainly limited responsiveness of the established parties to the issues of the New Politics was an important factor helping the emergence and success of the Green Party. However, there are noticeable inter-party differences that conform with our expectations: among issues of secondary relevance, SPD delegates consider environmental protection as the most urgent problem. The Liberals are – once again – split: support for nuclear energy and environmental protection obtained the same position on the Liberal list of political priorities. The Christian parties were clearly concerned with goals of the Old Politics (H. Schmitt, 1987, pp. 83ff.). However, things began to change somewhat in the early 1980s. A third survey, limited to CDU delegates, shows that by 1983, concern for environmental protection had gained considerable ground (H. Schmitt, 1987, pp. 88ff.).

The data indicate a certain degree of responsiveness on the part of the established parties to the changing political agenda. However, the study included only a few New Politics issues. Furthermore, the items were not designed to differentiate between varying degrees of commitment to New Politics goals. It would be erroneous, for example, to equate concern with environmental protection with support for ecological politics (see Chapter 7 for a discussion of the difference).[4]

GREEN PARTY DELEGATES: A SURVEY

This section is based on a survey of party congress delegates conducted by the author at the national party conference in Offenburg, 13–15 December 1985. Eight hundred and sixty-one delegates were officially registered;[5] 198 questionnaires were filled in. Since experience shows that not all registered delegates actually take part in Green Party congresses, we can assume a return of roughly 25 per cent.[6]

In order to facilitate international comparability of the data obtained, many questions were modelled on the Eurobarometer surveys. Unfortunately, this has led to a slight male bias, because the predominant use of 'male' endings in the questionnaire provoked some female delegates to refuse answers.[7] However, it is difficult to estimate the amount of error. Questionnaires returned by female delegates amount to 20.3 per cent of the total. If we assume that the delegate selection procedure does not produce a substantial bias in either direction, the proportion of female delegates should have been around one third (Kolinsky, 1988, p. 134).

There are other reasons for caution when extrapolating from results of this survey to the Green membership as a whole. The Green concept of membership is relatively informal. Unlike other parties, formal membership is not required for active participation in the party or for becoming a delegate for a party conference. Furthermore, there are indications of a built-in ideological bias that has encouraged fundamentalist over-representation at party conferences. For obvious reasons, mandates in local and regional parliaments are more likely to be held by Green Realists. The need for pragmatic, piecemeal politics is unlikely to attract many Fundamentalists, with their distaste for little steps. The link works both ways, however: even Fundamentalists may become more moderate through processes of institutional socialisation. Since time is a limited resource even for alternative politicians, those active in local and regional politics will find little attraction in spending their weekends on national party conferences. Given the severe shortage of active party members (Chapter 8), many mandate holders will nevertheless find it necessary to become delegates. In conjunction with the high membership delegate ratio, this suggests that a reasonable degree of representativeness of the delegates for the membership can be assumed.

However, there is another potential source of bias. Adherents of a particular political tendency may be less prepared to fill in survey questionnaires than others. Although this necessarily remains speculation, it may have caused a Realist bias in the sample. Fundamentalists, with their strong distaste for established politics, will probably be more inclined to dismiss survey research, since it is widely used by the established German parties. Whereas the delegate selection may work in favour of the Fundamentalists, therefore, their ideological reservations may have resulted in a slight under-representation in the survey. As far as the estimation of membership properties are concerned, the errors tend to cancel each other out. The remaining bias is hard to estimate. The Green Party congress, however, may have more fundamentalist delegates than are measured by the survey. In view of the extraordinary homogeneity that emerged for most questions, this is not a crucial handicap.

Most linkages and interrelations between social structure, attitudinal profile and electoral success, as well as the political performance of the Green Party, have been discussed in the chapter on party electorates. Therefore we can

Table 6.3: Social Composition of Green Party Delegates (%).[1]

	N	%
Self-employed	25	13.1
New middle class[2]	67	35.0
Worker	15	7.9
Student; services	46	24.1
Unemployed	24	12.6
Other[3]	14	7.3
	191	100.0

Missing cases: 7 (3.5%)

Notes:

1. Percentages in all subsequent tables are based on the number of valid cases. This is the most straightforward way of standardising across tables with varying numbers of missing cases. Furthermore, it corresponds to the presentation of the electorate data in Chapter 5. The category 'don't know' / 'no reply' was usually treated as missing. Exceptions will be mentioned specifically. All tables are significant on the 0.001 level (chi-square test).
2. The category 'new middle class' includes 'white collar worker' and 'executive, director' ('Angestellter' and 'Leitender Angestellter'). No specific category for civil servants ('Beamte') was included.
3. 'Other' includes farmers and fishermen, pensioners, housewives and house-husbands; 'services' includes men doing their military or social service.

concentrate the following analysis on differences between the Green electorate and party delegates – who can be taken as a reasonable sample of the membership as a whole. The data on the Green electorate presented in Chapter 5 was mainly from the 1990 Allbus survey, in order to be as up-to-date as possible. For the subsequent comparison of Green voters and delegates, however, the 1984 and 1986 Allbus surveys were used, because they were conducted around the same time as the membership survey. One caveat, however, needs to be issued at this point: it would be unreasonable to expect complete congruence between voters and party activists, because the profile of active party supporters will always be somewhat more pronounced. After all, they have taken a conscious, well-informed decision to get involved in party politics, whereas electoral choices are not necessarily made in the same manner.

THE SOCIAL BACKGROUND OF GREEN PARTY ACTIVISTS: IDENTITY OF VOTERS AND MEMBERS?

Occupation

Members of the various shades of the new middle classes are clearly the most numerous group among the delegates, closely followed by students and young men serving in military or civil duties (Table 6.3). Obviously, many individuals in this group are likely to come from a middle class background or to be oriented towards a middle class career. The dominance of new middle class values inside the Green

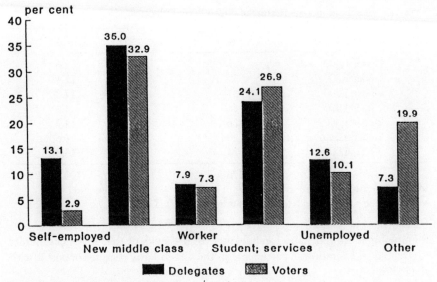

Figure 6.1: Social Composition – Green Voters and Delegates.
Source: Allbus, 1984; Conference Survey, 1985.

Party is highlighted even more if we take a closer look at the category of self-employed. Only four out of twenty-five are business owners, who are – as a social category – likely to be relatively distant from the ideas of the New Politics: their immediate dependence on the performance of the economy is not conducive to the development of New Politics-inspired political preferences. The others are self-employed members of the liberal professions who may not be all that different in their social and attitudinal moulding from members of the new middle class.

Although there was no specific category for civil servants, the identity of civil servants proved to be stronger than the categorising force of survey questions and a substantial number of civil servants mentioned their specific status on the questionnaire.[8] Some even noted their vocation as teachers. Taken together, these two groups represent 10.1 per cent of the total, which is a result worth reporting given the fact that this figure may underestimate the true number.

As was the case for potential Green voters, the unemployed are only slightly over-represented among Green Party delegates. Hence, there is little indication of an economically deprived counter-élite (see Chapter 5).

In the light of the self-proclaimed Green ideal of grass roots democracy, close similarity of the social profiles of voters and party activists is certainly a value in its own right. As far as social structure is concerned, the Green Party comes close to identity (Figure 6.1). Neither noticeable deviation causes any severe theoretical problems: The relatively large proportion of self-employed among Green Party delegates is owing to there being many delegates in the liberal professions. And the considerably larger proportion of voters falling in the category 'other' is mainly caused by the almost complete absence of pensioners from the Green Party conference. Given the 'ambience' of these conferences and the length of

Table 6.4: Household Income (Gross) of Green Party Delegates.

	N	%
Under 1,000	22	12.6
Under 2,000	37	21.4
Under 3,000	31	17.8
Under 4,000	26	14.9
Under 5,000	26	14.9
Under 6,000	8	4.6
Over 6,000	24	13.8
	174	100.0

Missing cases: 24 (12.1%)
Mean income per household (calculated from raw data): 3,600 DM.

the usual marathon debates (see Chapter 8), it is evident that it is much harder for the older generation to participate in the Green Party than to support it with the ballot paper.

Income

In principle, there are two ways of looking at income distributions: per capita and household income. Both methods give an imperfect impression of the actual financial situation of an individual. Household income does not control for household size (Table 6.4). Therefore, we cannot always be sure that individuals living in a high income household actually dispose of much money. A high household income may be a corollary of a high number of adult household members. Per capita income, on the other hand, tends to underestimate individual income because it does not differentiate between adults and children. Consequently, we need a joint interpretation of both tables in order to obtain a picture as close to reality as possible. In any case, survey data on income distributions need is to be read with particular scepticism, because people are often unaware of the difference between gross and net incomes. Furthermore, it cannot be taken for granted that they tell the truth. Nevertheless, there is no reason to assume that there should be a particular bias typical for Green activists or voters. We can therefore use the results for comparative purposes even if the absolute numbers may not be entirely accurate.

Most Green Party delegates live in family-sized situations, not in larger communes. The data is therefore comparable to that of other parties. The large number of people having a rather low per capita income can be explained by the large number of young delegates who are still studying, in the services, or at the beginning of their professional career (Table 6.5). It cannot be taken as an indication of deprivation or a lower social status (cf. Tables 6.3 and 6.7).

This interpretation is corroborated by the results given in Table 6.4. A large number of delegates live in high-income households with a monthly gross income of more than 5,000 DM (16.1 per cent). If we add those with 4,000 to 5,000 DM

Table 6.5: Income Per Capita (Gross) of Green Party Delegates.[1]

	N	%
Under 1,000	79	47.3
Under 2,000	48	28.7
Under 3,000	22	13.2
Under 4,000	12	7.2
Under 5,000	5	3.0
Over 5,000	1	0.6
	167	100.0

Missing cases: 31 (15.7%)
Note:
1. Computed from 'household income' and 'number of persons living in a household'.

per month, 29.2 per cent – almost one-third – live in very comfortable financial settings.[9] Again, the data do not support the argument that we are essentially confronted with an economically deprived academic counter-élite.

Unfortunately, the figures on income distributions are not directly comparable with the data on the Green electorate, because the Allbus survey measures net income. However, we can compare the underlying patterns of the respective distributions across the given categories. The figures in Table 6.4, representing per capita income, correspond roughly to the data on the Green electorate (Table 5.4). Both voters and party activists are most numerous in low income brackets – which can be explained by the age structure of the party. But considerable portions, presumably the older, have climbed up the income ladder quite a bit.

Education

A very high level of education of party delegates is common to all Bundestag parties: in 1979 the percentage of delegates from established parties with Abitur ranged from 64 per cent (SPD) to 82 per cent (FDP) (H. Schmitt, 1987, p. 132).

Although it is not entirely accurate to equate attendance at the highest-level educational institution with passing the final exam, it may be justifiable for comparative purposes. Furthermore, due to the required minimum age[10] of Green Party delegates, most of those who are still in education will either be close to their Abitur or already enrolled at university. Therefore, we can collapse the last three categories in Table 6.6 in order to obtain data that is comparable to the educational profiles of the established parties' middle-level élites and the Green electorate: 73.1 per cent of Green delegates have grammar school education. As is the case for all other parties, those active inside political parties tend to be more highly educated than the respective groups of voters (see Figure 6.2 for the Greens).

Table 6.6: Levels of Education of Green Party Delegates.[1]

	N	%
Hauptschule[2]	15	7.6
Mittlere Reife	38	19.3
Gymnasium	28	14.2
University	82	41.6
Still in education	34	17.3
	197	100.0

Missing cases: 1 (0.5%)

Notes:

1. Delegates were asked for the highest level of educational achievement or the last educational institution attended.
2. Unlike in most other Western countries the German education system is rigidly structured and distinguishes between three levels of school achievement: 'secondary modern school' (Hauptschule, 9 years); 'O levels' (Mittlere Reife, 10 years); 'grammar school' (Gymnasium, 13 years). In order to capture the difference between secondary school and O levels, delegates were specifically asked for this examination (Mittlere Reife), not for the type of school (Realschule).

Age

The age profiles of Green voters and delegates are almost congruent (see Figure 6.3). Two-thirds are 35 years of age or younger. Almost half of the Green delegates were socialised politically during the height of the extra-parliamentary opposition of 1968, the so-called APO period.[11] Six years earlier, in 1979, virtually nobody from the 'protest generation' (H. Schmitt, 1987, p. 132) was a delegate for one of the established parties. Evidently, this substantial lack of political integration and representation of a whole political generation is an important part of the explanation of the emergence and the success of the Green Party. After all, 1979 was the year when the Greens competed for the first time in a nation-wide (Euro)election.

One decade after the APO activists had called for the 'long march through the institutions', a mere 2 per cent of the protest generation had arrived at the Social Democratic Party congress (Table 6.7)! It is important to note, however, that we are not talking about the APO activists themselves: they were just a small minority of their own – 'affluent' – generation. But their vociferous political activity shaped the socialisation of those who were too young to participate actively in the student unrest: a 35-year-old Green delegate at the Offenburg conference was just 18 in 1968. The APO activists are submerged in the box of those who were between 36 and 45 in 1985. It seems reasonable to assume that at a Green Party conference the majority of this age-group is comprised of former APO combatants.[12] Frequently, they have been suspected of being the driving force behind the Green Party. But a brief glance at Table 6.8 shows that the Greens are not a party of former APO activists. They are only the third-largest group; behind the youngest cohort socialised during the period of the new social movements of the

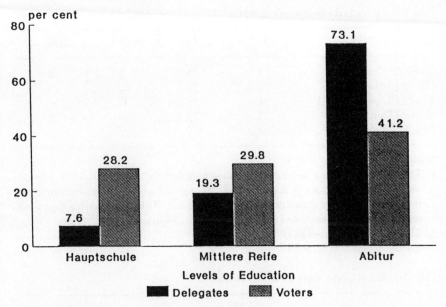

Figure 6.2: Education – Green Voters and Delegates.
Source: Allbus, 1984; Conference Survey, 1985.

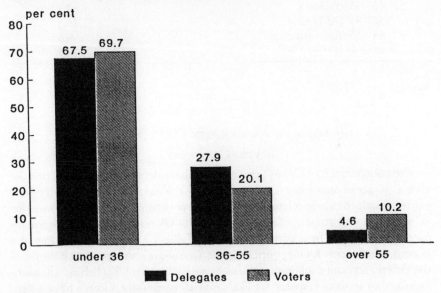

Figure 6.3: Age – Green Voters and Delegates.
Source: Allbus , 1984; Conference Survey, 1985.

1970s. However, their political experience has allowed them to play an influential role on both sides of the ideological trench warfare inside the party (van
Hüllen, 1990; Brand, 1987).

Table 6.7: Age of Party Delegates (1979) (%).

Age[1]	CDU	CSU	SPD[2]	FDP
Under 29 (Protest)	4	8	2	4
29 – 38 (Affluence)	17	22	25	28
39 – 49 (Reconstruction)	36	38	45	37
50 – 61 (Third Reich)	35	27	26	28
Over 61 (Weimar)	8	5	2	4

Notes:
1. The age categories are based on the assumption that the decisive phase of political socialisation takes place at approximately the age of 15. The categories correspond therefore with the important phases of German history: Weimar, Third Reich, phase of reconstruction, affluence, and protest (H. Schmitt, 1987, p. 133).
2. The data were collected in 1978–9.
Source: H. Schmitt, 1987, p. 132.

Table 6.8: Age of Green Party Delegates (1985).

	N	%
Under 26 (Movements)	45	22.8
26 – 35 (Protest)	88	44.7
36 – 45 (Affluence)	38	19.3
46 – 55 (Reconstruction)	17	8.6
Over 55 (Before 1945)	9	4.6
	197	100.0

Missing cases: 1 (0.5%)

THE BELIEF SYSTEM OF GREEN PARTY DELEGATES

a) Value Orientations

The concordance of Green activists on value orientations is almost breath-taking. It corroborates our argument that the phenomenon of New Politics parties is indeed closely related to the surge of postmaterialist value orientations in advanced industrial societies (Table 6.9). Obviously, such homogeneity cannot be matched by a party's electorate (Table 5.7). Apart from systematic reasons, which apply for all political parties (see above), the specific character of the Green Party can explain that the electorate is bound to 'lag behind' the party membership in some respects. Unlike catch-all parties, the Greens have a very distinct political profile that extends also to political style. This means that those who intend to engage in Green Party politics must be able to come to terms with this alternative style which predominates in internal party life. This may well deter many 'rational responders' from joining the party despite their approval of Green policies.

Table 6.9: Value Orientations of Green Party Delegates.[1]

	N	%
Postmaterialist	171	94.0
Mixed	9	4.9
Materialist	2	1.1
	182	100.0

Missing cases: 16 (8.1%)

Note:

1. Inglehart's four-item measure was used in the questionnaire; see Chapter 5, note to Table 5.7.

Table 6.10: Religious Affiliation of Green Delegates.[1]

	N	%
Catholic	37	20.0
Protestant	60	32.4
Other	2	1.1
None	86	46.5
	185	100.0

Missing cases: 13 (6.6%)

Note:

1. See Appendix 3 for full question.

As already mentioned in the preceding chapter, *religious orientation* is certainly as close to the core of an individual's personality as are political value orientations. Furthermore, both kinds of value orientations are interdependent (see Inglehart, 1977, pp. 221ff. and Chapter 5). Measurement of religious feelings, however, is not devoid of pitfalls. In the German case, a behavioural operationalisation would be misleading. Asking for formal church membership in West Germany does not yield much information: most people become church members through the decision of their parents to let them be baptised. Although there is a contracting-out procedure, many who are completely indifferent towards religion maintain their church membership from force of habit. Hence, the survey asked whether the respondent felt affiliated to a religious community, not whether he or she was actually a member.

For this reason, the data of Table 6.10 are comparable with the way in which the church affiliation of the electorate was measured (Table 5.8). In both cases, almost half of the respondents are fully detached from religious life. Among those who feel affiliated to a church, there is a noticeable Protestant overweight. In view of the engagement of some Protestant groups in various new social movements – notably the peace movement – this is not very surprising. However, the religious component of the Green Party is sometimes overemphasised by political commentators, as is shown by Table 6.11.

Table 6.11: Religion – Level of Importance (Green Delegates).[1]

	N	%
Great importance	9	4.5
Some importance	21	10.6
Only of little import	72	36.4
Don't know / missing[2]	96	48.5
	198	100.0

Notes:
1. See Appendix 3 for full question.
2. Includes those who claimed to have no religious affiliation ('keine Konfession').

Table 6.12: Democracy - Satisfaction Level (Green Delegates).[1]

	N	%
Very satisfied	1	0.5
Fairly satisfied	19	9.8
Not very satisfied	118	60.8
Not at all satisfied	56	28.9
	194	100.0

Missing cases: 4 (2.0%)
Note:
1. See Appendix 3 for full question.

Only 4.5 per cent of all party delegates can be considered to be strongly motivated by religious feelings. Together with those to whom religion has at least some meaning, they represent just 15.1 per cent of the delegates.[13]

b) The Attitudinal Profile of Green Delegates

Asked for their satisfaction with the operation of democracy, Green delegates reveal dramatic differences from Green voters. Whereas in 1986, the Green electorate was split down the middle when it was asked to assess the performance of the German democratic system (satisfied 50.4%; not satisfied 49.6%; Eurobarometer 25), almost 90 per cent of the party activists give the thumbs down (Table 6.12).

As was argued in Chapter 5, the response to the above survey question does not reflect a rejection of democratic governance. On the contrary, it indicates dissatisfaction with the actual realisation of democracy and with the results of the democratic process, that is, specific policies. It is nevertheless interesting to note that Green Party activists are substantially more alienated from the political process than Green voters. It could be speculated that this dissatisfaction with the way democracy functions in the Federal Republic represents an important motivation for becoming actively involved in politics. However, it is evident that the data do not tap the strategic antagonism inside the Green Party. Alienation from the political process does not automatically lead to the rejection

Table 6.13: Intra-Party Factions (Green Delegates).

	N	%
Don't know; no reply	36	18.8
Fundamentalists	23	12.0
Realists	65	34.1
Eco-Libertarians	4	2.1
Eco-Socialists	32	16.8
Other[1]	31	16.2
	191	100.0

Missing cases: 7 (3.5%)
Note:
1. Any other reaction to the question was coded 'other'.

of reformist, that is, 'realist', politics: Table 6.13 shows that there is a far more scattered distribution when it comes to attachment to party factions.

Throughout the 1980s, the public debate has referred to these four factions. Clearly, the main conflict was between Fundamentalists ('Fundis') and Realists ('Realos'), whereas the Eco-Socialists tended to coalesce with the Fundis and the Eco-Libertarians usually aligned with the Realos (see Chapter 7 for details). However, there is reason to suspect that the internal battle-lines were not as clearly drawn as the media coverage made them out to be. In order to obtain a complete picture the 'don't knows' were not excluded in this special case: they indicate that a respondent was not willing to identify with any of the factions. If we add those who reacted in any other but the pre-structured way to the question, 35 per cent of the delegates could not be assigned to one of the factions that seemed to dominate the internal Green debate. This result indicates that the factional strife in the Bundestag group and the federal leadership was not entirely shared by the party's rank-and-file. In December 1987 the so-called 'Basis' demonstrated substantial dissatisfaction with the ongoing trench warfare in Bonn when an emergency meeting was convened in order to find a 'modus vivendi' before the upcoming Land elections in Baden-Württemberg and Schleswig-Holstein (TAZ, STZ, 14 December 1987; Die Grünen, 1988a).

The reluctance of party delegates to identify with one of the party factions is expressed by a remarkable voting pattern at party conferences: motions that can be unambiguously assigned to a faction – so-called 'Strömungsanträge' – are often voted down irrespective of their actual political content. Very similar motions are often approved with large majorities – if they have been proposed by groups that cannot be identified easily with one of the dominant tendencies in the party.[14]

Irrespective of all these necessary qualifications, including a possible sample bias, it is an interesting result that, as early as 1985, the Realos seem to be the strongest faction – even if one allows for the fact that Eco-Socialists and Fundamentalists are most frequently found on the same side of the internal battle-lines.

Table 6.14: Left–Right Self–Placement of Green Delegates.

	N	%
Extreme Left	72	44.2
Left	72	44.2
Centre	17	10.4
Right	1	0.6
Extreme Right	1	0.6
	163	100.0

Missing cases: 15 (7.6%); Mean 2.5
Don't know/no reply: 20 (10.9%)

Table 6.15: Opinion: Income Differences Should Be Minimized(Green Delegates).

	N	%
Disagree completely	2	1.1
Disagree to some extent	10	5.5
Agree if anything	39	21.6
Broadly agree	71	39.2
Completely agree	59	32.6
	181	100.0

Missing cases: 17 (8.6%)

In the light of the apparent distance of many Green Party activists from any of these factions, it is not surprising that a centrist group (the so-called 'Grüner Aufbruch') gained considerable influence after 1987. In an attempt to overcome the exacerbating factional strife, it campaigned for a more consensual approach inside the party and tried to forge a broad 'centre-right' alliance. The centrist strategy had an overwhelming success at the Duisburg party conference of February 1989, where no outright proponent of fundamentalist positions was elected to the federal executive.

In any case, Green factionalism is obviously not directly motivated by conflicts over political goals or ideological positions: the subsequent tables show that the political preferences of Green Party delegates are exceptionally homogeneous – a phenomenon that is also typical of the Green electorate.

Although the Greens have always claimed – particularly in their early years – to be 'neither left nor right but in the front', only 10.9 per cent of the delegates consciously refused to place themselves on a left–right continuum (Table 6.14). The result shows that the Greens are clearly the most left-wing Bundestag party: 68.4 per cent of the delegates fall into the three most extreme left-wing boxes, whereas only 2.6 per cent are to the right of the centre (for the established parties, see H. Schmitt, 1987, p. 116).

As is the case for value orientations, the ideological profile of the Green electorate is – compared with the party delegates – less pronounced. Figure 6.4, which is based

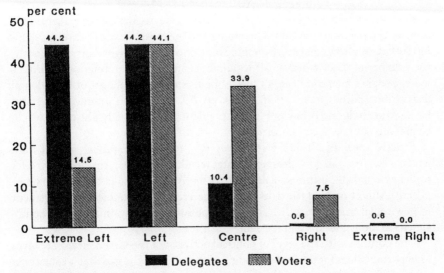

Figure 6.4: Ideological Profile – Green Voters and Delegates.
Source: Allbus, 1986; Conference Survey, 1985.

on a recoded 10-point scale, shows that the delegates have a clear lead over potential Green voters in the most left-wing category. Taken together, 88.6 per cent of the delegates, but just 58.6 per cent of the electorate, are left of centre.

Asked for their opinion on the existing income distribution in German society, Green delegates consistently opted for left-wing positions. The results in Table 6.15 are almost parallel with ideological positions. Like Green voters, party delegates are not indifferent to classic left-wing concerns in regard to distribution of income and wealth. It is interesting to note that female activists are more left-wing on average. With regard to their opinion on income distribution, however, they tend to be more right-wing than their male colleagues. Their understanding of the left–right continuum seems to be less dominated by an economic conceptualisation.

So far, we have discussed social characteristics, value orientations and attitudes of Green Party delegates. The data have shown that there are no differences between Green voters and party activists that could not be plausibly explained within the framework of our theoretical argument: since active participation requires a stronger identification with a party than voting, the ideological profile of party activists is normally more pronounced. The same reasoning applies to value orientations. Finally, it is a general pattern that activists tend to be higher educated than voters, because cognitive skills are an important precondition for active involvement in politics. With these exceptions, the profiles of both groups conform closely with our theoretical argument. However, one important aspect of our theoretical model needs still to be examined: the participatory behaviour of individual party members.

c) The Link to the Movements: Political Style

In the corresponding section on the party electorate, we have already mentioned some of the necessary caveats. The attempt to measure behaviour through opinion surveys is always plagued by a multitude of complicating factors. Frequently, the number of cases is too small to allow meaningful interpretations. Furthermore, people's memories cannot always be trusted. The concept of behavioural disposition (Barnes, Kaase *et al.*, 1979, pp. 59, 79) has an intermediate status between attitude and behaviour: the respondent is asked whether he or she would be prepared to take a certain action.

Strictly speaking, Table 6.16 mixes two types of empirical information: whereas the first category clearly measures recalled behaviour, the other two refer to behavioural dispositions. Taken by themselves the results are not very surprising. Almost none of the delegates is negatively disposed towards engagement in new social movements. It has to be emphasised once again that such homogeneity is rarely found in survey data.

The contrast with the level of political activism of the Green electorate gives us important clues for the understanding of the width of the gap that is sometimes visible between electorate and party élites. Only 3.3 per cent of the Green voters claimed in 1984 to be member of a citizen's initiative (Allbus, 1984). If the argument holds that frequent personal experiences with state repression make distrust of reformist politics more likely, it is not surprising that party activists are more fundamentalist than Green voters. As a result of their involvement in new social movements, they just had more likelihood of being drenched by police water-cannons than the average Green voter. Consistently, an overwhelming majority of the Green electorate has always favoured a coalition with the SPD, whereas this issue has always been highly contentious at party conferences (Forschungsgruppe Wahlen, 1983, 1987a).

However, Table 5.16 does not only tell us about the extent of personal overlap between new social movements and the Green Party. One can also infer the degree of approval for certain forms of political action in the Green Party. A repertoire of civil disobedience is typical of the political strategy of these movements.

Hence, a person who is willing to 'join' – which really means to participate – is clearly disposed to take such kinds of action. We can therefore conclude that almost all Green delegates are willing to use unconventional forms of political action. And a substantial part, those who are members, are very likely to have been involved in such activities.

AN 'IRON LAW OF SOCIAL OLIGARCHY'?

The analysis has shown that the memberships or middle-level élites of all German parties are characterised by a pronounced middle class bias. Furthermore, the data indicates a tendency for all parties to become socially ever more exclusive as one moves from the electorate towards higher echelons of the party hierarchy (Herzog, 1982, pp. 98ff.). The proportion of self-employed or highly

Table 6.16: Support for Social Movements (Green Delegates).

	SOS Nature[1]		Ecology Movement[2]		Anti-Nuclear		Peace Movement	
	N	%	N	%	N	%	N	%
Is a member[3]	54	32.3	38	21.5	51	28.5	98	53.3
Might join	104	62.3	137	77.4	127	71.0	84	45.7
Would not join	9	5.4	2	1.1	1	0.5	2	1.0
	167	100.0	177	100.0	179	100.0	184	100.0
Missing cases:	31	15.7	21	10.6	19	9.6	14	7.1

Notes:
1. SOS Nature Movements cannot be considered as new social movements (see Chapter 5). They are included by way of additional information. The result shows that Green activists are also active in 'conventional' environmentalist groups; see Appendix 3 for details.
2. The Eurobarometer surveys mention 'the Greens' as an example of the ecology movement. In the delegate survey, the national federation of environmentalist citizen initiatives (BBU) was substituted.
3. The question does not exclusively refer to formal membership, which rarely exists in such movements.

educated, for example, is higher among Green delegates than voters (Figures 6.1 and 6.2).

Not surprisingly, the social gap between party and electorate is widest in the case of the SPD. Whereas the party can still count on solid working class support at the ballot box, manual workers play only a secondary role inside the party, particularly beyond the threshold of ordinary membership. The FDP and the Greens, on the other hand, primarily appeal to a middle class constituency and are therefore 'automatically' more representative in social terms.

Whereas the substantive political representativness of the established parties could not be tested here, the data on the Green Party demonstrates a close congruence of voters and party delegates. It ought to be remembered, however, that survey data cannot portray the actual policy that is pursued by the parties. There is still a long way between the potential responsiveness of party delegates and political decisions made in Bonn by the national leaderships: the support for disarmament by Social Democratic middle élites (H. Schmitt, 1987, p. 75) contrasts sharply with the twin-track decision, put through by Chancellor Helmut Schmidt.

To a substantial degree, so-called 'Sachzwänge' (constraints of facts) explain such discrepancies. However, hierarchically structured political organisations have also significant socialising effects on those who are climbing up the ladder (Herzog, 1982, pp. 98ff.). The Green party organisation, still characterised by a low degree of formalisation and comparatively few hierarchical elements, should make Green MPs socially and politically closer to party delegates and voters.

There are indications which support this suggestion. A study which has collected relevant data on 235 Green parliamentary deputies[15] and members of the federal leadership (BUVO) between 1979 and September 1985 (Fogt, 1986) shows that 33 per cent of this party élite was female; in the Green parliamentary party of the tenth Bundestag (from 1983 to 1987), the female share reached 45 per cent, compared with an average overall Bundestag deputies of 8 per cent (ninth and tenth parliamentary term, i.e. 1980-7). This exceeds even the percentage of female Green Party members (Kolinsky, 1988, p. 134) – the Greens live up to their own goals concerning the equality of sexes.

Like Green voters and party delegates, most members of the party élite belong to the generations of the extra-parliamentary opposition (i.e. the protest generation) or the subsequent new social movements (54 per cent). Not surprisingly, two-thirds of the Green élite are active in new social movements (Fogt, 1986, p. 26). This contrasts sharply with the age composition of the parliamentary groups of the established parties: 45 per cent of them were socialized politically during the periods of reconstruction or the 'economic miracle' (Fogt, 1986, p. 18). On all levels, the Green Party is the prime representative of the two youngest generations.

This representation, however, is imperfect. As was to be expected from what we know about Green voters and delegates, only specific social groups like teachers and people working in medicine or in the social services tend to get involved in Green politics. Teachers, for example, were heavily over-represented among mandate holders in the early years of the Green Party.[16] Now, the figures have approached the Bundestag average – which is, of course, also characterised by a disproportionate presence of teachers (Fogt, 1986, p. 20; Emminger, 1985, p. 369). This occupational category is economically very secure and can therefore hardly serve as a good example of the 'counter-élite' argument.

On the other hand, the economically secure Green activists share their political struggle with a sizeable group that is characterised by insecure occupational status: Fogt includes all those who are unemployed, have frequently changed jobs, or work in the 'alternative economy' in this category (26 per cent) (Fogt, 1986, p. 21). However, the significance of this finding is debateable. After all, the autonomy to change jobs freely or the option of taking an occupation in the alternative sector may conform exactly with the aspirations of Green politicians who attempt to realise their political visions at least partially in their private lives. In social terms, the Greens are clearly both, the party of the economically secure and the insecure. Clearly, both categories share one important characteristic: they are socially distant from the dominant sphere of economic production!

This chapter has demonstrated that the Green Party, both socially and ideologically, is remarkably representative of its electorate. The party clearly comes close to our model of an ideal type New Politics party. As far as we can infer from the data, the 'law of social oligarchy' leads to a convergence of all parties. When we move up the hierarchy all parties tend to become highly educated and middle class. However, there remains a substantial difference. Whereas membership, middle-level élites, and élites of the established parties are relatively similar, Green activists and élites belong predominantly to a different political generation. Furthermore, the value profile of the Green Party is fundamentally different from that of the established German parties. Virtually all Green delegates are postmaterialists. Although the middle-level élite study does not directly measure value priorities, we can safely infer from the measures of New Politics orientations that none of the established parties is anywhere near such a value consensus.

NOTES

1. See section below for a discussion of a possible bias.
2. The figures were calculated from the numbers of conference delegates in 1978-9 (H. Schmitt, 1987, p. 70) and data from Poguntke with Boll, 1992.
3. This project commissioned two surveys of party conference delegates. The results for the established German parties have been analysed by H. Schmitt (1987).
4. Also, there is a danger of 'overloading' the concept of New Politics with issues where the link is less than obvious. This leads to party-specific versions of the New Politics which may in some cases represent little more than an Old Politics-inspired reaction to a new agenda that has emerged in society (H. Schmitt, 1987, pp. 99ff.).
5. An attempt was made to hand each of them a questionnaire. Also, questionnaires were distributed at the conference tables.
6. See Appendix for details on the questionnaire.
7. In 'established' German language the male ending often refers to both sexes.
8. The very low number of missing cases indicates that it was no problem for all respondents to assign themselves to one of the given categories in a meaningful way.
9. As already mentioned, most delegates live in normally-sized households. Therefore, we can assume that the figures are not significantly inflated by commune-type settings.
10. According to the party statute, the minimum age is 18, but three respondents were only 17.
11. See H. Schmitt, 1987, p. 133 for the grouping of age cohorts.
12. See also Fogt, 1986 on this problem.
13. See H. Schmitt, 1987, p. 132 for church attendance of party delegates of the established German parties. The data are not comparable. However, they indicate that the Green Party delegates are at least as remote from organised religion as Social Democratic and Liberal activists.
14. This statement is the result of the author's observation of several party conferences. See also, for example, TAZ, 29 September 1986.
15. On the Land and federal levels.
16. The 'outlier' was the Land parliament of Lower Saxony with 73 per cent teachers.

7. New Politics and Party Programmes:
The German Case

Whereas the lack of comparable data on party activists did not permit a systematic comparision between parties, this chapter will provide a comprehensive comparative analysis of the programmatic positions of the established German parties and the Greens.

Once established in the Bundestag, Green parliamentarians were successful in injecting new issues into the parliamentary debate (Ismayr, 1985) and attracting public attention through endless public meetings where all internal political, personal and procedural controversies were discussed. The dominant public image of the Greens quickly became one of a conflict-ridden party always manoeuvring on the brink of splitting up. Arguably, this is partly a result of the 5 per cent hurdle in German electoral law, which compels small party leaders to avoid secessions by dissenting factions in order to minimise the risk of parliamentary annihilation at the ballot box (Murphy and Roth, 1991). Consequently, any analysis of Green programmatic orientations must be put into perspective by a brief discussion of the causes and implications of Green factionalism.

For most of the 1980s, the landscape of Green factionalism has been dominated by the following four tendencies: Realists, Eco-Libertarians, Radical Ecologists and Eco-Socialists. Although the minority faction of radical feminists, who tend to approach virtually all political problems from a feminist perspective, frequently supports Fundamentalist positions, they represent a current in their own right. Since feminist positions are almost conventional wisdom in the Green Party, they are not very influential as a separate political force. Rather, feminism has penetrated all Green factions to a greater or lesser extent.

By and large, the Eco-Libertarians have tended to side with the Realists in these debates, whereas Eco-Socialists and Radical Ecologists formed the Fundamentalist camp (Murphy and Roth, 1991, pp. 412ff.). The principal conflict between these two camps is defined by their attitudes towards reformism (Kitschelt, 1985). Although this conflict is not unrelated to the left–right continuum, it is primarily motivated by a disagreement over strategies for accomplishing the goals that are shared by both sides. Whereas the Realists believe in the eventual success of piecemeal reform, the Fundamentalists fear the pacifying and demobilising effects of this strategy.

The choice of strategy also is related to different concepts of the state and the role of parliamentary politics. Many Fundamentalists adhere to various shades of Marxist-inspired views of the state as an agent of the capitalist system which they in turn hold responsible for the outlook of environment and society. From this perspective, the real power resides with those who run the industrial system, and politics is primarily seen as a phenomenon of the superstructure. This interpretation suggests that there is little to be gained from the attempt to attain political control over the state machinery. It would be more promising to challenge 'the system' directly though mass movements. This concept of societal 'counter power' (Gegenmacht) rests on the conviction that it is possible effectively to limit the power of state and industry through mass mobilisation. Furthermore, it implies that the parliamentary arena is not considered to be the place where important decisions are made. Instead, it is primarily regarded as a useful arena to voice political opinions and mobilise people for extra-parliamentary action (Frankland, 1987, p. 30f.)

The Realists, on the other hand, are influenced by the traditional Liberal concept of the state as a relatively neutral and powerful instrument of those who have gained political control over it. Unlike classical Liberals, however, green Realists are considerably more sceptical about the real power of parliamentary politics (Frankland, 1988, p. 101). They do not deny the power of the industrial system, but nevertheless they believe in the capacity of the state to influence the course of events. Consistent with their preference for extra-parliamentary politics, Fundamentalists have always sought to forge broad alliances. Whereas the Realists have kept a close eye on their (parliamentary) respectability, their opponents have been less willing to denounce new social movement activists who have become involved in violent confrontations with the police.

There are obviously also external, that is, party-system-specific or political, factors, which contribute towards explaining the existence and strength of these camps. Whenever governmental participation is out of reach, responsible opposition may not be very attractive. Consistently, the Fundamentalists gained influence in the party after the collapse of the first red–green coalition in Hesse in 1987. The possibility of an alliance between the Berlin Alternative List and the Social Democrats after the January 1989 election had inverse repercussions. It is apparent that the prospect of moderate, that is, 'realist', politics contributed to the fundamentalist defeat at the Duisburg party conference of March 1989.

As a result of spreading factional strife since 1987, a centrist tendency initiated by Antje Vollmer, the so-called 'Aufbruch', began to gain influence through its attempts to forge a 'centre-right' alliance. This change in the internal balance of power was accelerated by the debate over the Green position towards German unification (see Chapter 5), which caused considerable turmoil inside the party and led to significant defections on the élite level. Several prominent Green politicians left their party in order to join the ex-Communist PDS, but they virtually went alone. Similarly, only a few Green members followed the example of the Hamburg Eco-Socialist figureheads Rainer Trampert and Thomas Ebermann, when they left the party in April 1990 in order to resign from party politics altogether. Likewise, the attempt of the hard-line Fundamentalists led by the former party leader Jutta Ditfurth to launch a new project of the 'ecological Left' in May 1991 did not attract many Green Party members. Clearly, these developments corroborate analyses which emphasise, beyond strategic differences, a wide range of common political goals shared by large parts of the party. The fact that several previously very controversial statutory reforms were approved by the 1991 Neumünster party congress indicates that an alliance of Realists and Centrists and the undogmatic Left has now come to dominate the Green Party.

Obviously, a thorough analysis of Green factions would form a study of its own. Inevitably, such research would need to analyse the political biographies and traditions of these factions and relate them to the major currents of (sometimes specifically German) political thought as well as to the political history of the Federal Republic.[1] Here, only a few prominent aspects of Green factionalism will be highlighted. Basically, the following themes have dominated much of the factional debate of the 1980s: positions on the use of violence, the debate over possible coalitions, and the question of whether a state monopoly on the legitimate use of force should be accepted.

a) State Monopoly of Force

The above-mentioned basic cleavages have strong ideological connotations, but little immediate relevance to practical politics. However, due to their symbolic content they played an important role in the German debate of the 1980s. Since we are dealing with party factions, it is rarely possible to quote authoritative statements. Instead, we need to refer to selected public statements by the prominent Green politicians who act as informal spokesmen for the factions.

All three aspects are intimately related to the 'biography' of the Green Party as an offspring of various protest movements. Green identity has developed through an ongoing resistance against the policies of the prevalent parties in the Federal Republic. Such resistance sometimes involves the violation of existing legislation: in the struggle against the deployment of intermediate-range nuclear missiles or the construction of nuclear plants a higher-order legitimacy is set against the principles of the legal system. Continued involvement in such conflicts makes it very hard for some Greens to recognise state monopoly on the legitimate use of force as an abstract principle which may nevertheless be violated in order to induce political reform (Neumann, 1988, p. 4f.). The dialectic is not easily accepted by all Green activists. They find it hard to accept that the legitimacy of state action in the pursuit of certain policies must be acknowledged although the legitimacy of the policies themselves is questioned![2] This problem has frequently fuelled heated debates between Fundamentalists, who are reluctant to accept this principle of reformist politics, and Realists, who struggle for its unambiguous approval in order to enhance the political respectability of the party.

The debate is confused further by the ambivalent meaning of the German word for 'force', which can also mean 'violence'. Green politicians defending the state monopoly on force have frequently been accused by their own ranks of justifying violent state action such as police violence.

b) Violence

There is absolutely no dissent among Greens as far as violence against persons is concerned. Non-violence is one of the four basic principles of the party which are codified in the preamble of the federal party programme (Bundesprogramm, p. 5). The Greens pride themselves on being the only pacifist party in Germany.

Things become more complicated when violence against objects comes on the agenda. Again, this is related to the biography of the party. The 'destruction of destructive devices' has a long tradition in the history of civil disobedience, particularly in the pacifist movement. The second, more prominent aspect refers to the recurring debate over violence after incidents where peaceful demonstrations have turned violent. Knowing by experience that violent clashes are not always sparked off by protesters, many Greens have refused to denounce civil protesters' violence indiscriminately.[3] Prominent Green politicians have argued that peaceful activists have sometimes found themselves in situations where the use of violence was an understandable reaction of self-defence. In sum, the Greens are reluctant to denounce people who – against their own intentions – have been compelled by police actions to react violently.[4] However, this reluctance is far stronger in the fundamentalist camp, whereas leading Realists have repeatedly called for unambiguous denunciation of violence against people.

In the public debate, such a differentiated position lends itself to misunderstandings. For much of the 1980s, many SPD politicians have used this issue, in conjunction with the debate on the state monopoly on force, in order to rule out any co-operation with the Greens – a position which facilitated papering over the cracks opened by the strategic debate inside the Social Democratic Party. It would be misleading, however, to qualify the Social Democratic position as merely tactical. For historical reasons, the SPD has always been very much concerned with maintaining an image of a responsible party (see Chapter 9 for details).

c) Coalitions

Obviously, attitudes towards violence and the state monopoly on force are intimately related to choice of political strategy. Activists who have no confidence in piecemeal reform tend to be inclined towards radical extra-parliamentary action – which makes it hard to accept explicitly the state monopoly on force and to exclude violence-prone protest groups from protest activities. Consistently, Fundamentalists and Eco-Socialists tend to be extremely critical of possible coalitions with the SPD and prefer extra-parliamentary mobilisation over governmental responsibility. Realists and the small group of Eco-Libertarians are to be found on the moderate, reformist side of internal Green battle-lines. Not surprisingly, the heated internal debate over the merits and shortcomings of the 'rotation model' polarised the party along the same dividing line: reformists who aim at coalitions necessarily favour more personal continuity, which is clearly a systemic requirement of modern parliamentary politics. Those, however, who regard parliament primarily as a platform for extra-parliamentary mobilisation have no inherent interest in adapting to the organisational norms of parliament (see Chapter 8). As a result of the above-mentioned rearrangement of Green factions at the beginning of the 1990s, the debate over governmental coalitions has lost most of its antagonising thrust. The discussion has ceased to concentrate on the principle as such. Instead, the actual terms on which coalitions with the SPD, or even the FDP, should be considered have become the focal point of the internal debate.

In view of the bitter strife over short-term political strategies, there is suprisingly little disagreement over long-term political goals within the Green Party. Whereas it seems almost impossible to reach consensus on suitable means to accomplish it, the utopia itself is relatively uncontroversial. The following sections are based on a thorough comparative analysis of the basic programmes of all German Bundestag parties, which aims at identifying the particular issues associated with the growth of the New Politics, and establishing the current 'dimensionality' of party conflict and how this has been influenced by the Greens.

NATURE AND FUNCTION OF PARTY PROGRAMMES

The principal purpose of this chapter is a thorough analysis of the political identity of the German Greens and the crucial points of disagreement with the remaining German parties. One of the leading questions of this analysis aims at unravelling the reasons for the vigorous rejection of the Greens that characterises the positions of the established parties for most of the 1980s. Admittedly, there are differences between them, and a substantial part of the SPD has begun to alter its approach. In fact, the first, short-lived, red–green coalition in Hesse has demonstrated both the willingness of parts of the SPD to find ways of co-operation and the deep-rooted rejection of such moves by the right wing of the party. For the remaining German parties, 'Ausgrenzung' (keeping them out) is still the dominant mode of dealing with the Greens. Clearly, there are a variety of reasons for this, which basically add up to the argument that the Greens are typologically different from established parties. Nevertheless, the established parties themselves belong to different party families without having problems with forming coalition governments with each other.

There is, of course, some generational conflict involved, which materialises above all in questions of personal style and 'respectable' behaviour. However, it would underestimate politicians' quest for power and rationality to attribute much explanatory weight to these ephemeral differences. This chapter sets out to identify points of fundamental political disagreement that separate the Greens from all established parties that are the representatives of the West German consensus (Smith, 1982b, p. 67). However, before we turn to a comparative analysis of the basic party programmes of all German Bundestag parties, some reflection on the nature and relevance of such programmatic documents is necessary.

First of all, it is noticeable how much has been written on parties and party systems and how little on party programmes specifically. There are two possible explanations for this. Either most scholars agree that they are ephemeral to the universe of party politics, or it is rather difficult to assess their role and function, particularly in quantitative terms. In recent years, a cross-national study of party manifestos has intruded into this *terra incognita* demonstrating the relevance of this particular aspect of party research (Budge *et al.*, 1987).

Party programmes perform a multitude of internal and external functions. They help to attract voters and members, create party identity, are instrumental for internal faction fighting, and define the space for political action against potential dissidents and competitors in the party system (Narr, 1966, pp. 35ff.; Flohr, 1968, pp. 58ff.; Budge, 1987, p. 15f.; Kadan and Pelinka, 1979, p. 9f.). Basically, West German parties concentrate on three types of programme that differ as regards their scope, comprehensiveness, time perspective and the procedure of their drafting: basic programmes (Grundsatzprogramme), action programmes (Aktionsprogramme) and election programmes (Wahlprogramme).

Although this is a difference of degree, not of principle, it is relevant in the present context. Usually, basic programmes remain valid for at least a decade and are the result of a long-sustained process of internal debate on various organisational levels. They are intended to provide 'basic orientation and philosophy' for the party and are not influenced by short-term electoral tactics (Klingemann, 1987, p. 300). As a consequence, basic programmes tend to be less specific, less policy-oriented, less short-term, and offer fewer answers to the issues of the day than election programmes. On the other hand, they give a clearer image of the party's general ideas as to how the world should be organised or changed. This is also due to their main function as an authoritative statement of the collective political will of the party – with all the necessary compromise and fudging involved (Kadan and Pelinka, 1979, p. 11). Basic programmes are supplemented by specific 'action programmes' which offer short-term answers to immediate political problems. Election programmes respresent a selection of these two kinds of programmes (Klingemann, 1987, p. 300).

Arguably, election programmes are more influenced by external exigencies. Primarily, they are strategic documents aimed at influencing the party image according to the goals of those who plan the election campaign and providing the political 'ammunition' for party candidates (Budge, 1987, p. 18). Although they are normally approved by a party convention (Klingemann, 1987, p. 300) they tend to be – with the exception of the Green Party – more a product of the party leadership than   is true for basic programmes. Consequently, election programmes are more likely to be oriented towards the political profile of the party's prime ministerial candidate or leading figures. Hence, election programmes are more specific and policy-oriented, react more to the present political mood and are less representative of the whole party and of the party identity.

a) The Documents

Ideally, both election programmes and basic programmes should be included in an analysis of the programmatic orientations of political parties.[5] However, limitations of time, resources and accessibility of data unfortunately have precluded an analysis of election manifestos. Although this might have shown changes in the programmatic radicalism of the Greens and the reactions of the established parties to the Green challenge, it would have covered only the period 1980–90 – too short for true longitudinal analysis. Furthermore, as regards the leading theoretical question of this book – the difference between the Greens and the established parties – the analysis of shifting nuances over a short period of time would not have added much. It therefore seems legitimate to concentrate on the comparison of basic programmes, which are the most all-encompassing expression of a party's political *raison d'être*.

Naturally, the different basic programmes were formulated at different points in time. Although these documents are intended to reflect fundamental ideological convictions and long-term strategies for the future, they have been influenced by the issues of the day to a certain extent. Some political problems that dominate the contemporary debate seemed to be irrelevant when the Godesberg programme of the SPD, for example, was written in 1959. To compensate for this deficiency, more recent basic programmatic documents of the Social Democrats and the Liberals have been included in the analysis. In a sense they represent updates of the somewhat ageing basic programmes. This means that all parties have approved of fundamental statements in the mid-1970s or later, when New Politics themes were already highly topical. Consequently, the fact that some problems are hardly mentioned in some programmes cannot be attributed to the lack of salience of these policy areas at the time when the programme was written. On the contrary, the omissions can also be interpreted as political statements (Budge, 1987, pp. 24ff.; Budge and Farlie, 1983a, 1983b). The new Social Democratic basic programme of 1989 (Berlin programme) was consciously not used as a major point of reference, because it reflects the endpoint of the programmatic movement of the SPD throughout the 1980s and therefore cannot be used to grasp the deficient responsiveness of the established parties towards the demands of the New Politics which has contributed much to the electoral success of the Greens. In any case, fundamental political convictions are relatively immune to fast reorientation or erosion. Nuances may change quite easily; fundamental traits of political thought may not. Correspondingly, the SPD and FDP frequently refer in their more recent documents to their basic programmes in order to underline this continuity.[6]

In order to put the necessarily static picture which emanates from any analysis of basic party programmes into perspective and to add some dynamics to the argument, reference will be made throughout this chapter to areas where substantial programmatic shifts have been made by established parties in recent years. For this purpose, election and – where relevant – action programmes will be quoted. Obviously, the Social Democratic Berlin programme also provides several significant examples of substantial programmatic reorientation, which will be mentioned in the analysis. The combination of an analysis of basic programmes, which represent fundamental lines of political thought largely beyond short-term tactical considerations, and 'Zeitgeist' (although this is admittedly a difference in degree) with other programmatic documents and policy statements will hopefully produce a balanced picture of the parties programmatic tenets and political intentions. It will also allow us to identify policy areas where the established parties have undergone substantial programmatic change as a reaction to the Green challenge.

b) Can Party Programmes Be Taken Seriously?

The attempt to explore the political intentions of a party by reading its programmatic documents can be criticised on the grounds that parties themselves may not take them very seriously. Knowing that their chances of assuming sole governmental responsibility are not very high under German electoral law, they may be tempted to promise much more than they expect to realise in government. Furthermore, there are always manifold systemic obstacles that may conveniently be used as excuses for a party's inability to live up to the expectations it has aroused through its own programmatic rhetoric.

It may also be unfair to make comparisons between parties that have been sobered through disillusioning experiences of government and their competitors whose electoral failures have always spared them the effort of trying to match political intentions with reality. However, the purpose of the subsequent analysis is not to find out what a party will be able to do once it has assumed governmental office. More relevant to the identity and self-definition of political parties is what they would like to do if they were in office. In this view, programmes do constitute a certain kind of political reality because they define the boundaries of political compromise that will eventually be tolerated by the party's rank-and-file. Even if many of their goals are regarded as unrealistic by an overwhelming majority of experts, they will first of all determine the electoral appeal of a party and then affect its chances of entering coalition governments.

As indicated above, party programmes have important internal functions. As such, they are documents of compromise between various party factions influenced by related ideological traditions. Although the underlying causes for the growth of the New Politics are similar in all advanced Western societies, the specific political expression of its grievances is also partly moulded by country-specific factors like political culture and ideological currents. From this perspective, we must expect every country or even every political subculture to have 'produced' a slightly different New Politics orientation, just as Democratic Socialism or Christian Democracy does not mean exactly the same thing in France, Germany or Italy. In fact, it may not even mean the same within a given country! What we hope to achieve in this chapter is the description and analysis of New Politics-inspired ideological thinking in its specifically German variant. The picture that will be drawn will not be fundamentally different from the one we would get for other countries, but it will have some typically German nuances.

The major external function of all programmatic statements is to present a specific party image with which it is hoped electoral support can be attracted. It is this elective function which creates difficulties for our analysis. In trying to maximise support, programmes often become incoherent, sometimes downright contradictory. They tend to resemble warehouse catalogues where most people can expect to find something to their liking. In other words, unambiguous statements that make political priorities (i.e. winners and losers) clear are hard to find: all parties, for example, are for the preservation of the environment. Most of them, however, also argue for the stimulation of economic growth. The possible conflict between these two goals is not discussed in the documents. In many programmes, the real priorities are obscured by the clouds of an electoral 'catch-all' strategy.

Since similar or identical phrases can mean very different things for different parties, it is necessary to interpret single issue statements in the wider context of the programme and even the general character of the party. Interpretation is always context-bound if it wants to be comprehensive. Such a 'synthetic view' (Narr, 1966, p. 24) facilitates the exploration of the real political motives behind ambiguous and vague formulations.

Furthermore, one needs to keep in mind that the socially dominant perception of reality normally represents the starting-point for the formulation of programmatic positions. This means that all political actors relate their own normative preferences to this perception in order to arrive at political positions that are consistent with these preferences. It is this symbolic value of certain issue positions that is relevant for political debate. In some cases, it may be quite different from the real effects of such policies. To give an example: the expansion of the welfare system stands for egalitarian, left-wing politics. Although welfare systems may in some cases effect a redistribution from lower to higher income groups, the political perception of welfare policies has hardly changed (Esping-Andersen, 1985, p. 166). Necessarily, this symbolic value of political problems forms the basis of our subsequent discussion of the German party programmes.

The general linkage between reasons for the growth of New Politics and its substantive concerns has already been explored in the theoretical chapter. The more detailed analysis which follows will further explain why certain groups of the population are concerned with this specific set of political goals.

A COMPARATIVE ANALYSIS OF PARTY PROGRAMMES

The following analysis of the basic programmes of the CDU, CSU, FDP, SPD, and the Greens is oriented towards the major New Politics themes. In the section on economic policy, for example, attention has been focused on the interdependency of economic development and the ecological balance, rather than on other aspects. Inevitably, this means that similarities between the Greens and the established German parties on more traditional issues are somewhat undervalued. However, since the prime focus of this book is on crucial differences which are related to the New Politics, this does not affect the argument substantially.

This discussion is based on a synopsis of the programmes, which has been broken down into the following sub-categories: individualism; democracy and state; international relations and security policy; ecology; social policy; economic policy. The subsequent section headings correspond to the headings of the relevant tables in Appendix 4, which provide a detailed documentation of individual parties' positions on all relevant policy areas. Hence, no detailed references to the tables in the Appendix will be necessary throughout the following pages (see Appendix 4, Tables A4.1–7). The analysis has been largely limited to differences between the Greens and the most similar party for each issue area. Given that the programmatic differences between the established parties are well established by research (Rudzio, 1983; Kaack and Roth, 1980), this approach appears to be justifiable. Furthermore, we are concerned with providing evidence that the Green Party is programmatically distant from all other parties. We are not attempting to provide a complete ideological typology of the German party system from a New Politics perspective. Nevertheless, we have attempted to visualise the relative positions of the parties for some selected issues on the basis of qualitative judgement (Figure 7.1).

a) Individualism

Individualism refers to the concern with individual self-determination in the widest sense. Politically, it relates to the conflict between classical civil liberties and the tendency of governments to limit these freedoms to a certain extent in order to protect democracy from its domestic and foreign enemies. In its most pronounced form individualism stands for demands for 'state-free zones'. This slogan refers to the quest for the creation of social spheres that are completely free of state intervention and control. Frequently, such projects can be found within the realm of the welfare system: self-administered kindergardens, for example, or houses for battered women. In general terms, individualism means a general and deeply rooted distaste for any state interference in personal and social life (see Appendix 4, Table A4.1). This has profound results in many policy areas.

One of the most controversial issues that dominated the political debate in the Federal Republic during the 1970s was the so-called *Radikalenerlaß*, a decision by the Brandt government intended to prevent political extremists from entering into the German civil service. Legalistic reasons and German efficiency led to the creation of a sophisticated system of secret-service-aided screening of all civil service candidates. In 1979 the procedure was relaxed, but the principle remained untouched. Although the spd has declared in its 1987 election programme that it does not approve of the *Radikalenerlaß* (spd, 1987, p. 36), the Greens are the only relevant German party that explicitly argues for a complete abolition of the *Radikalenerlaß*.[7] Since this touches upon constitutional principles it means a very substantial difference to the other parties. Arguably, it was not without effect on the emergence of the Green Party that some spd-led Land governments have been more hardline executors of the Radikalenerlaß than Christian Democratic governments.

Also, the Greens are alone in their struggle for the full emancipation of various minorities. They argue for the abolition of discriminatory legislation on homosexuality and demand the preservation of the traditional life-style of gypsies. In their view, foreign workers ought to have equal social, political and legal rights with German citizens and should be entitled to a proportional share of jobs. The latter points would mean the abolition of most restrictions against immigration into the Federal Republic, a position that is rejected by all other parties to a greater or lesser degree.

The contrast between Greens and the remaining parties becomes most apparent if we focus on the role the concept of self-determination plays in a number of policy fields. With varying degrees of emphasis and enthusiasm all established parties propose some kind of co-determination schemes in the economic sphere (see Appendix, Table A4.4). In Christian Democratic thinking, such schemes are primarily regarded as necessary devices to create a sense of belonging within a company or bureaucracy. This attitude relates to the predominant Christian Democratic perception of society and all its sub-units as being organic bodies where all parts ought to be encouraged to play their due role.

By contrast, Social Democratic eagerness for co-determination is based on the ambition of subjecting all relevant social spheres to democratically legitimised control. From this perspective, co-determination means democratic control of external determination of the individual (i.e. 'Fremdbestimmung') – which itself is regarded as unavoidable. At least rhetorically, this position had changed by 1989. In the section on economic democracy in the Berlin programme, both possibilities are mentioned, co-determination and self-determination.

Liberal thinking, on the other hand, tends to give priority to the employers' or managers' need for self-determination. Hence, the FDP is generally not very sympathetic to the idea of co-determination.

Alternatively, the Green position amounts to a far-reaching reduction of authority structures which limit individual autonomy. They demand that those who are affected (as producers, consumers and neighbours) should have the right to decide themselves how, where and what to produce. This example from the sphere of economics serves to highlight the basic contrast between Green positions and the political concepts of the established parties. In fact, Green positions amount to the extension of Liberalism towards Anarchism: ideally, they would reduce the role of state or corporate control over individuals and their life-style as far as possible. Green demands for self-determined self-aid in all possible fields of social policy are inspired by exactly the same fundamental position (see Appendix 4, Table A4.5). A glance at Liberal positions highlights the difference to the FDP in this classic field of Liberal politics: The FDP considers individual self-determination to be already accomplished (see Appendix 4, Table A4.1), whereas the Greens see much room for improvement.

The leading principle of self-determination has also inspired the Green position on abortion: based on the conviction that abortion is never an easy choice for a women, they argue that this sphere of very personal moral considerations should not be subjected to legal prosecution. Significantly, the relevant paragraph of the Social Democratic Berlin programme of 1989 reads very similar (see Appendix 4, Table A4.1). In practical politics, however, things are complicated through constitutional boundaries which prevent the abolition of the relevant article on the statute book (§218). Whereas FDP and SPD want at least to defend the *status quo* (SPD, 1987, p. 35), there are strong tendencies in the Christian parties to implement more restrictive regulations.

b) Democracy and the State

The State

The above-mentioned Green positions on individualism would lead us to expect a very negative evaluation of state activities in general. However, Green attitudes towards the state are staggeringly ambivalent – at least at first sight. The Greens have nowhere formulated a clear statement on the role they have assigned to the state in their political edifice. This may be due to the problems they still have with accepting the state monopoly on the legitimate use of force – which can be explained by the history of the party as the outgrowth of social movements that had frequent and violent encounters with the police forces. On the other hand, state activities are frequently envisaged as means of controlling environmental legislation. Inevitably, this would mean an expansion of state bureaucracy and state power.

The paradox can be resolved by recalling the multifaceted and ambivalent nature and effect of state activity and state control. The political thinking of the established parties, however, is mainly unidimensional. Concentration on one preferred aspect pushes other possible approaches to the evaluation of the role of the state into the background. SPD, CDU, and CSU are united in a relatively positive interpretation of the role of the state. Naturally, the parties disagree in terms of the actual normative purpose of state activity. For the Christian Democratics, the state's real task is to secure order in society, which is seen as being complementary to individual freedom. Only in economic matters is exten-sive state activity and control regarded as detrimental to individual freedom. In the field of social policy, the specific Christian Democratic principle of subsidiarity (Subsidiarität) takes account of the ambivalence of an all-penetrating state. Here, Christian Democrats prefer to leave tasks to smaller, private or associ-ational units if they can cope with the problems at hand (see section 'e' for a discussion of the differences to the Green position).

Social Democrats, on the other hand, see the most important field of state activity as controlling private economic power and supporting the construction of a free society. Since the state is controlled by democratically legitimised elected bodies, so the Social Democratic reasoning goes, state interference with various social and economic activities is also legitimate.

Clearly, both concepts of the state are different and would deserve a far more thorough analysis than can be presented here. But they are very similar in one crucial aspect that is relevant from our perspective: the state is not seen as a principal constraint on individual freedom and the realisation of a meaningful life. Whereas the Left regards the state as an instrument for the accomplishment of greater individual freedom, the Right is convinced that a strong state is necessary to protect the masses from their own follies (Greiffenhagen, 1986, pp. 63ff.). At most, the Right regards it as a potential encroachment upon economic freedom.

A far more sceptical approach towards the expansion of state competences has always been an integral element of Liberal thinking. The classic Liberalism which has come to dominate the FDP in the 1980s prefers the state to be limited as far as possible: preferably to its indispensable functions of maintaining the legal edifice of society and guaranteeing internal and external security. In their programmes, however, the German Liberals are aware of the ambivalent role of the state in modern society as being a protection for and a threat to individual freedom at the same time. For them, the state's role as a guarantor of democratic participation rights leaves it with the obligation to make the realisation of these rights materially possible for the citizens. In other words, the state ought to provide a minimum material standard for all citizens.

The Greens distinguish between policy fields. In a way, they have not a principled but an instrumental approach to the role of the state. State control is rejected if it means bureaucratic control over individuals. But it is often viewed positively if it is applied to institutions, particularly if such control will serve Green ends. Although the Green utopia envisages a decentralised, self-determined economy, state power ought to be used to control the centralised economy until it has been restructured according to Green blueprints. Consequently, the Green programme calls for state funds for the development of alternative economic models (see Appendix 4, Table A4.4). Similarly, legal means are proposed for environmental protection. However, enforcement of new legislation means more state control and more state bureaucracy (see Appendix 4, Table A4.3). Other examples are redistributive policies through fiscal means or extensive state subsidies for the contruction of self-controlled, decentralised systems for self-help in the social sphere (see Appendix 4, Table A4.5). More generally, one of the state's most important tasks would be the creation of 'social spaces' where the population can manage its own affairs (Nullmeier, 1982, p. 352f.).

Direct Democracy

The concept of grass-roots democracy (Basisdemokratie) dominates all Green debates on democratic theory (see Appendix 4, Table A4.2). In a nutshell, it means a qualitative extension of the existing model of representative democracy. Again, the contrast with the established political scene is quite substantial.

The Christian sister parties are more or less explicitly opposed to any form of 'democratisation', whereas SPD and FDP argue – with different emphases – in favour of a 'spatial' extension of representative democracy. In concrete terms, they demand representative democratic control for social spheres that have so far been exempted from democratic practice to a large extent (like schools, hospitals, universities, companies). Only the FDP proposes some qualitatively new democratic tools: referendums initiated by government or parliament, and the right of citizens to initiate referenda. Those proposals, however, have never been put on the political agenda by the party. This may be explained by the deeply-rooted scepticism in post-war Germany about all the plebiscitarian procedures which played a role in the National Socialist regime. In the wake of the constitutional debate after German unification, however, things may change – particularly because the SPD, in 1989, followed the Liberal example of suggesting the introduction of plebiscites. This is another policy area where the challenge of the Greens has induced programmatic adaptation in the neighbouring established parties.

Unrestrained by such historical baggage, the Greens not only favour an extension of democratic rights. They also demand the introduction of qualitatively new elements that could be grouped under the label of direct democracy: decentralisation, far-reaching autonomy of lower units, self-governance, introduction of councils for social and economic affairs.

These demands are motivated by a deeply-rooted mistrust of all autocratic, hierarchical and bureaucratic structures which could lead to a distortion of the true will of the populace. To a certain extent, they are also inspired by the conviction that small units are more efficient – by analogy with the structure of eco-systems. As such, this is not only one of the cornerstones of Green ideological thinking. It is also reflected in their own party structure and in the style of political action Greens prefer inside and outside their party organisation.

This explains the difference from Christian Democratic concepts of decentralisation (SPD and FDP do not discuss this problematic in their programmes). For the Christian parties, decentralisation conforms to their understanding of state and society. It is influenced by the principle of subsidiarity that originates from Catholic social teaching. Together with an organic model of society, this indicates that all matters should be administered at their 'proper' place. Shifting certain decisions and actions to lower levels, however, does not automatically mean an extension of democractic control of society as a whole. Subsidiarity and an organic model of society do not mean that lower units ought to have any competences beyond their own genuine sphere of action. The tail of the 'organic' society is not meant to wave the dog. On the contrary, decentralisation, combined with a relatively non-participatory and centralised structure above the lowest levels, serves to shield big politics from participatory aspirations at the grass roots (Nullmeier, 1982, p. 353).

Green decentralisation turns this concept on its head. It differs from the Christian Democratic variant in two important points:

- The concept of far-reaching autonomy for lower units means that these bodies are not bound by political directives from higher-order decision-makers. They are entitled to decide for themselves as far as possible on their preferred course of action, whereas the Christian Democratic concept stresses the administrative, not the political, functions of lower units.

- The political initiative and power of these units is meant to extend beyond their own echelon. The Green Party argues for direct involvement of the grass roots in higher-level decisions, not only for representative influence upon them. This is reflected in demands for referenda and by the role attributed to citizens' initiatives and new social movements. Whereas all other parties accept citizens' initiatives as a complementary element of political life which may introduce an additional opportunity for co-determination, the Greens believe in the directly innovative function of these initiatives and movements. Finally, the Green demand for councils for social and economic affairs, which are envisaged as controlling investments on all societal levels, amounts to a substantial change in the institutional framework of West German democracy.

c) Ecology and Environmental Protection

The Meaning of Ecology

Green concern with the preservation – or better, reconstruction – of the ecological balance is often perceived to be the dominant, if not sole source of Green political thought and Green politics. The foregoing analysis of the Green approach to democracy and state, however, has demonstrated that ecological thinking does not make an overriding impact on these programmatic aspects.[8] This corresponds to our theoretical argument: New Politics is not only about ecology, it encompasses also a wide range of political issues including participatory democracy.

Nevertheless, ecology certainly has a central role for the formulation of Green positions on all policy areas that are related in any way to the sphere of industrial production. For ecological considerations may impinge on the volume and kind of industrial production with all its repercussions on the financial framework for other policy areas. In addition to these financial linkages, ecological thinking has inspired models for society to a certain extent: admiration for the subtle functioning of natural networks has led some people to attach a quasi-natural value to small, self-sufficient units. However, 'deep ecology' – as Capra calls it – is not the dominant current in Green programmatic thinking. Despite all Green rhetoric about 'holistic thinking', their positions on democracy and state are far more moulded by radical democratic and even anarchist traditions (Capra and Spretnak, 1984, pp. 30ff.).

In view of the important role of ecology in their thinking, it is useful to analyse the ecological orientation of all the German parties at this point. Before we go into details, an introductory point on terminological aspects should be made: ecological thinking is completely different from a concern with environmental protection. The latter means nothing more than the growing preparedness to prevent environmental damage through industrial production as far as is technologically and economically feasible. In concrete terms, it amounts to legal obligations for producers to install filters or to keep their emissions and industrial effluents within limits considered tolerable by parliaments or governments.

Contrastingly, ecological thinking means that the imperatives of the ecological system predominate over economic and technological arguments. From this perspective, ecologically damaging production must not be allowed at all if technological facilities for the control and absorption of most of the emissions are not available. Furthermore, criteria based on the non-renewability of natural resources are attributed a central importance in all economic decisions. More generally, this amounts to an alteration of the list of political priorities that have guided Western economic policy so far: profitability is no longer regarded as the most important, overriding principle. It has been moved down the list and overtaken by ecological considerations.

Growth

Attitudes towards economic growth are certainly the central criterion for identifying adherence to one of the above-mentioned positions. The evaluation of growth reflects a general assessment of the ecological problem. Given that further undifferentiated growth is likely to accelerate environmental decay, support for further unspecified growth clearly means giving first priority to economic imperatives. Implicitly, this means that ecological problems are considered to be of secondary importance. In this view, they should only be tackled within the boundaries of what seems to be economically feasible.

Until the late 1980s, all established parties were to be found on this side of the dividing-line – with nuances (Appendix 4, Table A4.3). They are united in their evaluation of growth as being the single most important precondition for the realisation of their preferred political ends.

Not surprisingly, Social Democrats emphasise the need for further economic growth in order to gain financial flexibility for the implementation of reformist policies while avoiding thoroughgoing redistributive steps. The other parties put more stress on the general conservation of the *status quo*, based on social security and affluence. Liberals, Social Democrats and the csu introduce the adjective 'qualitative' into the debate without specifying what exactly they mean. Since all these parties regard growth as an essential element of their politics, it obviously does not imply any fundamental difference from the position of the Christian Democratic Party.

On balance, the spd programme is slightly more sceptical on the whole issue. In its *Orientierungsrahmen '85*, the party mentions the possibility that there is limited potential for further growth. And it is the only established party that allows for the possibility that environmental protection is an inherent obstacle to economic growth. Hence, the notion that environmental imperatives might necessitate economic sacrifices is at least considered by the Social Democrats. Social Democratic uneasiness with this problem is highlighted by differential approaches in two recent documents: Whereas the 1987 election programme avoids the issue completely, the 1986 draft of a new basic party programme calls for the political selection of growth areas (spd, 1987, 1986a, VIII). Finally, the Berlin programme marks the endpoint of the changing position of the Social

Democrats on ecology. Their call for ecological necessities guiding economic decisions is almost an exact quotation from the Green programme which was written almost a decade earlier (see Appendix 4, Table A4.3).

By contrast, the remaining established parties fully adhere to the concept of environmental protection that has been analyzed above: from this perspective, environmental protection need not impede further economic growth, because such measures are subjected to the dominant logic of the economic system (Müller, 1987, p. 32). In concrete terms, this means that protective measures are only accepted as long as they do not interfere substantially with the goal of economic growth. Since this strategy is dominated by technological solutions – and not by a preparedness to be content with fewer material goods – new, additional fields of economic growth are possible and likely.

Here, the fundamental contrast is to be found between the Greens and the established parties. For the Green programme is still the only document which stipulates unequivocally that economic growth is destructive for the natural environment. Only if superior results can be achieved with equivalent or less consumption of energy and resources can growth be accepted. The resource consumption of industrial production assumes the same importance as the pollutionary outputs for the selection of fields of growth.

Clearly, this represents a severer standard than the rather vague distinction between general and qualitative growth (Eppler, 1981, pp. 47ff.). It means that criteria of future environmental conditions and resource stocks enter into present economic decision-making. The rejection of any further increase in resource consumption implies a 'partial dismantling and conversion of the industrial system' (see Appendix 4, Table A4.3): whereas the established parties argue for more cars with catalytic converters, the Greens demand fewer cars and more public transport. Again, this is a position which has, albeit less unequivocally, been adopted by the SPD in 1989. The example makes it clear: In the Green utopia, economic activities would be shifted to areas that help to maximise the utility of all consumed natural resources. In their programme the Greens explicitly assert that ecological imperatives have first priority and that economic goals can only be realised within their framework. Consequently, they argue for the prohibition of all substances and processes which have a substantially negative impact on the ecological balance.

Green rejection of undiversified economic growth is also inspired by a different understanding of quality of life. The established parties largely equate quality of life with standard of living. Green thinking, however, is influenced by the awareness of a growing conflict between these political goals. For this reason, they demand that the economic system has to be guided directly by the needs of the people as they are formulated by social and economic councils. Christian Democrats and Liberals do not address this possible conflict between quantitative and qualitative development, whereas the SPD, in 1989, refers rather vaguely to the problem that 'not all growth is progress' (see Appendix 4, Table A4.3).

In concrete terms, this would imply the selection of fields of production beforehand and according to politically discussed criteria. Under the present economic system, individual needs are only integrated in the process of economic decision-making by means of market research and the general allocative functioning of the market. However, it can be argued that needs are created to a considerable extent by marketing and advertising strategies.

Manifestly, it would be misleading to maintain that the established parties completely reject political influence on economic decisions. Such a position would mean an unrealistic denial of the enormous interdependence of the private and public sphere as it has emerged over the past decades in all welfare states. State subsidies, infrastructural and fiscal policies are well established and generally accepted tools of global economic steering (see Appendix 4, table A4.4). For the solution of environmental problems such a resort to market mechanisms is favoured by all established parties except the SPD, which is traditionally more disposed towards direct state intervention (CDU, 1989, § 28,29).

Implementation

The central principle of this political strategy is the so-called *Verursacherprinzip* (see Appendix 4, Table A4.3), which is mainly relevant for possible reactions to immediate environmental hazards and damages. All German parties adhere to this principle.[9] It means that those which cause environmental damage are made liable for its removal, or at least for some kind of financial compensation. The scope of application is obviously very wide. Air pollution, for example, rarely causes immediate damage. Long-term effects are hard to prove; and it is even harder to convince law courts of such causal links. The extent to which the application of this principle is envisaged is not explicitly specified in the documents. However, it is bound to be determined by the overall degree of a party's radicalism on this particular policy area.

Initially, the application of the *Verursacherprinzip* was limited to reactions to environmental damage. Meanwhile, the principle has assumed central importance for the environmental policy of all established parties. Generally applied, it entails the obstruction and promotion of fields of production via the market price: Producers would not only have to pay the costs for waste disposal and fees for the industrial effluents. 'Consumption' of all environmental goods, so the reasoning goes, should be made part of the cost calculation of producers. In concrete terms, it would result in payments for all kinds of pollutive discharges into the environment. Consequently, pollutive production would become more expensive and hence less competitive. The incremental substitution of environmentally damaging products and production processes by clean and resource-economising methods and goods would make the environmental balance sheet gradually more positive.[10]

From the Green perspective, such a system-conforming approach to environmental problems is insufficient because it does not completely preclude wasteful and polluting production. Such products will not disappear as long as profitable prices can be achieved on the market. Furthermore, market mechanisms may induce companies to shift such productions to countries where environmental costs are lower – analogously to what has happened to labour intensive industries over the past decades. Given the global scope of the ecological problematic and the global Green approach to its solution, this strategy is unacceptable to the Greens. Consistently, the Green programme calls for administrative and legal means in order to prevent hazardous production altogether. This represents a second, qualitatively new step: the *Verursacherprinzip* and its market-conforming solutions are not rejected, but they are regarded as relatively ineffective. Additional direct control and interference is favoured where market mechanisms are not capable of accomplishing the desired results. Again, the Greens are substantially less hesitant as far as direct state interference is concerned.

Energy

Due to the substantial dependence of industrial societies on energy supplies, energy policy occupies a pivotal position in all concepts of environmental policy. Until 1986, it has also been a field of fundamental conflict between all established parties and the Greens. Indeed, it was of constitutive importance for the emergence of the ecology movement and the subsequent foundation of the Green Party (Müller-Rommel, 1985a, pp. 55ff.; Klotzsch and Stöss, 1984).

The use of nuclear power symbolises the conflicting philosophies that underlie the Old and New Politics paradigms. Nuclear power stands for an unlimited confidence in man's ability to expand the boundaries of nature and to master highly complex technologies with an enormous and unprecedented potential for danger (Nelkin and Pollak, 1980, p. 129; Nelkin and Pollak, 1981). This belief in large-scale technological solutions for scarcity problems is combined with the conviction that cheap and secure energy supplies are essential for continued economic growth. As such it is typical of the Old Politics.

Contrastingly, the New Politics approach to the energy problem is mindful of the natural conditions that are the basis of all industrial civilisation. Natural and renewable sources of energy (wind, sun, water), in combination with extensive measures for energy saving, are favoured by its proponents.

The German parties' positions on energy policy and the nuclear power issue neatly reflect the line of division between Old and New Politics. Not surprisingly, all parties are in favour of energy saving. However, this is a rather vague statement which needs to be interpreted in the context of a party's overall environmental policy. None of the established parties was opposed to nuclear power before 1986 – which makes them clear adherents of the Old Politics in this regard.

Naturally, there are also diverse positions on this side. Whereas the Christian parties approve of nuclear power unequivocally, the Liberals call for a variety of energy sources to be used. The Social Democratic column on this issue remains blank as far as their old basic programme and the 'Orientierungsrahmen' are concerned. Recalling the party's internal friction over energy policy, this is not at all surprising. In the wake of the Chernobyl shock, however, the party officially committed itself to a phasing-out policy. It allows for a substantial period of time until the closing-down of the last nuclear station (ten years). This long period of time was chosen in order to avoid any dangerous upheavals in the smooth functioning of the economic system. Even this relatively modest schedule is made dependent on a broad societal consensus involving also those interest groups which are clearly supportive of nuclear energy. As such, it is consistent with the overall Social Democratic strategy to let political decision primarily be guided by economic, not by ecological, considerations (SPD, 1986b). Consistently, the Berlin programme is even more vague and does not specify any period of time needed for the eventual closure of all nuclear power stations.

The Green Party, on the other hand, demands the immediate switching off of all nuclear installations. Their radical approach is supplemented by demands for substantial effort to save energy. Inefficient electric heating systems should be banned, private transport be made less attractive, and alternative methods of energy production should be developed with high priority. Special emphasis is given to the construction of small, decentralised, manageable units of energy production which are capable of reacting flexibly to consumer needs.

Agriculture

Finally, we will focus on a field of environmental policy that is largely disregarded by all established parties: agriculture. The Greens are the only party to discuss in detail the connection between the intensification and industrialisation of modern agriculture and ecological problems. They emphasise the detrimental effects of the extensive usage of chemicals in contemporary agriculture and call for strict legal controls and severe penalties for offenders. Ideally, they want a chemical-free agricultural production. Since this would result in lower productivity, farmers should be entitled to financial compensation.

Evaluating the different positions on all aspects of environmental policy, it becomes apparent that the Greens are the only party that is prepared to alter the existing economic system substantially in order to combat the ecological crisis. By and large, all other parties prefer strategies that remain within the given systemic framework and its fundamental parameters such as economic efficiency, profitability and large-scale technological solutions. Although the SPD has undergone significant programmatic change in some selected policy areas, it is still far from having an integrated ecological orientation. Ecological demands are frequently counterbalanced by political goals inspired by traditional Old Politics. Only the Greens give unequivocal priority to ecological criteria and are explicitly prepared to accept possible economic sacrifices.

d) Economic Policy

The analysis of environmental policies has already demonstrated that ecological thinking necessitates substantial political interference with the functioning of the economic system. However, Green economic policy is not only motivated by ecological arguments. Radical democratic ideals and traditional left-wing strategies have also contributed to the formulation of an economic programme that is characterised by a frequently incoherent mixture of market-based instruments and state intervention. Since Green economic ideas have been analysed to some extent in earlier sections, it is possible to be relatively brief at this point and list basic normative convictions and their consequences as follows:

- ecological thinking;
- individualism and radical democratic ideals;
- general egalitarian orientation.

In part, the repercussions of these principles in the economic system have been mentioned above. The quest for self-determination gives rise to a self-governing model of economic production. We have already pointed out that ecological thinking leads to new criteria directing economic decision-making. Mono-causal explanations, however, are insufficient. Essentially, it is the combination of ecological and radical democratic orientations that explain the specific Green design for an economic system.

Small-scale Production

Large-scale units of industrial production are considered to be ecologically inefficient and detrimental. The spatial separation of labour from the life environment and the transport of goods from centralised units to dispersed consumers cause high energy and resource consumption (see Appendix 4, Table A4.4(c, d)). Simultaneously, large and centralised structures conflict with Green ideals of self-determination and democratic governance. Also, the analysis of eco-systems has given rise to the assumption that there is an optimal size for every structure. Growth beyond such a threshold will inevitably reduce the efficiency of that given unit, and it will have a negative impact on the overall system of which it is part (Capra and Spretnak, 1984, p. 85). The Green solution is an economy that is built upon decentralised, flexible and manageable units where employees live close to their workplaces and decide together with their neighbourhood on methods and objects of production (see Appendix 4, Table A4.4(a)).

The problem of size is an important point of disagreement between the Greens and the established German parties. None of them agrees with the Green proposition that there is an inherent value in small-scale units. Only in cases where companies have grown to the extent that they are in a position to prevent competition on the market is the size of enterprises regarded as a problem. State action, however, is only envisaged against further concentration. This means that the fusion of large companies may be prohibited if this would result in a dominant position on the market. All established parties demand such anti-trust control of the state in very similar statements. The Social Democrats even favour an 'europeanisation' of the state as a countervailing strategy against the internationalisation and centralisation of capital and production.

The Greens approach the problem from a completely different angle. They reject the control of one centralised structure by another one. In the word's true sense, they favour a radical solution by decentralising the economy. It is not the functioning of the market that worries them in the first place. Rather, they want to go a substantial step beyond the preservation of the *status quo* and demand that big companies should be broken up into smaller units.

The preference for small decentralised units of production is the central element of the Green economic philosophy. This particular field of Green programmatic thinking is still in a very nascent state and therefore far from having developed towards an integrated and coherent concept. However, it is quite obvious which aspects of the present economic system are vigorously rejected by the Greens. The most important characteristics are:

- large-scale units of production;
- democratically deficient, heteronomous organisation of production;
- separation of work and life environments;
- dominance of traditional criteria of economic profitability, as opposed to ecological considerations.

Co-determination Versus Self-administration

The above-mentioned aspects are clearly constitutive for the present economic system. They are not disputed in principle by the established German parties. Substantial change of these features would therefore mean a very fundamental alteration of the economic system as a whole. However, for this particular policy area, it is much easier to identify Green points of resentment than to depict a clear conceptual alternative. To an extent, the Green arguments are inspired by anarchist or autogestive traditions. They call for 'new forms of societal ownership' and propose 'models of self-administration' or 'democratic worker self-management of the companies' (see Appendix 4, Table 4.4(a, b)). On the other hand, they demand effective co-determination schemes and want to utilise the economic steering capacity of the state. Tax and fiscal policies are envisaged for the selection of production fields and the attainment of a more equal income distribution. Clearly, such proposals are very much in tune with conventional economic strategies as they are followed by the established parties.

The apparent incoherence is largely caused by the Green failure to distinguish explicitly between long-term goals and strategies to accomplish them. Partly also, it mirrors the relatively diverse ideological baggage that has been brought into the party by its founding movements and organisational predecessors. As already pointed out in the section on democracy and state, the Greens favour state power in order to pursue their goals. But they do not favour state power for principled reasons. This instrumental view of the state, that is, the dialectic of means and ends, differentiates them from classic anarchist approaches, which reject such a distinction.

As far as the general economic model is concerned, the conflict between Green and established models is clear and unambiguous. Due to the need for a short- and medium-term strategy, the Greens are also compelled to formulate positions on the management of the present economic system – as opposed to proposals for its conversion. Here, Green and Social Democratic positions are relatively similar. Both parties consider collective ownership of means of production and natural resources to be a 'legitimate form of public control' (OR '85, 2.3.6.; see also Appendix 4, Table A4.4(b)). Whereas the Social Democratic thinking is characterised by a generally positive evaluation of state power, decentralised solutions and self-administration are favoured in this context – very much akin to the Green position.

The difference, however, lies with the degree of autonomy such decentralised units are supposed to have. Social Democrats argue for substantial state intervention, whereas the Green (long-term) goal is 'direct-democratic economic steering'. However, no detailed suggestions have been made so far as to how such decentralised and relatively autonomous units could be co-ordinated in order to achieve favourable results for society as a whole.

Whatever the differences may be between SPD and Greens, their positions conflict clearly with the attitudes of the remaining German parties. The CDU, CSU, and FDP do not even mention the – constitutionally envisaged – possibility of public ownership. Additionally, the FDP and CSU are in favour of denationalising public services (see Appendix 4, Table 4.4(b)). Similarly, Greens and SPD are united against their competitors by demanding that industrial lockouts be made illegal (see Appendix 4, Table 4.4(f)). Also, both parties emphasise the need for more 'human' working conditions. In concrete terms, they advocate less routine work and more jobs which are intellectually and technically stimulating (see Appendix 4, Table 4.4(g)).

These examples indicate that the New Politics – and hence Green political philosophy – are not indifferent to traditional left-wing positions.[11] However, support for central demands of the labour movement does not mean accepting its existing form of organisation. Not surprisingly, the Greens keep faith with their radical democratic convictions and call for more grass-roots democracy within the unions.

New Technologies

The Green Party's general attitude towards new technologies is characterised by substantial scepticism. Unlike the other German parties who approve of new technologies either explicitly or implicitly,[12] the Greens propose strict criteria for their introduction. New technologies are only to be accepted where more and meaningful employment is created and environmental conditions are improved. Their introduction should be decided politically, on the basis of a societal cost-benefit analysis and the experiences gathered from a limited experimental phase.

Compared with the present procedure of handling technological progress, this would represent a substantial change of priorities. Corresponding to the overall normative preferences that guide Green economic thinking, social and ecological criteria would assume decisive influence for the acceptance of new technologies. In the present context, economic profitability is still of overriding importance. And it is not fundamentally questioned by the established parties, although the SPD stressed in 1989 the need for more political control over the introduction of new technologies (see Appendix 4, Table A4.4).

e) Social Policy

The pervasive Green principles of decentralisation, self-determination, personal initiative and a general egalitarian disposition have also moulded their social policies. Starting from a generalised support for the expansion of the 'social infrastructure' they favour supplementing central welfare systems by furthering decentralised self-help groups (see Appendix 4, Table A4.5). This preference for smaller units is also expressed by their demand for a larger number of small hospitals.

What has been pointed out earlier for the decentralisation of political structures becomes even more apparent in the realm of social systems: decentralisation alone is normatively ambiguous. It is also advocated by the FDP, which proposes a minimum of state-guaranteed social security and wants to leave all other tasks of social caretaking to private initiative. From such an unegalitarian perspective, the furthering of small networks, with only a minimal reimbursement of costs incurred by those who are engaged in them, amounts to a substantial withdrawal of the state from social policy. The Green approach is fundamentally different: convinced that self-help ought to be more than a cheaper alternative for the present social system, Greens want such initiatives to be embedded in a unified and egalitarian welfare system. Unlike the Liberals, they consider such private initiatives as complementary elements of the welfare system. They are considered desirable only in conjunction with the provision of sufficient material backing by the state.

With varying degrees of emphasis, the Christian parties also favour more private responsibility in the social sector. Again, the principle of subsidiarity comes to bear here. However, it is not complemented by egalitarian means. Corresponding to Liberal thinking, it is primarily aimed at the reduction of state responsibility for the solution of social problems.

Until 1989, Social Democratic social policy was best characterised by the slogan 'more of the same'. Social Democrats do not criticise the bureaucratisation and centralisation of many social services that have led to a rather impersonal and technical way of dealing with social problems. But they are in favour of an egalitarian expansion of social systems alongside the present organisational structures. However, the new Berlin basic party programme indicates a significant departure from old paths: the document calls for a combination of comprehensive social security systems and integrated support for self-help and neighbourhood groups.

In a nutshell, Green positions amount to a synthesis of the major traditions. As such they are unique to Green programmatic thinking. Greens share the right-wing distaste for the negative results of centralised and bureaucratised social care, but they combine it with belief in an egalitarian, left-wing basis on which such personalised, small-scale bodies of social care ought to flourish.

Equality

Green proposals for the creation of a unified egalitarian welfare system are far more radical than Social Democratic positions. In particular, their demand for the abolition of upper income limits for compulsory health insurance schemes would mean an end to the possibility of low risk/high income groups remaining outside the collective insurance system. At the moment, these groups benefit from low rates that are primarily the result of the obligation upon compulsory health insurance schemes to take care of the unemployed, students, and adults with children who pay nothing extra for their family. Furthermore, the Greens are the only German party which demands that all taxpayers (i.e. also civil servants) should have to pay contributions for health insurance and pension funds. Also, they want to integrate private and company-based insurance schemes into the public system, which would mean taking privileges away from those who are in high income brackets or who happen to be employed in strong companies with generous special pension funds.

Egalitarian ideas also inspire Green proposals for income policy. Here, the Greens' stance is almost identical to that of the Social Democrats. Both parties argue for redistribution means in order to arrive at a more just distribution of income and wealth (see Appendix 4, Table A4.5). This differentiates them from the remaining German parties, who maintain that the German socio-economic system makes for a fair distribution of income and wealth. Instead of redistributive steps, these parties favour wealth creation schemes that facilitate the participation of employees in the annual growth of societal affluence. Such schemes are not rejected by Greens and Social Democrats. However, they are regarded as insufficient since they do not usually alter the basic pattern of distribution in society.

Education

Education relates directly to distributive justice. Levels of education are decisive for the attainment of privileged positions in the social system. Even for a party that is in favour of a far-reaching abolition of such differences, educational policies are a suitable, complementary, medium-term strategy. Privileges cannot be abolished by means of an egalitarian education system. But their allocation can be made less dependent on already existing social stratification.

Consistently, the Social Democrats and the Greens are alone in their preference for comprehensive schools. However, the Liberals also emphasise the principle of equal chances in the educational system. Surprisingly enough, they are more outspoken on this point than the Greens.

The Role of Women

The struggle for the full emancipation of women in all spheres of society plays an important role in the Green concept for a future society. Manifestly, feminism has roots that date much further back than the relatively recent emergence of the New Politics movements. But the values and participatory orientations that have helped the emergence of these new social movements were responsive to feminist ideas. Oversimplifying, it could be argued that the emergence of the New Politics has resulted in a restatement and amplification of the feminist cause. However, this does not mean that the new feminist movement is just a product of New Politics. The relationship between the Green Party – as the political representative of the New Politics – and the women's movement is troublesome and intricate: many feminists do not share the other Green preoccupations although they may participate in the party for tactical reasons.[13]

If so, their tactic has been very successful. The Green programmes are the most feminist documents in the German party political landscape. However, the Greens are closely followed by the Social Democrats who also reject the traditional division of labour, with women being mainly responsible for housework and childcare even if both partners are fully employed (see Appendix 4, Table A4.5). Consequently, they demand part-time jobs for men and women, envisage joint child education and regard paid labour as an opportunity for self-actualisation on the part of women. Such proposals are shared by the Greens, who are nevertheless more radical in some respects: they are the only party which explicitly demands legal sanctions for discrimination against women and which calls for preferential employment of women whenever new jobs are being created.

As far as their basic view of male and female roles in society is concerned, the Liberals are relatively close to the red–green position as described above. They advocate in general terms the equal division of labour between men and women. However, the relatively brief mention of this would seem to indicate that it is not regarded as a very urgent and important issue from the Liberal perspective.

The Christian parties clearly occupy a more traditional position. To them, the most noble occupation of women remains their role as mother and housewife. Since equal rights of the sexes are constitutionally as well as politically sacrosanct, Christian Democratic statements are necessarily incoherent: both Christian parties advocate the full emancipation of women. But they also assume that it is usually the mother who is going to take care of small children. However, not least as a result of Green emphasis on this policy area, things have begun to change. The cdu has approved of a list of programmatic statements concerning 'women in family, at work and in society' where a more progressive view of the female role is laid down and it is no longer taken for granted that it is automatically the mother who is responsible for childcare (cdu, 1985, II.8 and 9).

f) Foreign Relations and Defence

Deutschlandpolitik

Three major aspects of foreign policy attract major attention from the German parties: defence, Third World relations, and the so-called 'Deutschlandpolitik', that is, relations with East Germany. Obviously, the latter issue represents the quite exceptional example of a political problem being completely resolved through the course of history. Nevertheless, Green dissent on this issue has always been noticeable and explains the uneasy acceptance of the inevitability of German unification by the party. Whereas all other German parties have payed lip-service at least to the constitutionally requested goal of 'reunification in free self-determination', the Greens abandoned what seemed to be a political ritual before 1989 (see Appendix 4, Table A4.6). Instead, they wanted to overcome the division of Europe and Germany through the dissolution of the military blocs. In contrast to the position of the established German parties, national unity never had an intrinsic value for Green political thinking: the Greens had called for a full recognition of the East German state (Die Grünen, 1987, 5.14).

However, there were also substantial differences between the remaining parties. Basically, the SPD and FDP limited their statements to brief quotations of the relevant paragraph of the preamble of the basic law. Furthermore, the Social Democrats had also begun to move away from the fiction of one German state in the second half of the 1980s. In their 1987 election programme 'two independent states' are mentioned, and it is left open how the claim to 'self-determination of the German people can be realised' (SPD, 1987, p. 8). The CDU and CSU, on the other hand, have always emphasised this point to a considerable extent. Clearly, the developments of 1989 and 1990 have rewarded the Christian parties electorally for what appeared to be little more than stubbornness just one year before.

Defence[14]

Defence represents a major point of disagreement between the Greens and the established parties. The ecologists are the only political grouping that is outspokenly pacifist in its fundamental approach to international relations (see Appendix 4, Table A4.6(d)). None of their central demands – the Federal Republic leaving NATO, dissolution of the military blocs, non-violent defence, unilateral disarmament – is explicitly shared by any other German party (Die Grünen, 1987, p. 5). This does not mean, however, that the remaining parties' attitudes are uniform. On the contrary, they align neatly along the dimension that has emerged for most political issues. As in most cases, the Christian Democrats occupy the most Old Politics-oriented position. They are predominantly concerned with security through strength, based on NATO, nuclear weapons and 'strong defence efforts'. Their security philosophy is based on the doctrine of mutual deterrence, which means that peace is best secured by military parity. Consistently, they reject any unilateral steps of disarmament.

All these principles are basically shared by Liberals and Social Democrats. However, they put more weight upon efforts to control the arms race and the pursuit of *détente*. Despite the party's commitment to NATO, the SPD argues for a long-term strategy to overcome the military blocs and accomplish a comprehensive European peace treaty (SPD, 1987, p. 8). Nevertheless, the fundamental antagonism is between the Greens and the rest.[15] It involves the conflict between two philosophies: unilateralism versus mutual disarmament.

Third World

For Third World policies, the main line of division runs between the SPD and the Greens on one side and the remaining German parties on the other. Both left-wing parties favour a true redistribution of world wealth which would necessarily entail sacrifices by the industrialised nations. Although the Green proposals are more detailed and specific, there is no difference so far as the underlying principle is concerned. The preparedness to incur real sacrifices in order to help the underdeveloped countries is not shared by the CDU, CSU, or FDP. Those parties want to rely on the established international economic system for the solution of the Third World problem. Conflictingly, the proposals of their opponents amount to a (at least partial) change in the world market system. In their view, this is necessary in order to alter the terms of trade substantially and to reduce the domination of Third World economies by the needs of the industrialised countries.

Europe

Support for European integration and the further development of existing European institutions is probably the most uncontroversial political issue among the established German parties. All of them favour the strengthening of the European institutions by giving them more decision-making powers. Of course, there are nuances: The Christian parties emphasise the principle of federalism, whereas the SPD argues for more centralised power in order to develop countervailing forces against the centralising tendencies of capital.

Green attitudes towards Europe are neither very surprising nor worked out in much detail. Greens regard the EC as the logical extension of the undemocratic and centralised structures of European nation-states. Consequently, their demands closely resemble those put forward in the national context: introduction of elements of direct democracy, decentralisation of the European structures, and the general demand for an EC policy which is guided by ecological considerations. However, the exact nature of the projected 'Europe of regions' consisting of autonomous, self-determined, interconnected regions is not described in any detail (see Appendix 4, Table A4.6(c)).

SUMMARY: THE GULF BETWEEN OLD AND NEW POLITICS

The comparative analysis of German party programmes has demonstrated the following:

1. Green programmatic orientations conform to the range of issues emphasised by the various elements of the New Politics syndrome.
2. Despite some programmatic adaptation by the SPD, Green positions in New Politics areas are still fundamentally different from the beliefs of all other German parties.

So far as the party system as a whole is concerned, Green programmatic thinking represents a substantial challenge to the legitimation of the established German parties. A considerable number of political demands represent restatements of

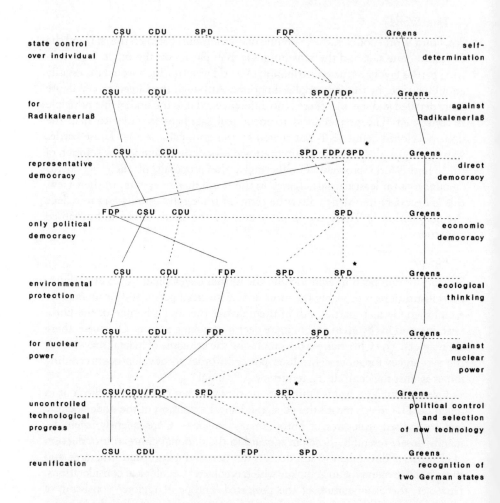

Figure 7.1: Programmatic Space between Parties.[1]

Note:

1. The figure represents a graphical depiction of the relative positions of German parties for selected policy areas. The distances are based on qualitative analysis; they have only ordinal quality and ought to be understood as a visualisation of major points of the preceding discussion. Starred positions are the 1989 positions.

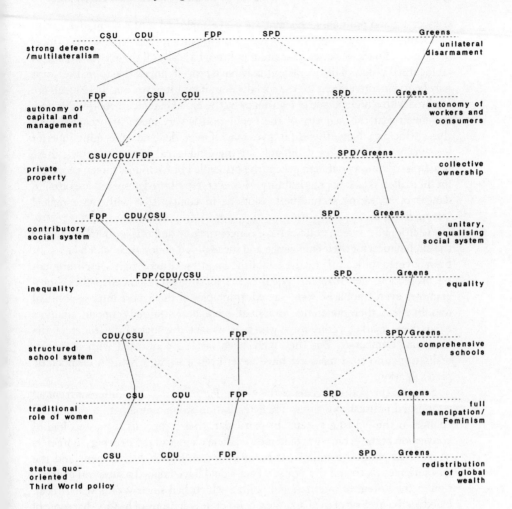

democratic and political ideals that are well established in the normative canon of German politics: openness, extension of participatory rights, grass-roots democracy, financial honesty, amateur politics; basically all these points relate to an idealised vision of democracy. It may have proved impossible to realise, or it may be too inconvienient for the socially dominant interests. But these ideals are credited with a high degree of legitimacy by the broad public. Of course, this does not mean that the majority of the population is very much preoccupied with these principles. Nevertheless, it gives many Green demands a seeming superior legitimacy, which makes it difficult for the established parties to attack these principles. The way out is to accept the principle but to dismiss Green proposals for their alleged lack of practicability. However, established proposals are often in danger of appearing second-best solutions in competition with more radical Green demands.

Additionally, Green policies have concentrated – and this is obviously part of the explanation for their emergence and success – on policy areas which have not been covered sufficiently by the established parties: citizens' rights, environmental protection, disarmament, equal rights for women. Ironically, Green programmes even emphasise some sacred principles of their most intense political foes. In effect, their preference for a small-scale, decentralised economy amounts to an ideal market economy – which is in fact the ideological tenet of the Christian Democrats. But they have been far less concerned with its actual realisation: anti-trust measures have never been a strong Christian Democratic preoccupation.

Some of the political goals of the Green Party are radically different from all established political positions. Their realisation would amount to a substantial change in the existing system. In particular, their proposals for an ecological conversion of the economy would mean radical change of the existing parameters of national politics. Similarly, their quest for unilateral disarmament and the dissolution of NATO and the Warsaw Pact would have implied a substantial alteration of the system of international politics which had since World War II been based on the freezing of the East–West conflict. It is an irony of history that some of these goals have been accomplished through the total collapse of the Warsaw Pact. It remains to be seen, however, whether Europe will become a safer place.

However, there are few things in politics that are not negotiable. In most cases it comes down to a question of time. Although the Greens are a system-transcending party in many respects, there is no reason to argue that there could not be agreements with other parties on short- or medium-term policies.

Our analysis has demonstrated that the SPD would be the 'natural' partner for the Greens, since it is the only party which is sufficiently close to Green programmatic positions in a number of policy areas (Figure 7.1). This is particularly true for social and economic policies. On the whole, the Greens tend to be more radical and egalitarian. However, the concordance extends only to policies that relate to the immediate management and improvement of the present socio-economic system. As far as the essentials of the New Politics are concerned –

ecology, unilateralism, participatory democracy and individualism – the SPD still tends to be closer to the Old Politics camp, although the 1989 Berlin programme has brought about significant movement towards the Greens. Figure 7.1 depicts the relative positions of the German parties on a number of policy areas. In some cases, the SPD has been located at two different positions to indicate the program-matic adaptation of the party to the Green challenge.[16]

Feminism is the second major policy area where Green and Social Democratic positions are relatively akin. As has been pointed out already, this can be explained by the fact that the emergence of feminism preceded the relatively recent surge of the New Politics.

It is the egalitarian disposition which places the Greens unambiguously on the far left of the political spectrum, including in the traditional sense of this concept. This is true despite resemblances between some Green positions and political strategies and goals that are usually found on the opposite side of the political scale: decentralisation, the preference for private initiatives, the dislike of bureaucratic solutions, personalisation of social care. Together with their apparent idealisation of nature which still provokes negative associations in post-Fascist Germany, such programmatic positions have often given rise to the suspicion that the Greens are really disguised Conservatives of a rather danger-ous, because a-historical, kind.

However, these political goals have to be interpreted in the context of fundamentally egalitarian orientations that are in many fields combined with the preference for autonomous and participatory solutions. This gives them a differ-ent, left-wing quality. Decentralised, autonomous models of economic and societal organisations resemble anarchist utopias. Their normative content is completely different from Conservative or reactionary orientations. What all these models have in common with the political right is a certain degree of formal – organisational – similarity.

Similarly, Green attitudes toward nature are not inspired by a mythical rela-tionship. On the contrary, the starting-point of the ecology movement has been the scientific analysis of the interrelated functioning of natural systems. Prima-rily, ecology is regarded as a scientific discipline that provides hard facts pointing to the necessity for a fundamental change in present-day politics. Ecology is not a kind of new religion for most Greens. Of course, this does not preclude the possibility that individuals with a mythical and irrational attitude towards nature may be attracted by the Green struggle for the preservation of the environment.

This is not to say that Green orientations towards nature are completely devoid of any spiritual content. The political commitment to the environment is not just motivated by scientific analysis. Clearly, a relatively unscathed natural environment also has aesthetic and emotional values – in this sense, the Greens are a spiritual movement. However, it could be argued that, from a different perspective and for people with another emotional structure, the sight of large industrial conglomerations or stringently structured concrete housing estates also arouses passion.[17]

The argument that the Green programme is mainly inspired by a cyclical resurgence of political idealism is therefore not entirely convincing. The criticism is mainly based on a seeming similarity between Green ideas and the 'Wandervogel' movement and the more widespread reaction against modernity that flourished in Germany after the turn of the century. However, the contexts of these movements are substantially different. Whereas the latter reacted against the introduction of modern technology and the victory of industrialisation, Green struggles are directed at the search for an industrial society that leaves the eco-system as intact as possible.

The 'idealistic' image of the Greens is mainly produced by the simple mechanics of political competition. Every movement that calls for fundamental change of the existing parameters of the social, economic and political system appears to be idealistic by default – because it lacks the legitimisation of already existing facts. It has to set ideas against the facts of an established system that has proved to function to at least some extent. Clearly, political forces which basically wish to remain within the given framework appear 'realistic' and rational, whereas any fundamental opposition is tainted by 'unrealistic' and 'idealistic' beliefs. In fact, idealism is little more than an empty box that is filled with normative content according to a specific historical situation.

Although the foregoing analysis has shown that the Greens are clearly distant from all established parties on most policy areas, it is worthwhile recapitulating fields of possible compromise with the established parties. As far as the Christian parties are concerned, affinities extend only to political 'labels' like decentralisation. It has been shown, however, that they have a completely different meaning in the context of Green programmes. Disagreements with the FDP over social and economic policies are likely to override 'programmatic neighbourhoods' in the field of classical Liberal themes in most cases of actual coalition politics. This leaves the Greens with the SPD as possible coalition partner. Both parties have similar locations on the traditional left–right continuum. However, they are still divided over a number of central issues associated with the New Politics like ecology, technological progress, direct democracy and unilateral disarmament. The SPD takes positions in these fields that are much closer to those of the other established parties than to the goals of the Greens. Nevertheless, it is still the party that is closest to the Greens. Bearing in mind that politics is the art of the possible, this could, in combination with the consensus on short-term social and economic management, provide a viable basis for red-green co-operation.

NOTES

1. Much relevant material is contained in studies that focus on the early history of the German Greens and its organisationl forerunners (Klotzsch and Stöss; 1984; Papadakis, 1984; Langguth, 1983; Brand, 1985; Brand *et al.*, 1984; Hallensleben, 1984, van Hüllen, 1990. For documentary evidence see Die Grünen, 1988a; Die Grünen, 1988b.
2. See the debate between the Green MPs Antje Vollmer and Otto Schily in *Der Spiegel*, No. 13, 1985, pp. 75ff.; also StZ, 5 January 1987.
3. Even conservative newspapers have criticised excessive police violence, and some

police actions have been declared illegal by law courts. See FAZ report on a demonstration at the nuclear site of Brokdorf; FAZ, 7 June 1976. Another example is the 'Hamburg encirclement', where several hundred citizens were surrounded by police forces for more than 12 hours: StZ, 13 June 1986; FAZ, 14 June 1986; *Der Spiegel*, No.25, 1986, pp. 95ff.; StZ, 7 March 1987.

4. Press photographs from demonstrations against the nuclear reprocessing plant near Wackersdorf show elderly people collecting and filling up beer cans for streetfighters (*Der Spiegel*, No. 30, 1986, pp. 32ff.)!

5. Action programmes are of secondary importance because they tend to be integrated in subsequent election programmes.

6. See Appendix 4 for list of documents.

7. For a more detailed discussion of this problem, see Smith, 1982a, pp. 204ff.; Lamprecht, 1982, pp. 78ff.

8. There are small minorities within the party who exclusively apply ecological thinking to all aspects of political life. However, they are not relevant for the character of the party as a whole.

9. The CSU does not mention this principle explicitly. However, the subsequent discussion will demonstrate that it is also part of the CSU concept (see also CSU, 1980, pp. 23ff.).

10. This method is also proposed by the Social Democrats. Although they do not explicitly mention the market mechanism in this context, they suggest environmental cost be levied on producers (Appendix 4, Table A4.3).

11. Cf. the discussion of the general left-wing quality of New Politics in Chapter 2.

12. According to the logic laid out above, omission is equivalent to non-opposition to the *status quo*.

13. See Brand *et al.* 1984, p. 118f. for the relation between Feminism and New Politics.

14. Naturally, the subsequent analysis cannot incorporate the breathtaking events in Eastern Europe after 1989, because none of the parties has been able to revise its programmes accordingly. Nevertheless, basic orientations towards this policy area are also reflected in the somewhat outdated programmatic statements that are the basis of this analysis.

15. Admittedly, there are quite substantial differences between the established parties that cannot be analyzed within the present context.

16. The starred positions are the 1989 positions.

17. Although this may seem to be an overstatement at first, it ought to be recalled that the domination of nature by industrial technology or the Bauhaus architecture was not only propagated on grounds of cost-effiency or the need for increased productivity.

8. The Challenge from a Participatory Party: The Organisation of the German Parties

INTRODUCTION

An important element of New Politics is shifts in participatory dispositions and behaviour, which coincide with related attitudinal changes. Their impact on party organisation will be analyzed in this chapter. Although the main focus will be on the organisational structure and the internal workings of the Green Party, all established parties are integrated in the analysis to some degree. Whereas this can easily be done for a comparison of internal party democracy on a formal level, a comparative approach extending to all aspects of internal party life would take too much space without advancing the purposes of this chapter too much. Consequently, the established parties have merely been used as reference points.

Two analytically distinct modes of participation are commonly distinguished: *Élite-challenging* political participation has gained considerable prominence in recent years. It means the direct involvement of the participant in specific political decisions (i.e. direct democracy) and can be explained by the growing disposition to use unconventional, sometimes even illegal, forms of political action in order to influence political decisions in the desired way (Barnes, *Kaase et al.*, 1979; Kaase, 1982). It is important to distinguish this type of political involvement from conventional, *élite-directed* participation, which is character-ised by generalised and reactive political behaviour. The individual chooses between alternative political packages that are usually presented by political élites (Chapter 2). No policy formulation is involved here. The most common form of this type of conventional participation is voting in elections.

The analysis of Green activists and electoral support has demonstrated that the party's social bases are disproportionately disposed towards unconventional, that is, *élite-challenging*, political action (see Chapters 5 and 6). Contrastingly, the social bases of the established parties are mainly characterised by preferences for élite-directed participation and representative forms of democracy, with the SPD having the largest portion of New Politics elements (Forschungsgruppe Wahlen, 1983; Müller-Rommel, 1984b). Contrary to Michels' assumption of rank-and-file lethargy (Michels, 1989, pp. 46ff.) and ensuing oligarchic tenden-cies, the Greens should therefore be significantly less hierarchical than estab-lished parties.

It seems reasonable to expect, that the attitudinal and participatory composi-tion of a party's membership should be reflected in its organisational outlook (Duverger, 1964, p. 165). Parties moulded by predominantely élite-directed participation and a political ideology geared to representative forms of democracy and trust in political élites are likely to provide few participatory arenas. Also, they should primarily rely on representative forms of élite-selection and policy formulation. Alternatively, New Politics parties should be characterised by a relatively low degree of formalisation (which hinders spontaneous participation) and easy access to internal decision-making and policy formulation. Furthermore, the anti-hierarchy ideology generic to New Politics should result in strong control of the party leadership by the base. In short, the internal organisation of the party should provide a good chance for the individual member to participate effectively in party politics.

In the case of parties that originated before the emergence of the New Politics, organisational inertia may well hinder a relatively straightforward translation of such shifts into a party's statute books. This is particularly true if participatory forces remain in a minority position. For this reason, all established German parties – including the SPD – are likely to be relatively non-participatory. The Greens have been founded recently, mainly by New Politics movements. Hence, there are no party-specific impediments against a participatory party structure. Obviously, behavioural and attitudinal dispositions should leave an even clearer mark on Green internal participatory culture and 'working modes' which will also be analysed in the sections below.

This chapter is primarily concerned with an assessment of the effects of these political preferences and participatory orientations on the organisational structure and the internal functioning of the Green Party. It represents also an evaluation of the Green's organisational performance and adaptation during their first decade of existence, that is, until the end of 1990. It is important to be aware of the fact that some of the statutory rules that are analysed in the following sections were changed or abolished in Spring 1991. However, the analysis of their nature and their effects is a necessary precondition for the understanding of the limitations to grass-roots democracy within the framework of a representative, parliamentary democracy. A final section will then discuss causes and consequences of the organisational reform after the Green defeat in the first all-German elections of 2 December 1990.

THE CONCEPT OF 'BASISDEMOKRATIE'

Central to Green organisational philosophy is the concept of 'Basisdemokratie' (grass-roots democracy or direct democracy). It is meant to be a model for society as a whole and represents the fundamental normative standard for all organisational efforts undertaken by the Green Party. Therefore, we will use this self-declared ideal as a 'yardstick' for our analysis. Clearly, the concept of grass-roots democracy has not been invented by the West German alternative movement. It relates to ideals of participatory democracy which have a long tradition in Anglo-American political thought (Pateman, 1980) and which are inspired by the Rousseauian ideal of creating a single identity of rulers and ruled (Greiffenhagen, 1973, p. 33). As such, they contrast with the 'pragmatic' model of representative democracy, which puts its emphasis on the inevitable difference between electors and elected. As Schumpeter pointed out, people should entrust politics to the politicians, accepting that this is their business and granting them the necessary confidence (Greiffenhagen, 1973, p. 19).

The philosophical principles of grass-roots democracy correspond neatly to the empirically observed shifts in values and participatory norms, that is, the desire for autonomy and direct participation: Political decisions should always be taken on the lowest possible levels, thus facilitating a maximum of direct in-volvement by those who will be affected by these decisions. At least in theory, it means the pre-eminence of the so-called 'Basis' (grass roots), the smallest organi-sational units (Bundesprogramm, Präambel, p. 5). Hence, it is different from models of decentralisation or subsidiary organisation which envisage a certain distribution of competences between various political levels.

Consequently, individual political power – where indispensable – should be limited and controlled as much as possible. This gives rise to the idea of collective leadership. Other principles of grass-roots democracy are mentioned in the pre-amble of the party programme :

> the central idea is the permanent control of all office and mandate holders and institutions by the grass roots (openness, time limits on mandates and party offices) and the permanent possibility of recall in order to make organisation and politics transparent for all, and to counteract the es-trangement of individuals from their grass roots. (Bundesprogramm, Präambel)[1]

Several means have been instituted by the Greens in order to prevent an estrangement between the grass roots and élites: the terms of office are limited (rotation), and party posts are not salaried (Bundesprogramm, V 1.3). Ten years of experience with a non-professionalised leadership, however, have led to an adaptation of ideals to political realities: the Duisburg party conference of March 1989 decided that members of the federal executive will be entitled to a salary (GB, 4/1989, p. 18; see below for a detailed discussion). By restricting the period of service, Greens hope to alleviate the inevitable social pressures and socialising effects which are concomitants of the exposed position of party élites and MPs (Duverger, 1964, p. 190f.). Also, rotation sets limits to the acquisition of personal prestige (Weinberger, 1984, p. 117). Such personalisation of politics is rejected by the Greens.

Additionally, 'amateur politics' is seen as a means of hindering the develop-ment of a professionalised party oligarchy. People are expected to run for office for political, not financial, reasons. The principle of public meetings further demonstrates the willingness to expose policy-making to full democratic control. To summarise, the concept of 'Basisdemokratie' comprises the following essen-tials:

- collective leadership;
- effective control of office and mandate holders by the rank-and-file ('im-perative mandate');

- rotation;
- openness;
- pre-eminence of the lowest unit.

'Basisdemokratie' is not an alternative model to representative democracy, but an extension: in all possible instances, representation is to be replaced by direct participation; in other cases, a maximum of information for the grass roots ought to be ensured. This is the leading perspective for our subsequent analysis of the internal structures and processes of the German parties. To put it succinctly we are asking: how direct-democratic are they? However, there are certain limits to the full translation of participatory ideals into political practice.

SYSTEMIC CONSTRAINTS

The organisational structure of all German parties is in many respects determined by relatively extensive and detailed legislation. The constitutionally required organisational conformity with 'democratic principles' (Grundgesetz, Art. 21) is laid out in great detail in the 'party law'. Furthermore, the electoral law regulates procedures of candidate selection and even specifies veto powers which the party hierarchy may use against certain lower-level nominations (Wahlgesetz, §21.4). The most important rules that relate to party organisation are as follows:

- a party conference must be convened at least every second year;
- membership or delegate assemblies are the decisive organs;
- the party leadership must be elected at least every second year (§9.1, Parteiengesetz);
- imperative mandate inside party organisation is illegal (§15.3, Parteiengesetz).

Hence, German parties are bound to be relatively similar in terms of their candidate selection procedures, organisational structure and units and the degree of democratic autonomy of lower-level units (for example the right to propose motions for higher-level assemblies, Parteiengesetz, §15.3).

This means, that all parties have a certain degree of internal democracy on the formal level. However, parties can voluntarily transcend this minimum level and move towards more direct democracy. It is here that we can expect the Greens to be substantially more democratic than established parties.

There are, however, also technical obstacles to 'ideal' internal democracy: party politics in a highly differentiated political system inevitably requires the formation of an organisation with a certain degree of representation, specialisation and exclusive decision-making. A party conference may be assembled in order to decide upon a coalition agreement or even the annual budget. But it is inconceivable for the federal executive or the parliamentary party to consult the rank-and-file on all important political moves. Similarly, it might be desirable on normative grounds to have general assemblies instead of assemblies of delegates. However, this is technically impossible for any party of significant size.

Comparing party organisations confronts us with a dilemma. Exclusive concentration on party statutes provides us with easily comparable 'hard' facts. The
results, however, may well be quite unrealistic, because the real working practices
of a party can differ widely from what statutory provisions were intended to
guarantee – or camouflage. But how to unveil the real functioning of a party
machine? Reliable quantitative indicators are rare and often almost impossible to
obtain, since parties are not always very enthusiastic about such research. In any
case, the influence and power of cliques or the degree of oligarchisation might
often be assessed more adequately by expert judgement than by quantitative
measurement. Thus, this chapter combines a comparative analysis of the formal
organisational structures of the German parties with a thorough study of the
internal functioning of the Greens, which is based on a wide range of sources:
documentary evidence, interviews, participant observation, and relevant publications of Green activists.

FORMAL ORGANISATIONAL STRUCTURE

a) Party

This section is not concerned with the detailed description of the various party
organisations, but with a systematic and analytical comparison of formal internal
democracy. The decisive criterion in this context is the lowest possible level on
which certain political initiatives are possible. This determines the openness of
access to political influences and decision-making. It would be of little value to
focus on higher levels: a party conference can always be convened by the federal
executive. But it makes a difference whether or not a certain number of individual members can also call it. It is in this case that party conferences can play a
decisive role in internal party politics. Table 8.1 compares the barriers individual
members have to overcome if they wish to have an impact on this arena of
decision-making. Additionally, the location of budgetary decisions is compared.
The figures represent relative positions of the parties for each aspect, that is, rank
orders ranging from most open (5) to least open access (1)[2].

The results correspond neatly to the hypothesis put forward in the first section
of this chapter. All established parties are relatively close to each other; no clear
rank order emerges. Ironically, the Liberals are somewhat more hierarchical, as
far as these four selected items are concerned. However, this might be a product
of the combination of a hierarchical concept of party organisation with relatively
low membership figures. This suggests the elevation of certain decisions to higher
levels in order to have them taken by 'relevant' constituencies. Clearly, the
Greens are the most participatory party. Due to their low membership figures,
(approximately 38,000 in 1989; Poguntke with Boll, 1992), important initiatives
can be taken by very few individuals: 10 per cent of all constituency organisations, the figure needed to demand the convocation of a party conference, would
not involve more than a few hundred members, if the respective organisations in
Saarland and Bavaria, where the rate of organisation is still relatively low,
decided to do this.

Table 8.1: The Location of Political Initiative in German Parties - Lowest Possible Entry.

Kind of action		CDU	CSU	FDP	SPD	GREENS
Convocation of extraordinary party congress	level:	1/3 of Land-organisations (§28.5)	3 regional conferences (§38.3)	4 Land-executives (§12.2)	2/5 regional executives (§21.1)	10% of district organisations (§8.4)
	rank order:	2.5	2.5	2.5	2.5	5
Budget decisions	level:	federal executive (§15-FO)	presidium (§24.2)	federal executive (§2-FO)	federal executive (§7-FO)	party congress (§12-FO)
	rank order:	2.5	2.5	2.5	2.5	5
Motions for party congress	level:	district executive (§6-GO)	district executive or assembly (§45.1)	5 district organisations (§11.1)	local organisations (§18.2)	20 members (§8.5)
	rank order:	2.5	2.5	1	4	5
Selection of federal delegates	level:	district or higher (§28.1)	district and region (§21)	Land-Party congress (§13.8)	region or sub-region (§15)	district (§8.1)
	rank order:	4	3	1	2	5
	average rank:	2.9	2.6	1.8	2.8	5

The Table gives the lowest possible levels for selected political initiatives (1 = highest level, 5 = lowest). The paragraphs refer to the relevant party statues from 1989: 'GO = standing orders (Geschäftsordnung); 'FO' = financial statute (Finanzordnung). No distinction is made between the competences of party leaderships and party conferences on the same level of organisation. The exception is the decision on the party budget, which has to be taken on the federal level. Since district organisations of the SPD sometimes play the role of Land organisations, both levels are collapsed into one category. The exception is the CSU, whose highest level is the Land - with a quasi-federal function: district and Land levels are kept separate here. The Land level is treated in the same way as the federal levels of all other parties.

However, the Greens' participatory party organisation involves other important elements:

Separation of Party Office and Mandate

A substantial degree of formal internal democracy may be almost neutralised by the emergence of a small party élite which is allowed to accumulate all the most powerful positions in the party and in the parliaments. Again, the Greens are the only party which strictly separates mandate and party office (§9.5).[3]

Office Accumulation

Whereas CDU and FDP have no statutory restrictions as far as the accumulation of party offices is concerned, the CSU and SPD have some limitations. The Social

Democrats do not permit more than two seats in executives above the local level, which facilitates the combination of two chairmanships.[4] Alternatively, the csu does not limit the number of seats in party executives, but allows only one chairmanship beyond the local level (§44.8). The Green principles are the most restrictive and inhibit any combination of offices beyond the lowest level (Bundesprogramm, p. 29). Strictly speaking, a paragraph in the party programme is not a binding statutory rule, but there have been no conspicuous violations of this organisational principle.

There are several other statutory rules which distinguish the Green organisational model. The Greens are the only party which

- explicitly stipulates the full political autonomy of the local organisations (§10): *autonomy;*
- gives its members access to meetings on all levels, including the federal executives and the parliamentary party (§5.2; §8.7, Ismayr, 1985, p. 301): *openness;*
- limits the terms of office in the federal executive to a maximum of four years, followed by a minimum pause of one year (§9.1, Frankland, 1987, p. 16): *rotation;*
- gives its working groups full autonomy and the right to propose motions for party conferences (§5.1; §8.5): *grass roots participation;*[5]
- has a collective leadership: three party leaders, who are called 'speakers', share power and responsibility. However, they do not have political dominance over the remaining eight members of the federal executive and normally consult them as far as possible, especially in controversial matters:[6] *collective leadership;*
- had no *professionalised leadership* (Bundesprogramm, V 1.3): members of the federal executive, for example, could only claim a moderate daily allowance for clearly defined political activities if they took place from Monday to Friday (Duisburg minutes, appendix 18). These rules were changed in March 1989: all eleven members of the federal executive were now entitled to a salary according to the payment structure of the public service (category BAT III). However, this is below the income of parliamentary assistants or members of the academic staff of the federal party headquarters, who are paid according to BAT IIa (GB 4/1989, p. 18);
- insists on sex parity for all party offices and gives women special veto powers for issues that are particularly relevant for women:[7] *equal rights.*

The debate over sex parity in elected offices demonstrates the impact the Greens have had on the established parties. Meanwhile, the spd has approved of a step-by-step approach towards a 40 per cent quota for all offices and mandates by 1994, and the cdu has committed itself to similar goals without formal regulations.

In sum, the principal organisational structure of the Green Party is as follows:[8] unlike other parties, the Greens have a collective leadership which is composed of three chairpersons (speakers), the treasurer, and the federal secretary (Schriftführer), who constitute the 'executive committee' (geschäftsführender Bundesvorstand). Together with six ordinary members, they form the federal executive of the Green Party. Members of the Bundestag, the European parliament or a Land parliament cannot be elected to the federal or a Land executive.

The federal executive is bound by decisions of the federal council (Bundeshauptausschuß), which is made up of delegates of the Land parties and the federal executive. It is the highest body between party conferences and meets at least every three months. An important task of the federal council is to guarantee communication between the grass roots, the leadership and the parliamentary party. Furthermore, it should determine party politics and is entitled to issue binding guidelines to the parliamentary party.

On the Land level, there are two different organisational models. In most cases, the highest body is a party conference, which is made up by delegates of the constituency organisations. The Land organisations of the 'city states' Hamburg, Bremen and Berlin and the Greens in Hesse adhere to the ideal of direct democracy by calling general assemblies, which are open to all members. In some cases, however, only issues of fundamental importance need to be discussed by general assemblies whereas everyday politics can be referred to assemblies of delegates. However, the gains in terms of easy access for ordinary members may be outweighed by the danger that a highly motivated core of activists can control party politics while members who are less committed – or who simply lack the time to go to frequent general assemblies – become increasingly frustrated (Hoplitschek, 1982; Heidger, 1987, p. 147).

b) Parliamentary Party

Legislative and technical constraints have set limits which even the most committed proponents of direct democracy could not ignore when setting up the party organisation. The result is a party statute which successfully reconciles these imperatives with the grass-roots democratic principles of the party. The true organisational philosophy of the Greens becomes even more obvious when we examine the way their parliamentary party in the Bundestag is organised. Strictly speaking, it was not organised at all for the first parliamentary term! Unconstrained by the need to organise a large number of people (as in the party), Green MPs refused in February 1984 to approve standing orders (Geschäftsordnung) which had been drafted by a select committee (RB 2, 1984, p. 10).

Obviously, this reflects deeply-rooted Green mistrust of formalised structures, which are considered to be the first step towards the inevitable emergence of an oligarchy. Manoeuvring between the Scylla of oligarchy and the Charybdis of chaos and/or informal, uncontrollable power centres, Greens generally tend to prefer the latter. Nevertheless, the need for efficiency often leads them to adhere to a certain procedural routine. By and large, the rejected standing orders were the basis of the parliamentary party's work. By not formally adopting them, however, it was always possible to resort to the direct-democratic sovereign, the plenary session.[9] When the new parliamentary party convened after the 1987 election, scepticism about formalities had been eroded through four years of parliamentary experience and the standing orders were formally passed. They can therefore be treated as being legally valid for our analysis.[10]

In any case, the most fundamental regulations concerning the parliamentary party had been imposed on it by a party conference decision in Sindelfingen, January 1983. All these rules, which will be described subsequently, are unique to the Green parliamentary party. Hence, no reference to other German parties is necessary.

Rotation

Although the rules were changed after the experiences of the first term in the Bundestag, rotation remained a central element of Green organisational philosophy throughout the 1980s. For the 1983–7 period, Green MPs had to resign from their posts after two years of service (Sindelfingen minutes, appendix). As the subsequent analysis will show, this caused too many practical problems. It was therefore decided before the 1987 Bundestag elections to permit Green MPs to serve one full legislative term. Nevertheless, the principle of limited terms remained intact. Furthermore, the left-wing Land parties of Hamburg and Berlin decided to adhere to the old procedure and exchanged their MPs in spring 1989 (GBU 3/1989, p. 10).

According to the original two-year rotation rule, the Greens almost completely changed their parliamentary team at mid term in 1985. All but one elected member of the Bundestag group resigned from their positions. The mandates were then taken over by a corresponding number of Green candidates who had occupied the subsequent positions on the respective Land lists for the general election. Most of these so-called 'movers-up' (Nachrücker) had been employed as parliamentary assistants from the beginning of the legislative term. Together with delegates from those Länder that did not elect Green MPs and the serving parliamentary representatives, they formed the parliamentary group of the Greens called *Die Grünen im Bundestag*. Internally, no distinction was made between MPs, their successors or delegates: everybody had equal rights and competences. After rotation, former MPs were expected to remain in Bonn, in order to take over the jobs of their successors and to support them in their difficult task of coming to terms with parliamentary rules and procedures.

Only Green MPs who were asked by a 70 per cent majority of their Land party conference to remain in office were allowed to do so – an exeption which did not occur in 1985 (RB 3, 1985, p. 9f.). The regulations valid for the first four years also prohibited rotation from Land parliaments to the Bundestag as well as more than four years of continous membership in the Bundestag group. The latter rule was somewhat ambiguous: a Green MP who did not serve as a member of the parliamentary group before or after rotation would have been eligible for the following legislative term. This would have been counterproductive, because it could have encouraged Green politicians to stay in Bonn only for the duration of their mandate. However, only very few MPs took advantage of this loophole.

As the Green Party has grown older, however, it has become apparent that statututory regulations have not always been kept up to date with political practice. The so-called 'Quer-Rotation' has become frequent. MPs who have completed their term in a Land parliament frequently managed to get nominated for the Bundestag (or vice versa), thereby undermining the idea of an amateur politics.

Obviously, the principle of rotation is highly precarious constitutionally (Stöss, 1984; Dicke and Stoll, 1985; Versteyl, 1985; Rebe, 1985). In Lower Saxony, for example, the president of the Land parliament refused to accept the resignation of Green deputies, on the grounds that they had not taken this decision of their own free will.[11] This example demonstrates the problem. By collectively deciding upon such principles, the Green Party runs the risk of being accused of constraining the free will of its MPs – which is constitutionally guaranteed. In the end, the constitutional court of Lower Saxony ruled that the resignations had to be accepted. But the Greens learned their lesson: when Petra Kelly refused to 'rotate' along with her colleagues of the Bundestag group, the parliamentary party reacted only mildly critical (RB 3, 1985, p. 7). Of course, this was also partly due to the fact that a conflict might have caused her to leave the parliamentary party which would have endangered its status as a proper parliamentary group.[12]

Parliamentary Allowance

Another basic Green tenet is the rejection of 'vicarious democracy'. Politics should be made by those who are affected by it. A means of at least symbolising such identity of representatives and represented is the limitation of the income of MPs: Green Bundestag deputies are expected to retain no more from their parliamentary allowance than the average wage of a skilled worker: 2,100 German marks per month net during the 1987–90 legislative term.[13] This already includes holiday and Christmas payments. Additionally, they are allowed to keep 500 marks for each person they have to support and a third (1,500 marks) of the tax-free expense allowance that is paid to every MP. Green MPs are expected to donate the rest of their income to special eco-funds in the Länder. These funds support alternative life-style and ecological projects (RB 3, 1985, p. 15f.; RB 2, 1984, p. 12f.; RB 1, 1984, p. 24; Ismayr, 1985, p. 301). Obviously, there are no legal sanctions a German party could use against its own MPs who refuse to comply with such rules. In view of the very low income limits, which hardly suffice to cover all the expenses related with being a member of parliament, it is therefore not surprising that there was a growing tendency among Green MPPs to keep more of their income (Diätenkommission, 1991).

According to the Sindelfingen decision, the successors/predecessors (Nachrücker/Vorrücker) had to be treated in the same way. Formally, they were employed by the parliamentary party. This led to technical problems with the expense allowance: whereas Green MPs received this money tax-free, non-MPs had to be financed out of the normal budget of the parliamentary party.[14] Paying the expense allowance net would have necessitated the detailed documentation of all actual expenses, a task which would have absorbed the bulk of the administrative capacity of the parliamentary party. It was therefore decided to pay the allowance as part of the normal income, that is, gross (RB 1, 1984, p. 3f.). Consequently, MPs ended up having more money available than non-MPs: a slight violation of Green principles, but nevertheless indicative of the severe technical and status-related problems involved in the attempt to treat MPs and non-MPs exactly equally (Sindelfingen minutes, appendix, p. 2; RB 1, 1984, p. 3f.).

Imperative Mandate

Due to the clear provisions of the German basic law, which guarantee the freedom and independence of MPs, attempts to establish something like an imperative mandate were bound to remain on the level of mere declarations of political will: the 1983 Sindelfingen conference approved of a motion stipulating that the members of the Green parliamentary party are bound by decisions of the party congress and the federal council (Bundeshauptausschuß). However, the sanction – expulsion from the Green parliamentary group – was hardly a credible option during the 1983–7 legislative period, because it would have deprived the party of most of its parliamentary privileges (see note 12).

Collective Leadership

In conformity with its principle of limiting formal power as far as possible, the Green parliamentary party has established a collective leadership. It is composed of three chairmen ('speakers') who have equal rights, the parliamentary manager (parlamentarischer Geschäftsführer) and his two deputies.[15] These six persons form the executive committee (Geschäftsführender Fraktionsvorstand). They are elected for one year and are allowed to stand for one re-election (§10.2 GO-PLP = standing orders).

Even this collective body has more technical than political power. The prime task of the three speakers is the representation of the Green parliamentary work in the political debate, which is obviously of considerable political importance (§4.2 GO-PLP). But internally, they have no real political leadership or power of co-ordination. They are mainly concerned with preparations for meetings of the parliamentary party and with personnel administration. Furthermore, all decisions of this body can be successfully opposed by at least three members of the parliamentary party, who can refer the issue at stake to a plenary session.

The genuine political centre of the parliamentary party is the extended parliamentary leadership (erweiterter Fraktionsvorstand), which also contains the chairmen of the working groups (Ismayr, 1985, p. 307; §5.2 GO-PLP). It can decide upon all matters which have not been dealt with in sessions of the parliamentary party.[16] This means that out of some fifty members of the first *Grünen im Bundestag*, twelve were able to participate in the proceedings of its power centre, which represents a considerable 'spreading' of political power. Additionally, plenary meetings of the parliamentary party are chaired by all members of the group in turn. Given the considerable opportunity for manipulation which usually lies with the chairmen of such meetings, this means that the parliamentary leadership is deprived of another important instrument of political control over its parliamentary party.

Openness

The Green parliamentary party adheres to another important democratic principle that has somewhat fallen into oblivion in other parties: all meetings are public. Only in exceptional circumstances, or when personal matters are debated, can the public be excluded by the majority of the group (§3.4 GO-PLP). Given the crucial role of public proceedings for any democratic control – it is the precondition – this represents a fundamental difference from the procedure of established parties: not only has the resulting compromise to be exposed to public scrutiny, but the whole proceedings have to take place completely in the open. However, this norm also reflects a certain distaste for the political instruments of bargaining and compromise which is indicative of the high level of ideological motivation within the Green party.

This discussion of the central organisational principles of the Green parliamentary party has demonstrated that the *Grünen im Bundestag* do – on a formal level – largely comply with the direct-democratic principles of openness, rotation, collective leadership, and non-professionalised politics. Any effective control of Green MPs by the party's rank-and-file, however, encounters clear limits in the German Basic Law. By contrast, all established parties are geared to conventional forms of party organisation, which stress representative forms of internal democracy.

THE PARTIES FROM INSIDE: WORKING PRACTICES AND POLITICAL CULTURE

As far as formal structures are concerned, the grass-roots democratic record of the Greens is quite impressive. It can be explained by the embedding of the party in the segments of society influenced by the New Politics. However, organisational structures only create a framework for the internal political life of a party. For any assessment of a party's democratic quality, what actually goes on is equally or more important. Two closely related aspects of these internal processes can be distinguished:

- *the internal political culture* of a party. This refers to the style of the political debate, the average intensity of participation, and the prevalent attitudes towards the party leadership, that is, deferential or not.
- *working practices*. This refers to the way formal structures are actually handled in the party. Where are the actual power centres? How much is really decided on party conferences? What is the influence of party working groups and associations?

Briefly put, we can expect profound differences between the old German parties and the Greens. Established parties are likely to have a relatively clear power structure with the major decisions factually being made by relatively small 'inner circles'. Alternatively, the predominance of participatory and anti-authoritarian attitudes in the Green Party is likely to result in a relatively diffuse power structure. Possessors of formal power – limited though it may be – will frequently be forced to impose decisions on informal groups in the face of grass-roots unwillingness to accept authoritative decisions from above. Hence, even in cases where it is not required by statute, many important decisions will be taken on lower levels or by larger constituencies. By contrast, established parties will experience pressures to refer decisions to lower levels only in exceptional circumstances or in cases of élite disunity.

This section will discuss the internal life of both party and parliamentary party. The internal political style is obviously not likely to be significantly different in different arenas of the same party, because it is strongly influenced by the participatory aspirations and normative convictions of party activists. Since there are no built-in mechanisms in the Green Party's structure which prevent access by specific groups to specific party arenas, this is a justifiable procedure. Also, the question of the location of the *de facto* centres of power and initiative can be determined only by focusing on all parts of a party at the same time.

Various analyses of the established parties have demonstrated that their internal life corresponds quite closely to their formal structures. Their formalised organisational fabric leaves relatively little space for the formation of informal power centres. It would therefore be superfluous to engage in a detailed empirical analysis of these parties. Instead, the results of these studies will briefly be summarised in the next section and then be used as reference points for the analysis of the internal life of the Green Party.

In any case, the formal structures of the established parties, which are, as has been shown, substantially different from Green Party organisation, point to a substantially different research question, that is, how well do their representative constitutions function? We are interested in the performance of the direct-democratic model of the Greens. Does it really correspond to the theoretical and statutory stipulations and really represent a significantly different way of organising a political party in a representative democracy?

THE REPRESENTATIVE MODEL: ESTABLISHED PARTIES

a) SPD

The oligarchic tendencies of the SPD party organisation have been well known since the classic work by Michels. Recent writers have come to similar conclusions. The federal leadership of the party has remained the power centre, and internal democracy is still subjected to the 'principle of unity', which means that the tradition of presenting a public image of party unity is still regarded as a positive goal in its own right. This goes together with a relatively intact federalism within the party: traditionally, the regions (Bezirke) have a powerful position within the Social Democratic Party (Heimann, 1984, p. 2,152). However, federalism does not mean substantial internal democracy in this case but competition between oligarchic élite groups. The predominance of the 'principle of unity' over internal democracy becomes even more apparent if we focus on the parliamentary party (SPD, 1991). Dissenting MPs are exposed to a multitude of pressures and disciplinary measures in order to ensure an image of party unity in the public. Whenever the majority or unity of a governing coalition is at stake, these means tend to be used with particular rigour (Sarcinelli, 1980, pp. 39ff.; Müller-Rommel, 1982c, p. 263; H. Schmitt, 1990, p. 154f.).

b) CSU

In a thorough study of the CSU, Alf Mitzel concludes that important decisions are rarely initiated by the representative organs of the party. Normally, they originate in the inner leadership, the parliamentary party of the Bavarian Landtag, or the group of CSU MPs in the Bonn parliament (Landesgruppe). Generally, internal participation is characterised by a 'fealty-like orientation' of the rank-and-file towards elected leaders and a 'pronouncedly authoritarian style of leadership' by the party élites (Mintzel, 1983, p. 706).

A good illustration of this point is the result achieved by Franz-Josef Strauß in his leadership re-election at the CSU party conference in November 1985: 967 out of 979 votes (98.8 per cent) were cast in his favour – which is still only the second best result in his career (StZ, 25 November 1985). The modernisation of the party apparatus, for example, was carried through with 'an almost complete exclusion of the organs of membership representation' by the party executive (Landesvorstand) and the general secretary of the CSU (Mintzel, 1977, p. 200). Modern communication technology has strengthened the inner leadership circle even further. When Franz-Josef Strauß died in 1988, the party leadership used the communication infrastructure of the party to prevent a controversial debate over his succession and ensured almost unanimous support for its candidate (Mintzel, 1990, p. 224). Above the level of constituency organisations, the CSU is today a modern, bureaucratic and centralised party. Only on the local level has it remained a traditional party of notables (Mintzel, 1977, p. 207). This is the result of an efficient organisational policy concerned with the promotion of functional efficiency and encompassing political presence of the party machine, not with the encouragement of membership participation (Haungs, 1983, p. 73). Basically, the party apparatus is a 'disciplinary instrument of the party authorities against party members' (Mintzel, 1977, p. 202).

Obviously, the personality of its long-serving leader Franz-Josef Strauß has contributed to the 'undeveloped state of internal party democracy in the csu' (Pridham, 1977, pp. 315ff.). Mintzel argues that, so far as the CSU has an explicit concept of democracy, it comes close to the élitist theory of democracy, which means the limitation of democracy to guaranteed choice between oligarchic leadership groups (Mintzel, 1977, p. 201f.). The high degree of oligarchisation is also indicated by the fact that most of the members of the executive

(Landesvorstand) hold mandates in the Landtag or the Bundestag (Haungs, 1983, p. 77).

c) CDU

Traditionally, the CDU is a party of strong federalist character. The foundation of Land organisations preceded the formation of the federal party, which took place only in 1950 – the year after Adenauer's assumption of office as chancellor of a CDU-led coalition government (Schmidt, 1983, p. 600). From the mid-1960s onwards, however, considerable efforts were made to strengthen the power of the federal party leadership (Pütz, 1985). In 1967, the position of general secretary was created. The holder has considerable control over the Land parties. He participates in the appointment of the managers of Land parties and associations (Vereinigungen) and has the right to issue directives on federal election campaigns to all bodies of the party (Schmidt, 1983, p. 602). At the same time, the federal party office was strengthened, and by the beginning of the 1980s about 200 staff were employed in the Konrad-Adenauer-Haus in Bonn. Together with full-time personnel on lower levels, the CDU then employed about 1,250 people (Schmidt, 1983, p. 604; Haungs, 1983, p. 72).

However, the participatory chances of ordinary rank-and-file members did not change to any considerable extent. Federal gains were made at the expenses of the Land 'barons' who had led their respective party organisations in the early years of the republic without much consultation of lower party ranks (Schmidt, 1983, p. 601; Scheer, 1977, p. 157). The influence of ordinary party members is normally confined to the lowest level (Pütz, 1974, p. 157) and party conferences are mainly for public relations and promotion of internal unity, not for true political decision-making. Accordingly, party conference decisions tend to be sufficiently vague to leave considerable political leeway for the parliamentary representatives of the CDU (Haungs, 1983, p. 68).

d) FDP

With some 65,000 members (Poguntke with Boll, 1992), the Liberals share some organisational difficulties with the Greens. On lower and middle levels, the organisational presence is relatively weak. Since the administrative structure of the Federal Republic makes for many elected bodies on communal and regional levels, the Liberals sometimes find it difficult to recruit enough qualified candidates. It is apparent that this means considerable participatory chances for the individual member. Simultaneously, the higher echelons of power are just as exclusive and oligarchic as in the other established parties (Dittberner, 1984, p. 1,374f.) The change of coalition partners on the federal level in 1982, for example, was decided and carried through by just a handful of top FDP politicians (Bölling, 1982; Vorländer, 1990, p. 271). Due to comparatively unconstrained access at the bottom of the party organisation, discontented members successfully pressed for the convocation of a special party conference on this issue. However, the *fait accompli* had by then defused the conflict. A return to the old government partner was politically no longer possible. Hence, the leadership survived the challenge.

This example demonstrates that the comparatively large number of opportunities on lower levels are not an expression of a radical democratic spirit inside the party. They are just the inevitable result of low membership figures: if only a few members take part in a branch meeting, ordinary members will find it easy to influence the debate even if they have no formal powers of determining the agenda. In fact, on the lower levels, the Liberals still resemble the old party of notables. Political influence has remained personalised because low membership figures make formalised procedures less important and permit a considerable degree of accessibility for ordinary members to party bodies (Vorländer, 1990, p. 271). The federal executive, on the other hand, is characterised by considerable office accumulation – almost all of its members hold senior positions in governments, parliamentary parties or their respective Land party organisations (Kaack, 1979, p. 72; Dittberner, 1987, p. 95f.).

The preceding – admittedly very brief – summary of research results on established parties has indicated their relatively oligarchic nature. More precisely, they rely strongly on formalised procedures which are heavily based on the principle of representation instead of direct involvement of the rank-and-file in specific decisions on all levels. Furthermore, power tends to be concentrated in statutorily envisaged small leadership bodies, which are responsible to elected party bodies and which are subject to regular re-election. Party conferences, for example, are characterised by substantial domination through the party leadership which determines the agenda and controls the proceedings. In a similar vein, candidate selection is the preserve of small groups of local functionaries (Niedermayer, 1989b, pp. 21ff.).

Hence, individual members are confronted with quite substantial obstacles if they want to exert influence on their own party. This is particularly true for specific policy decisions on higher levels. The situation is different on the local level, where all established parties are plagued by an endemic shortage of active members. To an extent, oligarchic groups are not the result of conscious strategies but simply follow from the low rate of grass-roots activity (ibid. p. 23).

By and large, established parties are characterised by a non-participatory internal culture. This does not mean that the established parties are necessarily less democratic than the Greens. After all, formalised if non-participatory structures may be regarded as a safeguard against the domination of internal party life by resourceful minorities who can (ab)use informal and loose structures to marginalise silent majorities. Although a normative evaluation of the advantages and shortcomings of these two different modes of organisation is beyond the focus of this book, it is worthwhile keeping this aspect in mind for the following analysis of Green practices.

*a) Competition at the Top: Parliamentary Party Versus Federal Executive and Federal
Council*

Theoretically, everything is clear-cut: according to the principles of grass-roots
democracy, the supreme power within the party organisation resides with the
'Basis' – the lowest level. In real life, however, the rank-and-file cannot always be
consulted when the political situation requires action. Strategic decisions of
fundamental importance are taken by party conferences or general assemblies
(Vollversammlungen). Hence, those Green politicians who are involved in the
formulation of the alternatives that are presented to assemblies exert considerable political influence. Political power is, after all, also the ability to define
political situations. Irrespective of all anti-élitist sentiments, it is inevitably a
certain exclusive – élitist – group of politicians which has the power to do so.
These may be the members of a group that negotiates over a possible coalition
agreement, or a programmatic commission of the party, or the party executive.
These groups are often in situations where they have to interpret or define
possible action alternatives which are then referred to the party sovereign for
decision. Obviously, such a group will be most influential if no one else has the
ability to make counter-proposals. The statement that the draft coalition agreement represents the optimum result is not falsifiable because nobody else was
present in the conference room.[17] In contrast, programmatic or strategic proposals can be challenged by others, because they involve no exclusive knowledge.

More generally, this means that bodies which are involved in practical politics
have a certain structural advantage over those who are mainly concerned with
programmatic and strategic work. Since the German political debate is highly
focused on parliamentary politics, parliamentary parties are the most frequent
beneficaries of this advantage. On the other hand, the Green Party is heavily
involved in extra-parliamentary activities such as participation in co-ordination
committees of various new social movements. This rival political arena gives
political weight to the federal executive of the party, particularly in times of
strong and active protest movements.

Apart from such situational circumstances, organisational and structural factors play an important role in enhancing or diminishing the power of various
leadership groups in relation to each other: power is related to access to media,
resources and statutory powers. From this perspective, the federal execution
(Bundesvorstand) is in a rather unprivileged position. Unlike the parliamentary
party it possesses almost no paid personnel.

Federal Executive

In 1983, more than eighty publicly-paid, full-time positions for parliamentary
assistants and secretaries, together with about fifty MPs and non-MPs, represented
a political centre of gravity which could not easily be counterbalanced by twelve

full-time employees of the federal executive. Only two of these were in genuinely political jobs; the others were occupied with administrative tasks, like posting information material.[18] Since the number of parliamentary assistants is linked to the number of MPs, the imbalance has even grown after the electoral gains in the 1987 election: in June 1989, the Green parliamentary party of the Bundestag had almost 200 full-time and part-time employees; more than 120 of them were parliamentary assistants.[19] The federal executive, on the other hand, could rely on 27 employees (Poguntke with Boll, 1992).

Until 1989, this imbalance was further aggravated by the fact that the members of the federal executive were not paid by the party. This led to the somewhat curious situation in which a body of largely unpaid weekend politicians who were dispersed all over the republic and could only claim moderate daily allowances (see below) tried to 'control' a fully professionalised parliamentary party (Kitschelt, 1989).

Due to lack of time, many tasks could not be fulfilled adequately by the federal executive. This was also true of any meaningful contact with the parliamentary party (RB-BUVO, 1985, p. 57), since unlike other parties, there is no personal overlap between different party arenas, which makes permanent communication between them even more important. Intermittent joint meetings of federal executive and parliamentary party are no substitute for continuous political co-operation – and this is hard to achieve if members of the party executive, who have to earn their living during the week, visit Bonn primarily at weekends, a time when Bundestagmembers are usually occupied with constituency work (RB 1, 1984, p. 23).

In the light of these experiences, it became apparent that the principle of amateur politics severely undermined the overall functioning of the model of grass-roots democracy ('Basisdemokratie'). The structural weakness of the federal executive resulted in a considerable overweight of the parliamentary party. Therefore, the 1989 decision to professionalise the federal executive can be understood as an attempt to sacrifice one element of the concept in order to enhance the viability of the experiment of grass-roots democracy as a whole. Nevertheless, the egalitarian thrust and the principle of dispersing power as much as possible was maintained by not differentiating between the three chairpersons (speakers) and the remaining eight members of the federal executive: all were to be treated equally (GB 4/1989, p. 18).

The Federal Council

The federal executive is assisted in its task by the federal council (Bundes-hauptausschuß), which is unprofessionalised and lacks independent organisational resources. The federal council (BHA), consisting of delegates of all Land parties and the members of the federal executive, is the highest organ of the party between party conferences. Again, there is no personal overlap with the Bundestag group. Hence the flow of information depends on the presence of representatives of the parliamentary party in the meetings of the federal council.

However, this was not always the case in the first year after the 1983 Bundestag election (RB 1, 1984, p. 23).

According to a party conference decision, rulings of the BHA are binding on the parliamentary party (Sindelfingen minutes, appendix 2). However, the federal council has no apparatus which could efficiently screen the activities of the Bundestag group (Frankland, 1988, p. 108). Consequently, control is largely reduced to controversies over an adequate political strategy against the SPD. Simultaneously, the parliamentary party has the personnel resources to influence many political and programmatic positions of the Greens in a way which determines also the strategic constellation, that is, the possibilty of co-operation with other parties. In their second report, for example, Green MPs resented the growing discrepancy between the Green programme and the programmatic results emanating from the co-operation between the federal working groups (Bundesarbeitsgemeinschaften) and the parliamentary party. They demanded that these 'experiences with parliamentary work' ought to be integrated in the Green programme (RB 2, 1984, p. 15). This demonstrates clearly the supremacy of the parliamentary party in terms of ideological and programmatic competence. Furnished with the self-confidence that originates from professionalised and resourceful work, they have demanded that positions they find plausible ought to be the standard for the party as a whole.

Media Attention

Media attention in a parliamentary democracy is normally concentrated on the parliamentary arena. Easy access to the mass media makes it easier for Green parliamentarians to influence internal debate in the party. The considerable political dominance of the parliamentary party was further amplified by the fact that most of the experienced and prominent party personalities were elected to the Bundestag and the Land parliaments. Due to the separation of office and mandate, they were therefore no longer eligible for positions in the party leadership.

The strict personal separation of parliamentary party and party has also had the unintended side-effect of institutionalising competition and mistrust between these bodies. Inevitably, parlamentarians are exposed to socialising influences and factual pressures which have an impact on their political thinking and behaviour (Duverger, 1964, p. 190f., Jäger and Pinl, p. 1985). Members of the federal executive and federal council are cut off from such experiences. Obviously, this represents a strong basis for effective self-control of the party against too much reformist adaptation. However, it also makes communication between parliamentarians and party leaders more difficult because they lack a common background. In theory, this should have become easier after the first term in the Bundestag, because former MPs should have become available for the party leadership. Experience has shown, however, that prominent Green members of the Bundestag managed to get elected to Land parliaments where they took over leading positions in their Green parliamentary party or even became ministers in Land coalition governments.

Unclear Powers.

The federal executive, and less prominently the federal council, suffers from lack of a clearly defined task. The federal executive has no genuine mandate for political leadership. It is supposed to be little more than a mouthpiece of the collective will of the grass roots. Obviously, this leaves room for interpretation and hence for political leadership and power. However, the pervasive grass-roots democratic philosophy within the party sets tight limits. A good example is the reaction to critical statements of the federal executive concerning the position of the Hesse and Saar Land organisations towards possible parliamentary co-operation with the SPD: the Hamburg conference (7–9 December 1984) approved a motion which asked the federal executive not to 'interfere through public statements with the competences of other organisational units of the party' (Grüner Basisdienst, 1/1985, p. 46). Effectively, this means that the federal party executive is not even granted a right to comment upon major political moves by lower-level party organisations. The sharp contrast with the established parties is obvious.

There is no mandate for the political leadership of the parliamentary party either. But a clearly defined field of political activity and a considerable resource base facilitate considerable political dominance over the party. The bitterness of conflicts between party executive and parliamentary group (or parts of it) needs also to be understood from this perspective. A structurally inferior position can only be compensated by stronger polemical attack.

However, what about the grass roots? The Greens have tried to limit the statutory powers of their leadership organs as far as possible. But the mechanics of the political system give them additional political prominence that can only be counterbalanced by an active grass roots which is capable of controlling the higher ranks and willing to do so. Does it exist?

b) 'Basisanbindung'

'Basisanbindung' (being tied up with the grass roots) is one of the favourite terms in internal Green debate: it means that all higher ranks should be in permanent communication with the rank-and-file. Ideally, all political initiative should come from below. On a formal level, ordinary Green members have far more power than members of established parties. Interestingly enough, the rate of participation in the Green party does not seem to be significantly higher than in established parties. Those who participate may use different action techniques, but they do not do so in greater numbers. Estimations range from 10 to 30 per cent of Green members taking part in meetings on the local or district (Kreis) level. Only 30 to 50 per cent of those are also available for party jobs or parliamentary mandates (Schaeffer, 1983, p. 78; Fogt, 1984, p. 104; Raschke, 1991a, p. 98).

These figures resemble results from a thorough membership survey commissioned by the SPD federal executive in 1977. According to the party functionaries, about 15 per cent were active members. A survey of the Northrhine-Westphalia

SPD in 1982/83 came to corresponding results. The chairmen of the local party groups counted 12 per cent regular participants and 13 per cent intermittently active. Party members saw themselves somewhat more active in the 1977 study: 25 per cent claimed active participation in party life and preparedness to stand for offices or parliamentary mandates. Altogether, 35 per cent were categorised as 'potentially active' (Becker and Hombach, 1983, p. 79f.).[20]

A study of Christian Democratic party members in 1977 yielded similar results. CDU members were asked for their role perception as party members. Obviously, such a question inflates 'participatory' responses even more. Of the respondents, 24.8 per cent saw their membership as concomitant with active participation and assumption of office or mandate, whereas 32.7 per cent stated that it entailed only occasional activity. Another 41.1 per cent regarded their role as being confined to purely passive support by paying their membership fees (Falke, 1982, p. 72).

For methodological reasons, it is not possible to compare the figures in a systematic way. Nevertheless, it is evident that a majority of Green members are inactive – just like Social and Christian Democrats, where 41 and 50 per cent respectively do not want to get involved in internal party life.

The low rate of participation is particularly detrimental for the Greens because they have the lowest number of members. After a steep rise in their early years, membership figures hovered around 40,000 throughout the second half of the 1980s. The voter–membership ratio on the federal level in 1983 was 86:1 (SPD 16:1, CDU 20:1, CSU 22:1, FDP 38:1) and had not changed substantially by 1987, when it was 74:1 (SPD 15:1; CDU 19:1; CSU 20:1; FDP 53:1) (data from Poguntke with Boll, 1992). The unconventional, extra-parliamentary traditions of the party have so far prevented clear membership recruitment strategies. Sometimes the party is even short of people to fill all the seats it has won in the elections to parliamentary bodies of all levels (Schaeffer, 1983, p. 78). Peter Glotz (then SPD manager) calculated that more than 7,000 Greens were elected to local parliaments at the end of 1984 (Bickerich, 1985, p. 13). This means that almost all Green activists hold a mandate. In many cases, control of local parliamentarians by the party is simply impossible because the active core of the local group will be almost identical with the Green group in the local assembly. To make things worse, the old guard, that is, the politically most experienced 'founding generation', was soon elected to the parliaments of the Länder or the Bundestag. The rotation principle, which was applied in different versions in the Land parties, inflated the need for parliamentary candidates. Qualified people who could have strengthened the party organisation were absorbed by parliaments: the Greens were overtaken by their own success. One obvious result was a gradual loosening of the rotation principle, which led to the above-mentioned 'Quer-Rotation'.

Nevertheless, there are in principle enough active local politicians to control the higher ranks of the party. However, since most of them are occupied with their own mandates, little time remains to effectively follow 'big politics' in detail. The result is that 'at most, the lowest level approves or protests' (Schaeffer, 1983, p. 78). Permanent communication between MPs and their constituency organisations is rather rare. The membership basis is too small. There are just not enough grass-roots activists who are not busy with their own local mandates and who could therefore afford the time to keep contact with Green MPs (Ismayr, 1985, p. 309; Schrüfer, 1985, p. 40). Green MPPs have resented this situation, because the concept of 'Basisdemokratie' embodies control by local groups as well as their initiative, support, and information. On the other hand, limited time, as a result of the immense workload in the national and Land parliaments, also sets natural limits to the amount of grass-roots contacts Green MPs can afford. Meaningful grass-roots control has to struggle with the overload and overcomplexity resulting from modern parliamentary work.

The Greens' dilemma is that they are – unlike other parties – committed to the ideological imperative of *specific* grass-roots control of parliamentary representatives and party élites. Established parties, on the contrary, content themselves with a *general* assessment of their élites' performance when it comes to the selection of candidates for the next election or leadership contest. Since it is technically impossible to realise the normative standard of detailed control, inability to do so finds its 'functional equivalent' in a general mistrust by ordinary members of those in positions of party prominence, the so-called 'Promis'. Unwillingness to grant unlimited confidence is a democratic virtue – but only to a certain extent. Trust is also an essential element of representation. Its lack in the Green party gives rise to a propensity to dismiss political proposals whenever they are a made by prominent party members.

In a sense, the low rate of organisation is not surprising. The core of Green voters comes from the New Politics groups of society who tend to have rather distinct participatory orientations. They are highly active, but they are not active in party politics. Their political passion is mainly reserved for single-issue initiatives and extra-parliamentary, unconventional forms of action (Poguntke, 1992c). They want direct immediate participation. Whenever they feel discontented with a certain political situation or policy, they want to do something about it without going through the painstakingly long process of organised politics: by forming a group with people who share their specific grievance and trying to exert political pressure directly, by collecting signatures, organising a protest demonstration, or occupying a building site.

Political parties are badly equipped to cater for such aspirations. Even a relatively open and democratic political formation cannot dispense with a vertical structure of organisational units and some levels of representative decision-making. This means that individual members have to go through a long process to win a party's support for a certain issue – and they have to compete with others who might not share their personal preoccupations. This holds true even on the local level. The organiser of a citizens' initiative against a new road construction project can be sure that only people who agree with this specific goal will join his group. A local party, on the other hand, even though it shares a general programmatic consensus, will often disagree over specific issues (Kaase, 1982, p. 185). This explains why it is difficult for the Green Party to recruit activists from the new social movements to party membership and active work inside the party, although there is strong affinity between their general political goals.

This dilemma undermines the crediblity of another cornerstone of Green organisational philosophy: the claim that the Green party is the 'parliamentary arm of extra-parliamentary social movements'. On the thematic level, the Greens are indeed the mouthpiece of the new social movements (Ismayr, 1985, pp. 299, 317f.; Frankland, 1988, p. 120). The Green parliamentary party has always been eager to declare solidarity whenever a concern of the social movements acquired some prominence. Furthermore, Green MPs donate large sums of money to the eco-funds which distribute it among alternative projects. Organisationally, however, all new social movements have insisted on maintaining their independence from a particular political party, because they have been able to mobilise supporters across almost the entire political spectrum (Pappi, 1989; Schmitt, 1990). Consequently, Green representatives have participated in co-ordination committees of various new social movements alongside delegates from other parties, the churches, trade unions and other movement initiatives (Kitschelt, 1989, p. 234; Schmitt, 1989, p. 591f.). Apart from these – rare – formalised linkages, informal contacts through overlapping memberships and joint extra-parliamentary activities have been the dominant mode of relationship between Green Party and new social movements.

However, a small membership basis means that a large part of Green party members are occupied with party-related activities like representing the Greens in parliaments and elected assemblies. Consequently, they lack time for active participation in social movements, which hinders a permanent, 'organic' exchange of information between party and movements. This problems is partially alleviated by institutionalised channels for this task, the 'federal working groups'.

c) Party Working Groups

In addition to their main organisational structure, German parties have developed more or less differentiated sub-systems. Unfortunately, there is some terminological confusion. Therefore, we need some definitions before we can proceed to the analysis of these organisations. In principle, there exist three types of subsystems:

- *ancillary organisations* in Duverger's sense (1964, p. 117f.), which are designed to cater for the social needs of members and/or supporters. They need not be considered here, since they virtually disappeared as a result of the attempt of the German parties to overcome the social divisions and subcultures which had troubled political life in the Weimar period.
- *affiliated organisations* are intended to guarantee the adequate representation of certain social groups within the party. They play an important role in the organisational philosophy of CDU, CSU and SPD, which define them-

selves as people's parties (Volksparteien) (Höfling, 1980b, p. 155). The CDU calls them 'Vereinigungen' (organisation or association), the CSU and the SPD 'Arbeitsgemeinschaften' (working groups). Greens and FDP have no such organisations, with the exception of the formally independent Young Liberals of the FDP. The organisational structure of such affiliated organisations is usually parallel to that of their party, with local, district and Land organisations. However, the strength of their links to their mother party varies within and between parties: in some cases party membership is required. Other organisations admit non-members, like the Junge Union or the CDA (Schmidt, 1983, p. 610f.).[21] In some cases, these organisations are formally independent. Interestingly enough, the latter is the case with one of the most powerful organisations of the CDU, the economic council (Wirtschaftsrat) (Schmidt, 1983, p. 616). Participation rights and influence in the respective parties is also quite differentiated, as we will see below.

• *commissions* are thematically defined and serve as expert groups for certain political fields. They lack a vertical structure and are usually quite influential on day-to-day party policies and programmatic development. Primarily, they do research and participate in the drafting of legislation or party programmes. Confusingly enough, the Greens call their commissions 'working groups' (Arbeitsgemeinschaften), whereas all other parties have named them commissions (Ausschüsse/ Arbeitskreise).

There is, however, an inevitable overlap between affiliated organisations and commissions because certain social groups are by definition particularly concerned with certain political fields. Furthermore, the organic development of CDU and CSU party organisations has led to a situation where the boundaries are not entirely clear: Local politicians are organised as an affiliated group although their concern is thematically, not socially, defined (Schmidt, 1983, p. 606f., Mintzel, 1983, p. 900). Alternatively, the CDU organises agricultural interests in a commission (Bundesfachausschuß für Agrarpolitik) which nevertheless has a vertical structure, just like affiliated organisations (Vereinigungen) (Haungs, 1983, p. 63).

The main reference-point for our analysis of these substructures is the degree to which they provide opportunities for direct participation in policy formulation. In other words: are there 'participatory short-cuts' through which individual party members can contribute to the drafting of bills or programmes without holding other senior positions in the party or depending on the nomination of a higher-level party body? In short, we are interested in the openness of party structures to direct, specific participation, not in the power of some sub-systems as such.

Affiliated Organisations

Affiliated organisations are irrelevant from this perspective. They are not designed for participation in specific policy formulation but for the representation of specific social groups and their general interests within the party. Furthermore, their vertical structure excludes direct participation of rank-and-file members in federal or Land politics. Before reaching the top level, all members have to go through the normal process of successive elections.

Affiliated organisations are frequently used as power bases for party careers. In the CDU, for example, members of such 'Vereinigungen' are over-represented in the party leadership (Höfling, 1980a, p. 145). The influence of organised sub-sytems must therefore not be confused with the participation of single members (Falke, 1982, p. 179). Similarly, almost all former leaders of the Young Socialists have advanced into senior positions in the SPD or its Bundestag group. Wolfgang Roth, for example, became deputy leader of the parliamentary party, Heidemarie Wieczorek-Zeul and Karsten Voigt became members of the party executive (Bundesvorstand) and the executive of the parliamentary party, and Gerhard Schröder was Prime Minister candidate for the Land elections in Lower Saxony in 1986 and became Prime Minister of a red-green coalition government in 1990.

Nevertheless, these organisations are subject to substantial control by the party leaderships. The Christian Democrats and their Bavarian sister party the CSU rely more on the moderating effects of financial dependency and grant their organisations quite substantial formal independence (Schmidt, 1983, p. 606f.; CSU-statute, §26). This explains why the economic councils (Wirtschaftsrat) of the CDU and CSU remained fully independent of their parties: financial independence gives them political autonomy and hence more political weight (Mintzel, 1983, p. 700; Schmidt, 1983, p. 616, Haungs, 1983, p. 58f.).

In contrast to the informal control exerted by the Christian Democrats, the Social Democrats prefer quite strict statutory controls. Sub-organisations like the Young Socialists are controlled by the party executives on the same level and hence have only restricted access to the public (Heimann, 1984, p. 2,154; SPD statute, §10).

Commissions

Thematically defined commissions could provide channels for direct participation. All parties have such commissions, which assemble expert knowledge on certain political issues. However, access, status and political autonomy vary considerably.

In the established parties, such commissions have the status of organs of their federal (CSU: Land) executives. They are set up and controlled by the party executives and mostly lack independent access to the public. In the CDU, the general secretary nominates the commission members;[22] in the CSU the executive has to approve the commission chairman and the commission executive.[23] In the FDP, he is appointed by the party executive.[24]

The commissions of the CSU have gained importance over recent years and have in some cases relegated corresponding affiliated organisations ('Vereinigungen') to secondary importance (Haungs, 1983, p. 66). Nevertheless, they can still be dissolved by the party executive. The same applies to another type of party commission, the 'Fachausschuß', which has virtually the same structure as a regular commission (i.e. 'Arbeitskreis') (csu statute, §27, §28).

Ideally, the Social Democrats would like to use their affiliated organisations as expert groups of the party on all organisational levels (Jahrbuch spd, 1982–3, p. 560). Nevertheless, they still have to rely on a large number of special commissions which can be set up and dissolved by the respective party executives (ibid). Like affiliated organisations, these commissions do not represent participatory channels for individual members of established parties. On the contrary, they are expert advisory bodies, primarily for the party executives. Usually, they are confined to the top levels of Land or federal party organisations. In all established parties they lack the right of independent formation and participation (see Falke, 1982, p. 167, for the cdu).

Green Working Groups

By contrast, the explicit purpose of Green 'federal working groups' (Bundes-arbeitsgemeinschaften) is to provide and maintain links between Green parliamentarians, local party groups and the new social movements which are sympathetic to the Greens (Ismayr, 1985, p. 310). They are largely integrated in the work of the parliamentary party.[25] Although co-operation with the Bundestag group is not free of the usual conflicts and rivalries, there are examples of good co-operation between parliamentary party and working groups in the process of developing parliamentary initiatives (rb 2, 1984, p. 15). Other working groups, however, have preferred to act as lobby organisations for specific policy interests without wanting to get involved in the actual drafting of policy proposals (Kitschelt, 1989, p. 186).

As a result of legal problems, the structure of the bags (federal working groups) needs further differentiation. Working groups of the party must be distinguished from groups advising the parliamentary party – a distinction that has not always been very clear. This is necessary because all working groups have been financed by the parliamentary party, which is legally obliged to use its public funds exclusively for parliamentary purposes (rb 3, 1985, p. 15).

Unlike their counterparts in the established parties, these groups are open to anybody who feels competent to participate.[26] Furthermore, working groups were given the right to propose motions to the federal party conference in 1986. From our perspective, this is the most important difference: the federal working groups provide individual members with unhindered access to the formulation of specific policy proposals. No specified nomination or selection procedure is involved. Additionally, they are open to activists from the various social movements (rb 1, 1984, p. 25). The autonomy of such groups is guaranteed by the party constitution (Green statute, §5.1). Federal executive or other party organs have no political control over them. The Greens are the only party that has institutionalzed a participatory 'short-cut' that allows transmission of political ideas and initiative directly from the grass roots or the social 'milieu' of the party to its parliamentary activities. Given what has been said earlier about the problems of the Green party in recruiting active members, the institution of working groups is potentially an important means of maintaining the political viability of a party that is based on the 'anti-party' groups of society.

A PARTY OF THE COUNTER-CULTURE?

The political culture of a party is the sum of attitudes, values, traditions and modes of behaviour that mould the political and social life inside a party and its behaviour as an entity in the political process. Since this chapter is concerned with party organisation, we will attempt only to portray the internal political culture of the Green Party. It will be analysed in terms of the Green concept of the role of politicians and politics; the attempt to create new forms of parliamentary party organisation; and the role of women inside the party.

a) Green Politics and Green Politicians

Green democratic consciousness is moulded by the ideal of 'Basisdemokratie'. It comprises the concept of 'identitäre Demokratie' ('identity democracy'), which postulates identity of rulers and ruled. Clearly, this is not a particularly new or original invention. Working class parties have been committed to this model of democracy with varying degrees of emphasis during their radical phases. By contrast with the Socialist parties, Green commitment to 'identity democracy' is not only the result of theoretical considerations, but also the outgrowth of deeply-rooted anti-establishment sentiments. This is not surprising in the light of the findings about the social bases of Green politics: its core is formed by anti-establishment groups (see Chapters 5 and 6). Consequently, Green politics is characterised by a general attempt to retain alternative forms of politics and life-style throughout the political life. The theoretical justification is that form and substance of politics cannot be separated: only alternative forms of politics – so the argument goes – can achieve alternative policies.

No Privileges

Green politicians are therefore expected to live the life of their grass roots, at least in material terms. In particular, great attention is given to Green politicians not having structural advantages in the internal life of the party. We have already mentioned the severe limitation on parliamentary allowances for Green MPs and the fact that members of the federal executive could only claim a rather moderate daily allowance. However, this allowance was only paid if they fulfilled duties related to their membership in the federal executive. Furthermore, the rule applied only from Monday to Friday (Duisburg minutes, appendix 18). Personal political work, for example participation in the party conference of the relevant Land, was not covered. As mentioned above, the principle of non-professionalised politics no longer applies to members of the federal executive, who are now entitled to a salary.

When competing for political influence within their respective organisations, all other party functionaries have to incur the same financial sacrifices as ordinary party members. They can still capitalise upon their image gained in such an exposed position. However, unlike their colleagues in established parties, Green party élites do not enjoy the structural advantage of being able to live from politics – another disadvantage they have vis-à-vis the parliamentary group. Furthermore, the separation of office and mandate excludes a possibility open to middle-level élites in established parties: the combination of a Landtag or Bundestag seat, for example, with the office of unpaid district leader (Falke, 1982, p. 80).

The proceedings of party conferences are another example of the attempt to limit structural advantages accruing from senior positions. All speakers' lists on federal party conferences are usually drawn up by lottery (despite a different procedure laid down in the standing orders for federal conferences!). Unlike those of established parties, debates are not dominated by prominent party members. Every delegate has the same chance to express his or her opinion. From a democratic point of view, this is certainly an achievement. However, a considerable price has to be paid in terms of quality of the debate and its structure. One proponent and one opponent of the motion under consideration have the right to open the discussion. But the remaining speakers are selected purely by chance. To some extent, intellectual quality is sacrificed to democratic purity.

Furthermore, members of the federal executive have very little formal control over the agenda of party conferences. In conjunction with the pronounced élite-challenging thrust of party activists, this leads regularly to unstructured proceedings where many delegates are no longer fully aware of the precise alternatives that come to vote. This is mainly the result of an excessive use of motions on a 'point of order' (Geschäftsordungsanträge), which can be proposed at any moment (Heidger, 1987, pp. 147ff.). Green Party conferences exemplify the danger that a lack of formalised procedures may enhance individual chances for participation while threatening the democratic quality of the proceedings as a whole. Interestingly enough, however, the rules of the established parties concerning motions on 'points of order' or 'emergency motions' (Dringlichkeits-anträge) do not differ substantially – without corresponding effects. Ironically, parties with fewer participatory (i.e. more deferential) activists can 'afford' participatory rules without risking counter-intuitive effects.

Problems of Collective Leadership

A similar dilemma arises from the institution of collective leadership. From a radical-democratic point of view, collective leadership is certainly positive. However, it can have almost paralysing effects in conjunction with the internal dynamics of a political party. There is no party without factions. Normally, a representative of the broad centre will be elected. He has the task of integrating the extreme wings of the party. A collective leadership, however, is likely to be composed of representatives of the most important factions. These party leaders are likely to retain a prime loyalty to their own faction because the task of integration has been externalised by establishing a collective leadership representing the dominant political currents. Furthermore, their position in the party depends primarily on the support of their own wing, not on the approval by a large majority of the whole party. Hence, there is some incentive for a member of the collective leadership to seek a higher profile at the expense of his colleagues and the performance of the collective leadership as a whole. Paralysis of the collective body is a likely result. This was precisely the case with the federal executive for 1985/86 (RB-BUVO, 1985, p. 57), for example, and the problem was epitomised by the performance of two of the party speakers on the evening of the first all-German elections of 2 December 1990. When asked to comment upon the failure of the West German Greens to overcome the 5 per cent hurdle, every statement by Heide Rühle was vigorously rejected by her fellow party leader Renate Damus in front of running TV cameras.

Anti-élitism

The profound anti-authoritarianism and the general anti-establishment senti-ments prevalent among the Green social bases have left an imprint on the internal style of the party. Whereas party leaders in established parties normally enjoy high respect, sometimes almost deference, Green party élites are not pampered by such grass-roots admiration. A high degree of education and partici-patory orientation makes Green party members feel that there is little party élites can do better than they themselves. Hence, prominent leaders in the party are constantly threatened by the élite-challenging behaviour of their rank-and-file. Media attention and political prominence earned by extraordinary performance is often heavily criticised by the grass roots as being contradictory to the prin-ciples of 'Basisdemokratie'. Whoever deplores the media attention given to party élites and their alleged neglect of grass-roots contacts can be sure of earning thunderous applause on a party conference (Raschke, 1991b).

Another outgrowth of alternative culture is the principle of public meetings, which is applied throughout the party. Obviously, this represents a democratic virtue. However, it leads inevitably to an increasing frequency of informal meet-ings where the real decisions are prepared or even taken. Sometimes compromise between different positions is much easier if essentials and possible points of compromise can be made clear in small, exclusive circles. Here, potential trade-offs can be discussed freely, without the need to anticipate the likely reactions of the respective followers on every preliminary proposal. Consistently, party activ-ists have reported that a break for a cigarette is sometime of vital importance in breaking deadlocks in Green Party meetings (Schaeffer, 1983, p. 85; Fischer, 1984, p. 125).

All these features are unique to the Greens. The anchorage of the Green party in the counter-culture is further exemplified by the picture Green party confer-ences offer to the observer. Being used to the image of a uniform mass of, until recently, predominantely male delegates dressed in pin-striped suits that domin-ates meetings of established parties, an unprepared visitor might well wonder whether he has ended up in a general meeting of a students' union. At second sight, however, the higher average age of the assembly and the mass of TV cameras and journalists would reassure our imaginary observer that he had found the right meeting.

The 'ambience' of Green party conferences has been reported many times by bewildered journalists: children playing in the assembly hall, delegates knitting with biologically produced wool and sleeping in mass quarters like gymnasiums; the alternative style of clothing and a very controversial – frequently personal – style of debate that is the expression of the Green commitment not to suppress emotions. Nevertheless, this style is more than a picturesque gloss on proceedings. It demonstrates our earlier point about the great importance that is attributed by the Greens to the way in which politics is conducted. This does not mean that all Green delegates sleep in sleeping bags and travel by public transport. However, the dominant spirit in the party confronts those who do not live what they preach with difficulties of legitimation.

b) Alternative Style in Parliamentary Politics

The Green parliamentary group represents an explicit attempt to transplant the alternative style of grass-roots initiatives into the framework of a bureaucratised institution (Sindelfingen minutes, appendix 1). Therefore, the general limitations of subcultural intrusion into an established system can be analyzed within this quasi-experimental situation.

In conformity with the egalitarian and anti-authoritarian ideals of the alternative culture, Greens had intended to establish a 'hierarchy-free zone' within the federal political process. A central element of a completely new form of parliamentary organisation was to be the so-called 'office community' of MPs and non-MPs in the 1983–7 legislative term: Green parliamentarians and their successors (after rotation: predecessors) were supposed to form a team with equal rights and responsibilities inside the Green parliamentary party. The successor would co-operate with the MP and hence be able to take over his place after rotation without long periods of 'apprenticeship'. Additionally, his task would be alleviated by support from his predecessor: ideally, the persons on the parliamentary benches would be swapped, but the internal structure of the Green group would remain largely unaffected (RB 1, 1984, p. 5; RB 3, 1985, p. 7).

In reality, parliamentary structures and institutional arrangements proved too strong to be neutralised by internal arrangements. We have already mentioned the first violation of the principle of equal treatment, in regard to the different expense allowances for MPs and non-MPs. A wide range of other privileges is reserved for MPs and could not always be provided for non-MPs. Access to the Bundestag driving service and the special rights that accrue from a special MP passport are two examples that attracted public attention.

However, all these privileges are relatively marginal compared to the fundamental formal difference: only MPs are admitted to the plenary session of the Bundestag and – what is more important – to the meetings of the parliamentary committees (Geschäftsordnung des Deutschen Bundestages, version of March

1983, §69). Since the German parliament functions through committee work, non-MPs are effectively cut off from important first-hand information and involvement in policy-making. Their information depends largely on their ability to maintain good relations with their MPs. It is evident that minutes are not an equally good source of information.

Obviously, the attempt to create a non-hierarchical parliamentary group has definite limits when the rules of parliament create first and second class members. However, the major obstacle against its realisation proved to be the fact that MPs and their 'deputies' rarely shared the same fields of interest. Positions on election lists are decided on political grounds and areas of specialisation normally have very little influence on the selection process. The ideal of functioning office communities was doomed to failure since co-operation was often not possible due to diverse fields of interests (RB 1, 1984, p. 5; RB 3, 1985, p. 7). In principle, the problem could have been alleviated by deciding upon the membership in Bundestag-committees after rotation at the beginning of the legislative term. Non-MPs could have then formed office communities with MPs specialising in similar policy areas. However, organisational difficulties at the beginning were too overwhelming to allow concentration on such 'distant' problems.

Additionally, competition between MPs and their prospective successors was institutionalised by an unfortunate decision of the 1983 Sindelfingen party conference. It was stipulated that MPs could only hold on to their seats if a 70 per cent majority of the respective Land party conference approved of the exception (Sindelfingen minutes, appendix 1). However, this did not occur in 1985 (RB 3, 1985, p. 9f.). It was particularly this 70 per cent rule which rendered any non-passionate debate about the merits of rotation impossible: any critical remark by serving MPs about rotation was immediatedly interpreted as pure power politics in order to undermine the chances of non-MPs ever succeeding them. The conflict is epitomised by a dissenting statement of non-MPs on the problem which was appended to the report of the parliamentary party: the functioning of office communities was evaluated far more positively in this paper than by the MPs (RB 1, 1984).

Alternative style also has an impact on the way parliamentary assistants are integrated into the work of the parliamentary party. Although they have no political mandate, they find it hard to accept the authority of MPs and non-MPs as – de facto – employers, because they often come from the same alternative milieu. Hence, they expect the Green faction to function like an alternative grass-roots initiative. Green MPs who refuse to integrate assistants into the political decision-making process have been heavily criticised for 'authoritarian' or 'established' manners (Jäger and Pinl, 1985, pp. 148ff).

To summarise, the Green parliamentary party is far from being a non-hierarchical organisation. Serving MPs clearly occupy the top of the power pyramid, followed by non-MPs (until 1987) and the parliamentary assistants who are subordinate to varying degrees, depending on their jobs. Nevertheless, the Greens have succeeded in establishing a fundamentally new way of organising parliamentary work: they have kept faith with important elements of alternative political style like public meetings, collective leadership, limitation of MPs' income and a very low degree of formalisation and hierarchisation. The latter point is also illustrated by the fact that the parliamentary leadership has changed every year, at least to a considerable extent.

c) The Role of Women

In conformity with the party's ideological convictions and due to the role of the women's movement as one of the forces that participated in the foundation of the Green party, women play an important role on all levels. According to the Nuremberg *women's statute* (see above), they are entitled to 50 per cent of all party offices and parliamentary mandates. In addition, the women's statute gives women a suspensive veto on all issues that are of special relevance to women. A preparatory motion of the Offenburg conference in December 1985, which made it obligatory to have 50 per cent of all paid party jobs occupied by women, was passed without any substantial debate. This may reflect true conviction on the part of male party members. It could also indicate a certain degree of opportunism or resignation of male politicians faced with a vigorous and well-organised feminist campaign within the party. The latter is sometimes claimed by the feminists. However, as a matter of fact, Green women have achieved a degree of formalised power inside the party which is obviously far greater than in any other German party.

Furthermore, the Greens were the first – and so far the only – party to have a completely female parliamentary leadership. Correspondingly, they hold an impressive record of female representation in both their Bundestag fraktion and in the federal leadership. Between 1979 and 1989, 21 out of a total of 55 elected members of the executive committee were women. The figures for the federal executive were 48 out of 117. As a result of the regulations stipulated in the women's statute, the figures have increased significantly after 1986. Similarly, the first Green contingent in the Bundestag was still dominated by men (18:10), whereas the second Green parliamentary party had a female majority (25:19) (Poguntke with Boll, 1992). By contrast, no established party has ever elected a female party leader.

GOODBYE TO BASISDEMOKRATIE?

It is beyond doubt that the exceptional circumstances of the first all-German elections have significantly contributed to the totally unexpected and spectacular electoral defeat of the most successful Green party in Western democracies (Chapter 5). Virtually overnight, all issues that normally work in favour of the Greens had been removed from the political agenda (Kaase and Gibowski, 1990). Arguably, however, Greens' inability to react coherently to the changing political environment and their half-hearted campaign have made independent contributions to their disastrous performance at the polls. Both factors are clearly related to the peculiarities of the Green organisational structure. The strict separation of party arenas stifles intra-party communication and induces polarised public debate. As a result, swift adaptation to quickly changing political circumstances is hard to achieve. Furthermore, the role of the federal council as a kind of 'watchdog' of the federal executive which claims power but no responsibility for the effects of certain actions and disunity among the members of the collective leadership paralysed the election campaign. As a result of the factional stalemate on the federal level, party élites opted for an 'easy way out' and resorted to the ideals of *Basisdemokratie* for campaigning: the federal party organisation reduced its role in the Bundestag election campaign to a minimum and left most of the initiative – and funding – to lower party levels (Boll and Poguntke, 1992).

Consistently and not surprisingly, Green reformists skilfully exploited the election shock to initiate substantial structural reform aimed at drawing lessons from a decade of alternative politics and making the party politically more efficient. Already before the Neumünster party conference of April 1991, pragmatist majorities in several Länder had used the momentum of the shock of 2 December 1990 to streamline their party organisations by partially giving up the strict separation of office and mandate in order to improve the flow of communication between party arenas through personal overlap.

On the federal level, the federal council (BHA) was identified as a major organisational incentive for factionalism (see above). It consisted only of delegates elected by the Land party conferences and the federal leadership and was supposed to 'supervise' the federal leadership. As a result of the strict separation of office and mandate, neither experiences from parliamentary politics nor of Land leaderships could influence the decision-making of the BHA. Not surprisingly, the BHA could never really fulfil its envisaged task of co-ordinating Green politics.

Consequently, the Neumünster conference decided to abolish the federal council and substitute it by a *Land council*, which is designed to guarantee the flow of information between different party arenas. This required a partial abolition of a sacred principle of *Basisdemokratie*, that is, the separation of office and mandate. The Land council consists of between two and four delegates from each Land party (depending on membership). One of them must be a member of the Land leadership; another one should be a member of the Land parliament. The federal executive, two members of the Green Bundestag fraktion, one Green member of the European parliament and two delegates of the federal working groups complete this body, which no longer has the authority to issue binding decisions for the federal executive. Instead, it has been limited to an advisory role (§8a, federal statute of June 1991).

Another major reform failed by a narrow margin. A motion to open one-third of the seats in the federal executive to members of parliament missed the required two-thirds majority. Hence, there is still no overlapping membership of parliamentary party and federal executive. Before this – very likely temporary – victory by organisational purists, the conference had approved of reducing the federal executive to nine members (instead of eleven) and the number of party speakers from three to two. Also, it abolished the position of federal secretary (Schriftführer) and introduced a *political manager* (politischer Geschäftsführer), who is also member of the executive committee. Whereas this moderate stream-lining of the federal leadership hardly signifies a major departure from the original model of grass-roots democracy, the abolition of the rotation principle for this party body is more significant. Until 1991, members of the federal leadership had to take an obligatory break from office after four years. Finally, financial constraints have forced the Green Party to give up another tenet of *Basisdemokratie*. There will be two categories of members of the federal executive, unpaid ordinary members and professionalised members of the executive committee.

Inevitably, this raises the question of whether or not the Greens still adhere to an alternative organisational model. It is certainly true that the 1991 reform represents a significant reorientation of the dominant organisational philosophy inside the party. The bitter defeat of December 1990 led many diehard believers in true grass-roots democracy to accept the need for sacrificing some of their participatory ideals to the creation of a more efficient organisational structure. After all, the Greens are becoming electorally more dependent on their own *political performance* – despite the fact that they appeal to political ideals which are structurally anchored in specific segments of society. However, even after the 1991 reforms, the participatory ideals and the counter-cultural political style of the Green social bases have left a substantial imprint on the organisational structure and the internal political life of the party. The Greens are still the only German party without office accumulation, with a collective leadership, a pronouncedly participatory and élite-challenging internal political culture, special veto powers for women, and extensive grass-roots rights to propose motions on federal party conferences. Furthermore, the federal working groups (Bundesarbeitsgemeinschaften) represent unique channels for injecting grass-roots initiative and knowledge into parliamentary policy-making.

Nevertheless, after more than a decade of experience with their experimental attempt of institutionalising direct democratic structures within the framework of representative democracy, the Greens have moved somewhat towards the estab-lished parties. Clearly, the structural imperatives of the political system have taken their toll. From the outset, constitutional and technical reasons have reduced the imperative mandate to a mere declaration of political will. It was an ironic 'revenge' of the parliamentary system that the parliamentary group of the 'anti-party party' acquired considerable political prestige and rewards. This was partly due to generous state funding and absorption of the most qualified political personnel into parliamentary politics. Consequently, professionalisation of the federal executive seemed to be the only possible remedy against the domination of the party by its parliamentary group. Hence, the attempt to rescue one organisational principle (i.e. the predominance of extra-parliamentary politics) entailed the departure from the ideal of amateur politics and hence a significant move towards the organisational model of the established parties. In similar vein, the mechanics of the political system have forced the Greens to reconsider the rotation principle and the separation of office and mandate.

Inherent problems of *Basisdemokratie* have also become apparent over the course of the 1980s. The very low degree of formalisation of the policy process in the Green Party has proved to have ambivalent effects. It provides the rank-and-file with considerable participatory opportunities. But it entails considerable risks for the transparency of decision-making. Ordinary rank-and-file members might not always be able to see through the behind-the-scenes manoeuvring of the party élites. However, the open and non-formalised party organisation facilitates the revocation of decisions that have been pushed through by manipulative means. Given the fact that a high degree of formalisation in established parties does not exclude élite manipulation, it can be argued that the Green party organisation represents democratic progress.

In a nutshell, 'Basisdemokratie' is more than a catchword in the political debate. The full realisation of the concept of *Basisdemokratie*, however, is hindered to some extent by the weak membership basis of the party. It is also inhibited by some mechanisms generic to the parliamentary system, which in the long run could represent the greatest problem for Green identity. In fact, there are good reasons for the argument that the high degree of complexity typical of advanced industrial societies structurally prevents a full realisation of the concept. In order to arrive at decisions which are consistent with their own normative convictions, political élites need to acquire expert knowledge. Furthermore, the complexity of problems requires specialisation: to an extent, even MPs have to rely on the specialised knowledge and judgement of other members of their parliamentary party.

Unless many active and highly educated members at the grass roots can afford the time to keep up with the level of information of their party élites and MPs, they will rarely be able to challenge their decisions effectively. Clearly, this makes meaningful, *specific* grass-roots control very difficult. Instead, it may become evident, that the ideal of *Basisdemokratie* can primarily lead to a higher intensity of *generalised* grass-roots control. Of course, this would also require a growing willingness of ordinary party members to trust their élites.

NOTES

1. 'Kerngedanke ist dabei die ständige Kontrolle aller Amts- und Mandatsinhaber und Institutionen durch die Basis (Öffentlichkeit, zeitliche Begrenzung) und die jederzeitige Ablösbarkeit, um Organisation und Politik für alle durchschaubar zu machen und um der Loslösung einzelner von ihrer Basis entgegen zu wirken.' (Präambel (Entwurf) Bundesprogramm, 2nd edition)
2. For legal and administrative reasons, German parties largely correspond to the administrative structure of the Federal Republic. The principal levels are as follows: Ortsverband (local branch); Kreisverband (district organisation, which is comparable to constituency organisation, although there may be more than one constituency in a district); Bezirks/Landesverband (regional/Land organisation; one Land organisation usually consists of several regional organisations); federal level.
3. Unless noted otherwise, all subsequent references to statutory articles refer to the 1989 versions of the respective party constitutions.

4. Decision taken by Parteirat, Vorstand, Kontrollkommission, 18–19 May 1981 (SPD, 1982).
5. The working groups of the FDP have the right to propose motions to the party congress via the federal executive (§24). However, they are no autonomous bodies but creatures of the federal executive.
6. Interview with Robert Camp, federal executive staff, Offenburg, 15 December 1985.
7. Frauenstatut, approved by Nuremberg party conference, 26–8 September 1986.
8. See below for 1991 changes.
9. Interview with Georg Dick, press secretary of the parliamentary party in Bonn, Bonn, 6 March 1985.
10. There are slight differences between both versions; our analysis is based on the draft version of 1983.
11. Cf. *Die Grünen im Landtag informieren*, No. 10, 1984, Hanover.
12. See the standing orders of the Bundestag (Geschäftsordnung), version of March 1983, which stipulates that a parliamentary group must have 5 per cent (=26) MPs in order to have full rights as a 'Fraktion'. After the secession of Gerd Bastian, the Green parliamentary party had 27 members (the figures include MPs from Berlin).
13. For the 1983–7 legislative term, the allowance was 1950 German marks.
14. For the sake of brevity we will call successors/predecessors of MPs (Vorrücker/ Nachrücker) non-MPs. This corresponds to a term that was used in the Green Bundestag group: 'Nicht-Mandatierte'.
15. In German parliaments, the leader of a parliamentary party is in charge of maintaining the voting discipline. He is comparable to the whip in the English system. A parliamentary manager (parlamentarischer Geschäftsführer) is responsible for technical affairs concerned with the parliamentary proceedings. His most important task is to ensure adequate speaking time for his group in parliament and to negotiate the agenda with his collegues from other parties.
16. It is not clear whether decisions of this body can be opposed in the same way by three members of the parliamentary party. The draft standing orders offer two alternative formulations. However, it can be assumed that controversial issues will always be decided in plenary sessions – in conformance with grass-roots democratic principles (see §4.5, GO-plp).
17. Yet another example for the importance of public proceedings for democratic control – and its ambivalent consequences. The first rounds of negotiations with the SPD in Hesse were staged publicly, but it proved to be too difficult for both sides to make concessions when always being scrutinised by a suspicious public. Hence, later negotiations took place behind closed doors.
18. Cf. RB 3, 1985; interview with Robert Camp, federal executive staff, March 1985. There was some change in the number of members of the Bundestag group, because few ex-MPs decided not to stay full-time in Bonn. The federal executive hired assistants on a short-term basis for special purposes, like the support for the movement against the nuclear reprocessing plant in Wackersdorf. See RB-BUVO, 1985, p. 23.
19. Information of the press office of *Die Grünen im Bundestag*.
20. The diversity of results can be explained by the difference between observed behaviour and self-classification. To a certain extent, the latter always reflects internalised norms of the respondent. Participation is part of the concept of membership and has the character of a positive norm. Hence party members will tend to exaggerate their actual involvement in the party.
21. Junge Union = Young Christian Democrats; CDA = Christlich-Demokratische Arbeitnehmerschaft, which is the representative of labour interests in the CDU.
22. Ordnung für die Bundesfachaussüsse, BFAO, §3 (standing orders for federal commissions), printed in: CDU Statut.
23. See CSU statute §27.3; the CSU calls its commissions 'Arbeitskreise'.
24. FDP Geschäftsordnung für die Bundesfachausschüsse (standing orders for federal commissions), §3.1.
25. On the Land level, they are paralleled by 'Landesarbeitsgemeinschaften'.
26. Interview with Torsten Lange, member of *Die Grünen im Bundestag*, Bonn, 6 March 1985. For other parties, see Höfling 1980a, 1980b; Schmidt, 1983; Mintzel, 1983; Haungs, 1983; Heimann, 1984.

9. Green Political Action: Stretching the Limits of Legitimate Forms of Participation

The preceding chapter has shown that both normative convictions and behavioural aspirations need to be considered when trying to explain the party organisation and internal political style of the German Greens. Normative pre-dispositions, for example with regard to the preferred model of democracy, have a direct impact on organisational structures. In a comparable way, behavioural norms and dispositions are relevant for actual behaviour. However, political behaviour has a normative dimension which goes beyond the kinds of action techniques which are considered to be useful or legitimate. Unconventional participation is not just characterised by the use of a certain repertoire of action techniques but also by a distinct motivation: whereas conventional participation tends to be *élite-directed*, unconventional action is often used to *challenge* the élites in power or the policies pursued by them.[1]

Barnes, Kaase *et al.* have used the criterion of legitimacy to distinguish between conventional and unconventional action techniques. Forms of partici-pation which meet with distinct disapproval by sizeable minorities mark the beginning of the realm of unconventional participation (Barnes, Kaase *et al.*, 1979, p. 70). Aspects of legality are only of very secondary importance in this respect (Kaase, 1976, p. 185).

However, this approach necessarily disregards the kind of political goal that motivates a specific type of action. Obviously, this is the only method of obtain-ing reliable cross-nationally comparable data. In most cases, the goal involved will have little bearing on the population's judgement on a certain political action. It is possible, however, to think of political situations that justify means that would clearly be rejected by a large majority of the population in normal times: politically motivated assassination is the most extreme example. We will see below that disruptive action by the peace movement met with more tolerance than similar activities by other groups.

Furthermore, political tactics and opportunism may sometimes lead party élites to tolerate or even endorse substantial disruptions of the public order which they would otherwise denounce forcefully. Franz-Josef Strauß's active solidarity with lorry-drivers who blocked the roads leading through Austria to Italy is a frequently mentioned example of the flexibilty of the boundaries of legitimate action. Another, more recent, example is the reaction of the Social Democratic authorities when protesting steel workers paralysed the entire Ruhrgebiet on 10

December 1987: nobody was prosecuted, whereas temporary blockades of missile bases regularly led to trial and – in most cases – to a sentence for coercion[2] (*Der Spiegel*, January 88, pp. 41ff.).

The examples show that any empirical analysis of party behaviour needs to attempt the identification of boundaries of action that are not transcended by parties under 'normal' circumstances. Also, it is important to distinguish between tolerance after the event and active, supportive participation in such activities.

POLITICAL ACTION AND THE MECHANICS OF THE PARTY SYSTEM

The analysis of the organisational structure of the Green Party has demonstrated that the – New Politics-inspired – behavioural dispositions of the membership have left a clear imprint on the internal political style of the Greens. The same reasoning leads us to suggest that these dispostions are bound to have a discernible effect on the way the party behaves as a collective actor: if most of the party members are prepared to use unconventional forms of political participation, the Green Party as a political organisation will endorse at least some of these action techniques. Legal and ideological reasons, as well as the constraints of party competition, may induce Green Party élites to refrain from giving support to some of the most extreme forms of action, particularly if they are clearly illegal. Since they have to deal with a pronouncedly anti-élitist party membership they can seldom be sure that such decisions will be respected by party militants. Results from the empirical analysis of party behaviour need to be judged in light of this qualification.

A second line of reasoning leads directly from the 'organisational history' and political anchorage of the Green Party to the same expectation: the Greens are the 'child' of the new social movements and adhere to a self-proclaimed role as their spokesman. They transported their ideals and goals into the realm of parliamentary politics (Ismayr, 1985, p. 316, Cornelsen, 1986; Gatter, 1987; Chapter 7). Organisationally, the party has institutionalised channels which facilitate the participation of activists from the movements in the political and parliamentary life of the Green Party. Resort to unconventional forms of political participation is a constitutive characteristic of new social movements (Roth, 1985, pp. 44ff.). It would be surprising, therefore, not to find such a political style in the way the Green Party acts in politics.

The dynamic of party competition suggests that neighbouring parties – in the 1980s particularly the SPD – may have been inclined to imitate certain action techniques in order to absorb parts of the electorate that are politically oriented towards the agenda that is thematised by these movements. As the analysis of programmes, electorates and activists shows, the Social Democratic Party appeals also to moderate New Politics proponents (see Chapters 5, 6 and 7). Their minority position within the party in conjunction with a relatively oligarchical organisational structure suggests that the leadership will be able to contain and control unconventional aspirations within the party. A party that is still predominantly rooted in an Old Politics milieu and electorate is constrained by the preferences and limits of tolerance of those who represent the dominant portion of a party's social bases. Electoral strategy, on the other hand, makes it advisible for the Social Democrats to present themselves as a party that is not entirely aloof from all forms of unconventional participation. After all, the image of a party is not only determined by its political and programmatic positions. Aspects of political style may be even more important for some voters.

However, the leeway for manoeuvre beetween Old and New Politics is also restricted through a historical legacy of German Social Democracy. A constituent trauma of the SPD is the party's fear of being identified with anti-national, anti-statist elements. This dates back to the nineteenth century anti-Socialist legislation of Bismarck and was revitalised by the division of Germany after 1945 and the establishment of a Communist East German state under the ideological flag of 'real existing Socialism'. It was the common ideological root in Marxism which made the SPD vulnerable to suspicions of not being entirely favourable of the existing 'free democratic basic order' in the Federal Republic (Smith, 1982a, pp. 214ff.). Consequently, the SPD has always been very eager not to cause any doubts concerning the party's integrity as a 'responsible' party. Strict adherence to the law and 'Staatstreue' (loyalty to the state) are hallmarks of Social Democratic identity (Greiffenhagen and Greiffenhagen, 1981, p. 156f.). Clearly, efforts of the Social Democrats to develop links with the movements were the logical result of the dynamics of party competition. In the light of this legacy, however, they are likely to avoid illegal activities or forms of action that are considered illegitimate by a substantial part of the population.

As far as the remaining established German parties are concerned, we can exclude the CDU and CSU, as both parties are clearly embedded in the Old Politics (H. Schmitt, 1987; Chapters 5 and 6). Neither the party membership nor the exigencies of party competition will therefore push for unconventional action. The position of the FDP is – once again – less clear. In the 1970s and the early 1980s (until the change of coalition partners), the FDP was a substantially different party with a modest acceptance of moderate New Politics demands (Soe, 1985, pp. 171ff.). Almost from the beginning of the electoral history of the Greens, however, the FDP has been in a coalition with the CDU/CSU. This strategic move caused a substantial turnover of the party's electorate and membership which produced a strong majority for Old Politics-related classical Liberalism in the party (Dittberner, 1987, p. 95). Moreover, electoral politics no longer compelled it to compete for New Politics votes. On the contrary, the FDP pursued its usual strategy of poaching in the hunting grounds of its coalition partner, in recent years the CDU/CSU.

On the grounds presented so far, we can expect only the SPD to have become infected by protest politics to a considerable extent in the 1980s. We will therefore focus our analysis on the SPD and the Greens in the 1980s, referring to the remaining parties as necessary.

It could be objected that excluding the 1970s misses out a period when the new social movements were already very active. However, it was exactly the lack of response of the Bundestag parties that led to the foundation of the Green Party. It seems therefore that established parties were not open to unconventional action at the élite level in this period (Bürklin, 1984, pp. 102ff.). On the mass level, however, there were signs of erosion in the SPD – and to a lesser extent the FDP – that eventually led to the exodus of New Politics-oriented members: many members of the Green élite are disillusioned ex-Social Democrats (Fogt, 1986, p. 23). Since we are not primarily concerned with historic developments but rather with the contemporary state of the German parties and the party system, we will limit our analysis to the 1980s.

SPD AND GREENS: SIDING WITH THE MOVEMENTS?

The unit of analysis of this book is the political party. We have shown that the Greens as a collective actor are characterised by specific properties that distinguish them from other parties. Correspondingly, the primary focus of the following analysis of political style is the élite and/or collective level, that is, the authoritative decision of the party to endorse, actively support or denounce certain action techniques and political activities. The behaviour of individual party members who violate the guidelines of the party is not directly relevant from this perspective. However, relevant in so far as their dissidence can be interpreted as signs of change that is taking place at the grass roots of a party and, probably, moving upwards towards the higher echelons of political power.

As already mentioned, the question of party style involves fundamental decisions of the party or the party leadership on various kinds of political action. It is therefore possible to concentrate on a qualitative analysis of party positions for some prominent examples. Subsequently, we will analyze the political action style of the Greens and the Social Democrats using as examples three important political conflicts of the 1980s: the peace campaign; the struggle against nuclear power and the construction of a nuclear reprocessing plant; and the boycott movement against the national census.

a) The Peace Movement

The emergence of the new peace movement in West Germany was largely a reaction to the NATO 'twin-track decision' of December 1979. Protest against the projected modernisation of medium-range nuclear missiles in particular, and the arms race in general, reached a first height in October 1981, when more than 300,000 rallied for a mass demonstration in Bonn. From the beginning, the nascent Green Party actively supported the peace movement. Delegates from the party leadership participated in its steering commitee (Koordinationsausschuß) (Roth, 1985, pp. 67ff.; Papadakis, 1984, pp. 134ff.).

Despite prominent dissidents, the SPD remained loyal to chancellor Helmut Schmidt's policy of adhering to the NATO decision. Whereas the German federation of trade unions (DGB) prohibited the participation of its members in the peace rally of October 1981, the SPD took a more liberal stance. After long debates, a majority of the party leadership turned down Helmut Schmidt's desire to outlaw the participation of Social Democrats. However, the comrades were advised to stay at home (WR, TAZ, 19 October 1983). Obviously, this decision did not mean that Social Democrats were opposed to peaceful demonstrations as political method. It just highlights the pronounced distance between the Social Democratic leadership and the peace movement when the SPD was still in government.

Two years later, the government and the majorities in the SPD had changed: the SPD had become an active participant in the peace movement's steering commitee and Willy Brandt was the main speaker at the peace demonstration of October 1983 (FR, 19 October 1983). However, solidarity with the newly adopted ally (FR, 15 June 1983) reached clear limits when it came to illegal action. Temporary blockades of missile bases were considered legal and were therefore regarded as acceptable (SPD, BUVO, PR. 579/83). Prominent SPD politicians participated in blockades of the Pershing II base near the Swabian village of Mutlangen (*Der Spiegel*, No. 17, 1988, pp. 59ff.).

However, when the peace movement began in 1984, with the fervent support of the Green Party, to seek direct, if non-violent, confrontation with soldiers in manoeuvre, the SPD distanced itself (BR, 11 September 1984; SPD, BUVO, PR. 373/ 84; Greens, BUVO, PR. 16 August 1984). The SPD was also opposed to a defence-tax strike (Rüstungssteuerboykott), which was actively supported by the Greens. Several Green MPs participated in this strike (Greens, PLP, PR. 260/83; 563/83; 545/83). Another conflictual point was the debate over political strikes against the stationing of the nuclear missiles. Whereas the Greens called for such strikes, the Social Democratic leadership denounced political strikes on legal grounds (Sozialdemokratischer Pressedienst, 29 June 1983; Greens, PLP, PR. 432/83).

The examples show that the SPD followed the expected – legal – strategy. However, given the widespread public support for the goals of the peace movement, the party was prepared to go to the utmost limits. In May 1988, the German High Court (Bundesgerichtshof) ruled that blockades of missile bases have to be prosecuted as coercion – irrespective of the intentions of the protesters (STZ, 14 May 1988). Consequently, the SPD found itself on the other side of the legal fence, a situation the party has always tried hard to avoid. After all, the party had always argued that peaceful blockades were not illegal. The Greens, on the other hand, did not refrain from breaking laws as long as they considered their own action legitimate.

b) Nuclear Power (Wackersdorf)

The second fundamental political turn-around of the Social Democratic party after their loss of governmental power was accelerated by the Chernobyl catastrophe. At their Nuremberg party conference in August 1986 they called for a ten years' phasing out of nuclear energy production (SPD, 1986b, pp. 827ff.). Before this decision was taken, the party was already opposed to plans for the construction of a nuclear reprocessing plant near the Bavarian village of Wackersdorf. It was argued that initiating the 'plutonium circle' would multiply the risks of nuclear technology. Also, the immense investments would predetermine a future nuclear path in national energy policies.

From the beginning of the protest against the Wackersdorf project, the SPD actively supported the resistance movement. The SPD head of the administration of the relevant administrative district (Landrat), Hans Schuierer, tried hard to throw a spanner in the works. The project was vigorously pushed by the CSU Land government under Franz-Josef Strauß. The Social Democratic Prime Minister candidate for the upcoming Bavarian state election actively engaged in the anti-Wackersdorf movement (SA, 15 December 1985; SZ, 14 October 1985).

Not surprisingly, Green protest dates further back and was even more determined. As early as May 1983, the Green parliamentary party called for a demonstration against the project (Greens, PLP, PR. 100/83). In December 1985, a national Green Party conference was interrupted for one day in order to drive collectively to the Wackersdorf site and symbolise support for those struggling against the project. Green MPs also participated in the occupation of the building site (Greens, PLP, PR. 814/85).

There were hardly any differences of principle between the SPD and the Greens. Both parties supported the protest movement against the Wackersdorf project. Gradual differences, however, became visible in the aftermath of the Chernobyl catastrophe. The Russian accident led to a sudden resurgence of the anti-nuclear movement all over the Federal Republic. Several mass demonstrations in the spring and summer of 1986 were accompanied by mass violence (Der Spiegel, No. 31, 1981, pp. 56ff.). Whereas the Social Democrats have been very eager to distance themselves unambiguously from all violent action, the Green Party was not entirely unambiguous in all instances: the Hamburg GAL, for example, approved in June 1986 of 'all forms of resistance' against the nuclear state (Der Spiegel, No. 30 1986, p. 36). Whereas this appears to have been an accidental majority that can never be precluded due to the informal and loosely structured organisation of the party, it points to an ongoing dispute within the Greens. Although there is no dissent about disapproving violent action against people, there is no consensus on the necessity of denouncing all violent action by protesters (see Chapter 7).

In the light of – often personal – experience of violent and sometimes illegal police action, many Green politicians can at least understand violent reactions by protesters.[3] Others argue that it is necessary to reject violence regardless of such considerations in order to interrupt a self-perpetuating spiral.

c) The National Census

In March 1982, the Bundestag unanimously passed a bill that prepared the legal ground for a national census in Spring 1983. Concern about looming infringements of civil liberties is a prominent theme of the New Politics. It was therefore no surprise that the planned census sparked off a heated debate about the protection of personal living conditions from state curiosity. The SPD approved of the need for a census but criticised several operative details that were seen to collide with data protection and personal liberties. Hence, the Social Democrats called for a moratorium that should allow for changing the law accordingly (SPD, PLP, PR. 29 March 1983). The Green Party, on the other hand, quickly joined the grass-roots movement against the census and supported the – illegal – call for a boycott. In April 1983, the constitutional court repealed the law because it violated several constitutionally guaranteed personal freedoms (Hubert, 1983).

When a revised census law was passed and May 1987 was selected for the undertaking, the Green Party was again left alone in its rejection of a census on principle. Its support for a boycott was denounced by all other Bundestag parties as a call to break the law (STZ, 24 September 1986; 17 February 1987). Further Green activities were met with legal sanctions: the Green parliamentary parties of the Bundestag and several Land parliaments installed so-called 'hot lines' that were used to advise people planning to boycott the census on their legal rights. These lines were cut off by the respective parliamentary presidents (STZ, 13 March 1987). Also, several Green MPs were prosecuted for calling for a boycott, because this is illegal (STZ, 23 April 1987). The conflict culminated in a raid on the Green national headquarters in Bonn, where the police searched for anti-census posters and information leaflets (STZ, 27 April 1987).

The conflict over the census demonstrates once more the limits of SPD action. When the party was critical of the census in 1983, it concentrated on legal arguments and refrained from support for the boycott movements. Correspondingly, the prime criticism of the Social Democrats in the second debate of 1986/7 was directed at the fact that the Greens advocated illegal action, not at their arguments against the census as such.

RÉSUMÉ

The case studies have clearly carved out the crucial dividing line between the Green and Social Democratic parties. The SPD is very careful not to transcend any legal boundaries. Accordingly, the only case in recent history when prominent Social Democrats found themselves on the wrong side of the legal fence was in the peace movement. Resistance to the deployment of new nuclear missiles was a popular cause in these years and the legal status of the blockades was unclear. Significantly, the SPD used primarily legal arguments to justify these forms of action.

The Greens, on the other hand, have no reservations about getting involved in illegal action as long as they consider their cause legitimate. However, the form of action needs to conform with the Green definition of non-violence. To conclude, the Green Party has introduced a new style of political action into the realm of party politics. Whereas the claim for supremacy of legitimacy over legality has so far been the preserve of extra-parliamentary movements, it has now become a regular feature of the political style of a parliamentary party. This highlights the 'split' identity of the Green Party: for a party represented in parliament, the arena for seeking redress would clearly be the Bundestag. Nevertheless, the Greens at the same time behave like a protest movement, that has no means of fighting against policies other than resorting to protest action.

Whether or not such a political style undermines the stability of parliamentary rule is a question that cannot be answered here. It might be argued that the authority of parliament is undermined when even parliamentary parties no longer accept the pacifying effect of binding decisons made by majority rule. A counter-argument would be, however, that the Green Party serves as a kind of safety valve which allows those who are vigorously opposed to certain policies to identify with members of established political institutions.

NOTES

1. For the difference between élite-challenging and élite-directed participation see Chapter 2.
2. The German legal term is 'Nötigung'
3. On 8 June 1986, several hundred demonstraters were encircled by the police in Hamburg. They were forced to remain on the site for many hours without being allowed to contact anybody. Later, courts ruled that the entire police action was illegal and awarded compensation to the victims (*Der Spiegel*, No. 25, 1986). For another example of extreme police violence, see *Der Spiegel*, No. 20, 1988, p. 115f. on Wackersdorf events.

10. Conclusions

Elsewhere, we have argued that the German Greens belong to a new party family that has made substantial inroads into Western party systems in the 1980s (Poguntke, 1987b; 1989b). The analyses of this book have been guided by the attempt to provide thorough empirical evidence for the proposition that the German Greens do indeed represent a new, distinct type of political party, which is primarily the product of shifts towards the New Politics. It has been shown that they are clearly rooted in identifiable, New Politics-prone sections of society, that their voters and activists share a theoretically expected set of political preferences and behavioural dispositions, and that the party's programmatic and organisational profile is clearly in tune with the characteristics of the New Politics. Nevertheless, the German Green Party is not only a product of the relatively uniform upsurge of New Politics in all advanced industrialised societies. The party has also been moulded by specifically German factors ranging from legal requirements concerning party organisation to particular ideological and cultural traditions. As such it is a German version of a New Politics party.

When talking about party types, distance from neighbouring parties is of crucial importance. On all relevant aspects, we could find substantial distance between the established German parties and the Greens. Despite intrinsic and structural impediments to adaptation, however, there have been signs of movement from both sides of the great divide. Gradually, the Greens have begun to adapt to the most imminent systemic requirements of parliamentary politics. Also, after long and painstaking debates, they have accepted the need for entering governmental coalitions and taking responsibilty for running a system they still want to change substantially. On the other side, the Social Democrats have undergone significant programmatic change which they are beginning to convert into practical politics in several coalitions with the Greens on the Land level. Nevertheless, the SPD is still torn between its traditional working class clientele, which adheres to the Old Politics, and its middle class voters with New Politics preferences. Consequently, the Social Democrats can hardly go much further towards the New Politics side without risking substantial losses among their traditional electorate. Clearly, the Social Democratic capacity to absorb the Green electorate is limited by the need to maintain and consolidate their appeal to the more traditional segments of society.

Our analysis of the German Greens corroborates the theoretical argument, which is essentially comparative: postmaterialism and related behavioural dispositions produce only a potential base for a New Politics party. These dispositions go through a 'filter' of situational, frequently class-related factors before they actually lead to voting for, or engagement in, such a party. Furthermore, there are additional aggregate factors whose importance is frequently underestimated in regard to the success of New Politics parties. The most important is the existence of a related set of political problems. Although it is certainly true that perceptions of the saliency of these issues are influenced by attitudinal dispositions, there are a number of ecological problems, and the whole question of disarmament, which are – in principle – regarded as relevant by large majorities of all Western publics. It is not only a new set of political priorities among segments of Western mass publics which has put these themes on the political agenda. Due to their 'objective quality', they have an agenda-setting capacity of their own and can therefore be understood as independent causal factors for the emergence of New Politics parties.

The emergence of New Politics parties represents a major structural innovation in Western party systems, based on a new dimension of political conflict. Unlike the 'frozen' structure of political conflict so brilliantly depicted by Lipset and Rokkan (1967), this new dimension is not primarily based on homogeneous social groups with well-defined social or economic interests. Instead, it rests on individual preferences that may have been moulded through quite diverse processes. Social position is obviously still an important factor, but the socialisation experiences of certain generations and the overall historical situation have gained more weight.

A GREEN FUTURE OR A FUTURE FOR THE GREENS?

It is unquestionable that the political success of the Greens, that is, their coalition relevance on all levels of the political system, has had important repercussions on German politics. The advent of the Greens has fundamentally changed the political agenda of the Federal Republic. Ecological problems, the role of women in society and the debate over the arms race have dominated the political debate throughout the 1980s. All established parties have felt compelled to adapt programmatically to the Green challenge – not least because many of their demands are directed at the improvement of collective goods like the environment. The analysis has shown that, consistent with their respective positions in the party system, Christian Democrats and Liberals have largely resorted to semantic adaptation whereas the Social Democrats have substantially altered several programmatic positions. By strengthening the intra-party bargaining power of the New Politics wing inside the SPD, the Greens have acted as catalysts of Social Democratic transformation.

There has also been change in practical politics. Cabinet portfolios for the environment and women's issues have become a regular feature of federal and Land governments. Environmental legislation has been improved and expenses for new military equipment are met with increasing public and parliamentary resistance. In their own organisations established parties have begun to promote the role of women, either through formalised rules, as with the SPD, or through intra-party campaigns, as with the CDU.

When the Greens began to take seats in the first Land or local parliaments, their advent was accompanied by many critical comments asking whether their challenge to the all-party consensus on several policy areas and their unconventional political style would not endanger the stability of West German democracy. Although much of this critique was politically motivated, the analyses of the Green electorate have shown that Green voters are more distant from the political system. Nevertheless, it is plausible to argue that it was precisely the electoral success of the Green Party which has contributed to the integration of a segment of the electorate which was, arguably, on the brink of being alienated from the political system.

Ironically, the Greens are in danger of falling victim to their own success. After a decade of organisational existence and established parties' adaptation, the Greens depend increasingly on their own political performance. This is to say that they are no longer automatically regarded as the only proponent of the New Politics. Moderate New Politics adherents, in particular, begin to regard the Social Democrats as an increasingly credible alternative. On the other hand, Social Democratic dependency on support from the Old Politics electorate forecloses a strategy which would appeal to radical New Politics voters. This segment of the electoral market will remain the preserve of the Greens – as long as they are capable of mobilising it. Since they have, after more than a decade, inevitably lost much of their rebellious aura, it will require more political fantasy and imagination than in the past to capture the imagination and support of people who do not regard party politics as the sole means of making their demands heard.

From this perspective, the Green failure to overcome the 5 per cent hurdle in the Western part of the united Germany is particularly detrimental, because it has reduced the political visibility and relevance of the Greens on the level of federal politics. During the crucial phase of implementing unification, the Greens have no real voice in the Bundestag – only two out of the eight members of the East German alliance of Greens and citizens' movements are members of the Green Party. Nevertheless, sixteen German Länder provide ample arenas for political relevance, and soon after the disaster of 2 December 1990, the Hesse Greens formed a Land government with the Social Democrats. The structure of German federalism means that participation in Land governments entails increased visibility on the federal level through the Bundesrat and the possibility of correcting or even obstructing federal policies.[1]

Here, the Greens are likely to benefit from the fact that they have fundamentally altered the format of the (West) German party system and hence the balance of power and the strategic options of parties in parliament. Although the hope (or fear) of the early 1980s did not materialise, that is, the FDP was not relegated to secondary importance in coalition politics, it has emerged that, at least on the Land level, the Social Democrats are likely to find themselves in positions where they can choose between several coalition alternatives. And in many cases, the Greens will be part of the game of coalition building. No doubt, Green governmental participation will be eased by the results of the swift organisational reform, which has substantially reduced the built-in potential for faction fighting by institutionalising communication between party arenas and creating a clearer allocation of power and responsibility inside the party. In addition, the exit of the radical wing has led to a pragmatic majority in the party which is capable and willing to take advantage of opportunities for reformist coalition politics – and hence political visibility.

Also, the future may hold a more favourable agenda for the Greens. As the economy takes off in East Germany, which is among the most polluted regions in the industrialised world, ecological problems will become increasingly salient. Although the arms race has been ended by spectacular disarmament treaties between the United States and the late Soviet Union, peace is likely to remain on top of the list of political problems for years to come. The debate over the German role during the Gulf War and a more assertive international role of a united Germany in the future have indicated the potential for future conflict between parties that reject the use of military violence as a means of international politics and parties who regard military action as a legitimate last resort. The war in Yugoslavia and the increasing ethnic tensions in the republics of the former Soviet Union demonstrate that there is likely to be much future conflict potential.

Furthermore, organisational consolidation suggests that the Greens are here to stay. Once a party has managed to gain a significant electoral foothold, it becomes viable in its own right. Instead of being just a dependent variable, susceptible to the impact of social forces, it begins to mould society according to its own preferences, acting as an 'agent of socialisation'. In the German case, the chances for survival are enhanced by generous state finance which allows parties to generate a dense organisational network independently of financial support from members or donors.

A PARTY OF INDIVIDUAL PARTICIPATION

Finally, some speculations concerning the historical significance of the New Politics party come to mind. They relate primarily to the organisational dimension of our ideal type. It is possible to conceive of certain types of party organisation as corresponding to certain stages of societal development. Whereas the party of individual representation was the party of the liberal bourgeoisie, the party of mass integration served the political organisation of the newly enfranchised masses (Neumann, 1956). Obviously, the social status and background of the parties' clienteles goes a long way in explaining organisational differences. The educated bourgeois in a period of non-mass politics needed no strong party organisation to have an impact on political decision-making. Workers, on the other hand, had to compensate for their lack of individual resources through mass membership and organisational strength.

The period of post-industrial politics is characterised by the emergence of a new kind of citizen who can dispense with strong organisation because he or she is well educated and highly resourceful (Barnes, 1984). In addition, skilful use of modern means of mass communication can function as a functional equivalent to communication through organisational channels, which were an important means for opposition movements of getting their message across. A party corresponding to the social structures of post-industrial politics would need to combine mass membership (we are still in the era of mass politics) with channels for maximal individual input – conditions our new type of party attempts to fulfil. Talking in such ideal-typical terms does not, of course, imply that each historical period simply adds a new type of party while the older types remain unchanged.

Parties have adaptive capacities, and all parties of individual representation, that is, Liberal and Conservative parties, imitated the mass organisation techniques of the working class and denominational parties to some extent – not least for electoral reasons. However, many of them still show traits of their earlier structure which distinguish them from 'genuine' parties of mass integration. Correspondingly, we can expect established parties to move towards the New Politics side without risking the alienation of their core support. The analysis of the German parties has indicated that the SPD is already on the move, programatically and organisationally. From this perspective, the Greens could be a 'trend-setter', indicating a wider development towards the 'party of individual participation'. There may not even be a specific ideological profile attached to this development. Whereas, in earlier historical periods, parties were based on specific social groups with particular interests, the 'individualistic society' seems to allow for more variation.

NOTE

1. The conflict between the Green minister for the environment in Hesse and his colleague in Bonn over the permission for a nuclear fuel plant in Hesse in late 1991 and early 1992 is a prominent example of the opportunity structure of German federalism.

Appendices

1. THE DATABASE AND FORMAT OF TABLES

'Allgemeine Bevölkerungsumfrage der Sozialwissenschaften' (Allbus). The database has been made available by the Zentralarchiv für empirische Sozialforschung, University of Cologne.

Allbus 1980 was conducted in January and February 1980;
N 2955
Allbus 1982 was conducted from February to May 1982;
N 2991
Allbus 1984 was conducted from March to June 1984;
N 3004
Allbus 1986 was conducted from March to May 1988;
N 3095
Allbus 1988 was conducted from April to July 1988;
N 3052
Allbus 1990 was conducted in spring 1990.
N 3051

In addition to the Allbus, the Eurobarometers 21 (March/April 1984: 986 cases), 25 (March 1986; 987 cases), and 31a (June 1989; 1202 cases) were used. Both survey series include West Berlin, where the party preference for the city parliament was asked. According the special status of West Berlin, the city parliament elected delegates to the Bundestag before German unification. They had limited voting rights in the Bundestag.

Allbus data was used unweighted, Eurobar: national weight 1.

Format of Tables

All tables are based on the 'second vote' party preference (Zweitstimmenpräferenz) of the electorate of the Federal Republic and West Berlin. 'Don't know', 'would not vote', 'no answer' were coded missing. NPD, DKP and 'Other Parties' have always been excluded from the tables because they have very small frequencies and are irrelevant for our argument (see Table A1.1). The marginals have not been adjusted, in order not to distort the 'true' electoral strength of the parties as it would be ascertained at election day through the calculation of the 'valid votes'. Hence, the rows do not total 100 per cent and the column 'potential voters' (p.v.) includes all respondents who report a party preference. This provides a more accurate image of the distribution of social characteristics and attitudinal orientations among the German electorate than excluding all respondents with preferences for smaller parties. Due to the varying number of missing cases for different variables the party strength varies insignificantly.

Only column percentages are given, because row percentages do not control for party size. Only exceptional results will be reported in the discussion.

Significance levels are only mentioned in the text if they are lower than 0.001.

Table A1.1: Party Strength (Zweitstimme) – Federal Republic of Germany (including West Berlin).

N Column percentage	1980	1982	1984	1986	1988	1990
CDU/CSU	930	1,137	1,003	848	777	871
	39.4	48.8	43.9	38.2	37.2	35.0
SPD	1017	685	913	947	943	1051
	43.0	29.4	39.9	42.6	45.1	42.3
FDP	262	272	112	178	143	241
	11.1	11.7	4.9	8.0	6.8	9.7
Greens/AL[1]	137	216	246	234	191	268
	5.8[2]	9.3	10.8	10.5	9.1	10.8
Others	17	18	12	14	35	56
	0.7	0.7	0.5	0.6	1.7	1.8
Valid N	2,363	2,328	2,286	2,221	2,089	2,487
Missing cases	592	663	718	874	963	564

Notes:
1. The Alternative List in West Berlin acted as a Green Land party. Since 1985 they have attained formal status as a Green Land organisation (GBD, 1-2, 1986). A separate Green Land organisation remained insignificant and was finally disowned by the federal party because of alleged infiltration by right-wing extremists.
2. Due to tactical voting induced by the candidature of the CSU-leader Franz-Josef Strauß, the Greens gained only 1.5% at the Bundestag election of October 1980.

Source: Allbus

Table A1.2: Election Results (excluding West Berlin).

	1980		1983		1987		1990[1]	
	%	seats	%	seats	%	seats	%	seats
CDU/CSU	44.5	226	48.8	244	44.3	223	43.8	319
SPD	42.9	218	38.2	193	37.0	186	33.5	239
FDP	10.6	53	7.0	34	9.1	46	11.0	79
Greens	1.5	–	5.6	27	8.3	42	5.0[2]	8

Note:
1. All-German Elections
2. The Greens ran as two separate parties. The West German Greens obtained 4.8% of the vote and missed the West German 5% hurdle by 0.2%. The East German Greens fought the election in an alliance with the citizens' movements, which reached 6.1%. Two members of their Bundestag group are Greens.

2. INDEX CONSTRUCTION

The indices are based on the assumption that the single variables have equal importance. The variables were combined in an additive index, in order to measure the various facets of a given problem (cf. Friedrichs, 1973, pp. 165ff.). Cases with one or more missing variables were coded as missing. The statistical significance of differences of index means was tested through t-tests, because the index represents an interval scale (Blalock, 1981, p. 193). N is sufficiently large to relax normality assumption (ibid., p. 227). The condition of independence of the subsamples is automatically met, since they were selected from a single larger sample (ibid., p. 224). The direction of the differences could not always be specified beforehand and equality of population variances could not be assumed; hence the two-tailed test with separate variance estimate was applied (Norusis, 1982, p. 47f.).

Justice-index (Allbus, 1984)[1]

'Generally speaking, the economic profits are shared out in the Federal Republic in a fair way.'

'Even if one tried one could hardly diminish social differences further than in the Federal Republic.'

'The Federal Republic is an open society. Achievement in life depends no longer on family background but on personal talents and educational success.'

'Generally speaking, I consider the social differences in our country as just.'

'There is still the old antagonism between property owners and the working population. The class background determines the personal situation.'
* Agree completely
* Agree to some extent
* Disagree to some extent
* Disagree completely

The last variable was recoded in order to have the same polarity as the other variables. All variables were dichotomised and an additive index was constructed.

Index: 'Environment: Opinion' (Allbus, 1988)

'Now a question concerning our environment. Would you please tell me according to this list to what extent the environment in general is affected through
* noise from aircraft?
* leaded petrol?
* industrial waste in inshore waters and the sea?
* nuclear power plants?
* air pollution through industries?
* noise from traffic and air pollution through cars?

---

[1]Allbus questions: translation by the author; Eurobarometer questions: translation taken from English language questionnaire.

- A great deal
- A fair amount
- Not very much
- Not at all.'

Variables were dichotomised and the positive categories were combined in an additive index.

Index: 'Environment: Relevance' (Allbus, 1988)

'To what extent do you feel personally affected in your own environment through [questions as above]?'

3. SURVEY QUESTIONS (CHAPTERS 5 AND 6)

Religion: Attitude: Personal Rating

'As far as religion is concerned would you like to indicate your attitude about religion on this scale (SHOW CARD). Position 1 shows that you consider yourself as someone who is not at all religious. Position 10 shows that you consider yourself as someone who is completely religious. Would you please indicate, on this scale 1–10 where you think you are on the point of view of your religion.' (from Eurobarometer 25, 1986)

Religious Affiliation (Table 6.10)

'Do you feel affiliated to a religious community? If yes, which one?'

Religion: Level of Importance (Table 6.11)

'Do you personally feel, irrespective of how often you go to church, that religion is of great importance, some importance, or only of little importance in your life?' (from Eurobarometer 21)

Class Conflict

'It is often said that there are conflicts of interest between the different groups in in Federal Republic, for example between men and women, etc. Not all of them are equally strong. I will now name several of such groups. Would you please indicate on this list whether these conflicts are very strong, strong, fairly weak, or whether there are no conflicts.

• between capitalists and the working class.' (from Allbus, 1990)

Funtioning of Political System (Table 5.14)

'All in all, what do you think? How well or badly does our political system function nowadays? Which of the following statements is closest to your own opinion?

• It functions well and needs no change.
• It functions fairly well, but needs some change.
• It does not function well and should be changed in many respects.
• It does not function well at all and needs complete change.'

Satisfaction with Democracy (Table 5.15)

'Let us now consider democracy in the Federal Republic of Germany. Generally speaking, how satisfied or dissatisfied are you with democracy, as it exists in the Federal Republic of Germany?

• very satisfied
• fairly satisfied
• somewhat satisfied
• somewhat dissatisfied
• fairly dissatisfied
• very dissatisfied.'

Satisfaction with Democracy (Table 6.12)

'On the whole, are you very satisfied, fairly satisfied, not very satisfied, or not at all satisfied with the way democracy works in the Federal Republic?' (from Eurobarometer 21)

Income Differences: (Table 6.15)

'I will now ask your opinion on a number of items. Will you please, for each item, select on this list the answer which best describes your own opinion.
    "Differences in incomes must be reduced as far as possible".

- disagree completely
- disagree to some extent
- agree if anything
- broadly agree
- completely agree.'

(from Eurobarometer 21)

Trust in the Bundestag (Table 5.16)

'Now I am going to read out a list of public institutions and organisations. Would you please tell me how much trust you have in each of these institutions and organisations. Please use the following scale: position 1 means that you have great trust; position 7 means that you have very little trust in these institutions and organisations. Would you please indicate, on this scale 1–10, where you think you are with regard to your trust in these institutions and organisations?'

Social Movements and Party Support / Activists (Tables 5.11, 5.12, 6.13)

'There are a number of groups and movements seeking the support of the public. For each of the following movements, can you tell me
    a) whether you approve (strongly, or somewhat) or disapprove (somewhat, or strongly)?
    b) whether you are a member, would probably join or certainly would not join?'

Minority Rights Index (Table 5.13)

'The next question concerns immigrant workers in the Federal Republic. There are some sentences concerning immigrant workers on this list, which one has heard already somewhere. Please indicate on this list to what extent you agree with each of them. Value 1 means that you disagree completely; value 7 means that you agree completely. You can grade your opinion with the intermediate values.

- Immigrant workers should adapt their way of life somewhat more to that of the Germans.
- Immigrant workers should be sent home when jobs are getting scarce.
- Political activity in Germany should be forbidden for immigrant workers.
- Immigrant workers should choose their spouse among their compatriates.'

4. A SYNOPSIS OF GERMAN PARTY PROGRAMMES[1]

List of used basic party programmes:

FDP

F = FDP Bundesvorstand (ed.), Freiburger Thesen, Bonn; approved by the Freiburg conference, 25–7. 10. 1971. 'E' stands for introduction, 'Th.' for thesis.

K = Kieler Thesen 1977. 'Ka' = first section ('Wirtschaft im sozialen Rechtsstaat); 'Kb' = second section ('Bürger, Staat, Demokratie'); 'Kc' = third section ('Bildung und Beschäftigung der jungen Generation'); roman numbers stand for chapters. Published in Günter Verheugen (ed.) (1980), *Das Programm der Liberalen*, (Baden-Baden: Nomos).

S = FDP Bundesvorstand (ed.), Das Liberale Manifest, Bonn; approved by the Saarbrücken conference, 23–4. 2. 1985. For international relations a separate party conference decision from Saarbrücken, February 1985, has been used because this policy area is not discussed in much detail in any of the major programmatic documents.

SPD

No specification = Vorstand der SPD (ed.), Grundsatzprogramm der SPD, Bonn; approved by the party conference at Bad Godesberg, 13–15. 11. 1959.

OR = Vorstand der SPD (ed.), Ökonomisch-Politischer Orientierungsrahmen für die Jahre 1975–1985, Bonn; approved by the Mannheim party conference 14. 11. 1975.

B = Grundsatzprogramm der Sozialdemokratischen Partei Deutschlands, approved by the Berlin party conference, 20. 12. 1989. In Vorstand der SPD (ed.), Protokoll vom Programm-Parteitag Berlin, 18–20.12.1989, Bonn (mentioned for significant change only).

CDU

CDU Bundesvorstand (ed.), Grundsatzprogramm, Bonn; approved by the 26th federal party conference, Ludwigshafen, 23–5. 10. 1978.

CSU

CSU-Landesleitung (ed.), Grundsatzprogramm, Munich; approved by the March 1986 party conference.

Greens

No specification = Die Grünen (ed.), Das Bundesprogramm, 2nd edn, Bonn; approved by the Saarbrücken party conference, 21–3. 3. 1980.

S = Die Grünen (ed.), Gegen Arbeitslosigkeit und Sozialabbau. Sinnvoll arbeiten – solidarisch leben, Bonn; economic programme of the party, approved by the Sindelfingen conference 15–6. 1. 1983.

[1]For the sake of brevity, quotes have not been used widely. By and large, the substance of the relevant paragraphs has been paraphrased by the author.

Table A4.1: Individualism.

(civil liberties v. state interference or surveillance; more police powers; rights and protection of minorities; abortion; divorce[1])

---

a) Civil Liberties and the Role of the Individual

CSU: *fully in favour of 'Radikalenerlaß' (p. 23); *for a 'militant democracy' ('wehrhafte Demokraties') (p. 22); *only a strong state is a liberal state' (p. 23).

CDU: *fully in favour of 'Radikalenerlaß' (116); *commitment to domestic security ('innere Sicherheit') without mentioning the possible conflict with civil liber- ties (124); *data protection: citizens need to be protected against the abuse of their personal data (125).

FDP: *everybody must be able to move freely and unguarded; *more data protection: citizens should decide on the uses of their personal data (S9); *'the Liberal Party will always side with the individual against the institution', wants to defend the freedom of the individual against heteronomy (Fremdbestimmung); *wants to defend the self-determination of the individual in state, legal system, society and economy (F, E. Th1).

SPD: * co-determination is seen as participation in rule (OR 2.3.2); *decisions by the state mean coercion, i.e. heteronomy (Fremdbestimmung), which cannot be abolished but can be democratically legitimised (OR 2.4.1); * civil service employees should have special commitment to the constitution, but spirit and practice of the 'Radikalenerlaß' should be overcome (B, p. 49); * abortion problem should not be a subject of penal law (B, p. 19).

Greens: *fully opposed to the 'Radikalenerlaß' and all other means and methods of state surveillance; *against infringements upon the rights of defence lawyers; *for a non-violent police force (V.1.5); *opposition to the wholesale encroachment on civil liberties (V.1); *abolition of all laws restricting freedom of expression; *for a special anti-trust legislation for the mass media (V.8); *wants to realise the principles of grass-roots democracy, which mean a far-reaching autonomy of the individual and the basic units of society; *self-determination is seen as being far from satisfactorily realised (I); *abolition of any discrimination against homosexuality (V5.3); *abortion should be legal (V2.7).

---

b) Immigrant Workers

CSU: *immigrant workers should have the same rights and obligations in economic life as citizens of the Federal Republic; *in favour of a reduction of the number of immigrant workers in West Germany (p. 51).

CDU: *nothing specific on this topic (105).

FDP: *'everybody should be entitled to his own preferred life-style without any discrimination' (S9).

SPD: *for solidarity with immigrant workers in economically difficult periods also (OR 2.3.3); *against increasing the numbers of foreign workers during future economic booms (OR 4.1.2).

Greens: *unrestricted political activity for foreigners; *right to vote in local elections (V.5.1); *preservation of the traditional life-style of gypsies (V.5.2); *social, legal and political equality for foreigners and legal enforcement of a propor- tional share of jobs for immigrant workers (S II.3).

---

[1]It is indicative that abortion and divorce are not explicitly mentioned in most programmes. Appar- ently, after legal changes in the 1970s, these issues were regarded as too contentious for a renewed debate in the context of party programmes. Nevertheless, the issue of abortion is being kept alive by vigorous minorities in the Christian parties.

Table A4.2: Democracy and the State.

(participatory democracy v. representative democracy; role of decentralisation; role of the
    state)

---

a) Role of the State

CSU: *for a strong state that has the power to protect the freedom of the individual
        (p. 17); *state competence should be guided by the principle of subsidiarity
        (Subsidiaritätsprinzip) (p. 18); *state has a realm of its own, beyond society (p.
        22); *commitment to political leadership (p. 20), but also for a withdrawal of
        the state in order to give citizens more freedom (pp. 25ff.)

CDU: *the state is an institution above society, like a referee (115); *state guarantees
        basic rights of the individual (114); *for political leadership, even if this means
        working against the dominant public mood (116); *'new social inequalities'
        ('Neue Soziale Frage'): State is the advocate of the common good and takes
        care of the interests of the unorganised (100).

FDP: *state action secures and endangers personal freedom (S17); *scepticism about
        too much state power (S5); *state generates preconditions necessary for the
        realisation of participation rights (Ka Th1).

SPD: *state controls private economic power and furthers the development of a freer
        society (OR 2.4.1); *state is not autonomous and above society (OR 2.4.2),
        not neutral, but dependent on societal forces, i.e. 'relative autonomy'(OR
        2.4.4); for the expansion of public responsibility in several areas (OR 2.4.1);
        *active role of the state in the moulding of societal conditions in the public
        interest (OR 2.4.1).

Greens: no explicit programmatic statement on this point.

---

b) Democracy

CSU: *generalised rejection of 'democratisation' (p. 18).

CDU: *commitment to representative democracy and free mandate; *consideration
        of referendum (117).

FDP: *democratisation of state and society by means of representative organisation;
        *in the realm of society, democratisation by means of functional representa-
        tion (F. p.11, FE Th. 3); *extension of representative system through referen-
        dum and petition for a referendum (S 18); *in favour of free mandate (S 19);
        *striving for the democratisation of large organisations (S 18).

SPD: *committed to the expansion of parliamentary democracy (OR 1.11); *demo-
        cratisation means co-determination (OR 2.3.2); *socialism can only be realised
        through democracy, democracy can only be fully achieved through socialism
        (p. 5); *democracy is a way of life (as opposed to merely a political procedure
        (OR 2.3.2); *against imperative mandate (OR 3.2.4); *democratisation of
        interest organisations is necessary (OR 2.4.8); * referendum and petition for a
        referendum should be introduced (B, p. 47).

Greens: *social and economic councils on all levels should decide on public invest-
        ments and budgets on the respective levels (V. 12); *principled priority of the
        lower unit, direct democracy according to the organisational model of the
        Green party (I); *petition for a referendum and referenda should be introduced;
        *abolition of 5% hurdle (V.12); *democratisation of political parties according
        to the Green Party model (V.1.3).

c) Citizen Initiatives

CSU: ——————

CDU: *initiatives represent inspiration for office holders; *programme emphasises concern of initiatives with particularistic interests (199).

FDP: *initiatives are 'normal' in democracy, but no alternative to political parties: the constitutionally determined institutions have to make binding decisions (KbI, Th. 6).

SPD: *citizen initiatives are regarded as a chance for co-determination (OR 3.2.1).

Greens: *attempts should be made to attain goals not only through the parliamentary system, but rather, grass-roots movements should take care of problems themselves (S I.5).

d) Decentralisation

CSU: *transfer of as many duties as possible to the local communes (p. 27); *emphasis on 'principle of subsidiarity' (p. 18).

CDU: *no relevant statement; only general commitment to 'administration close to the citizen' ('bürgernahe Verwaltung', 126).

FDP: ——————

SPD: ——————

Greens: *far-reaching decentralisation and simplification of adminstrative structures (V.1.2); *decentralised units should have as much autonomy as possible (I:preamble).

Table A4.3: Ecology and Environmental Protection.
(role of growth; ecology v. economy; nuclear power; political implementation)

a) Growth

CSU: *in favour of further economic growth, because this is the precondition of social security and fairer distribution of material wealth (p. 40); *'reasonable' balance between economic and ecological imperatives (p. 59); *'hence qualitative growth is to preferred over quantitative'; *'limits to growth have to be drawn at the point where environment or landscape is threatened or even destroyed' (p. 59); *if there are conflicting goals, environmental protection should have priority in cases of serious damage of the environment – this applies particularly when public health is affected (p. 63); *environmental protection offers new fields for economic production (p. 63).

CDU: *economic growth is the precondition for secure jobs, social security, less conflict over redistribution, developmental aid; *'where economic growth results in unacceptable damage to the natural environment, such growth must, as a last solution, be sacrificed' (84); *growth and technological progress are indispensable and are not irreconcilable with environmental protection (87).

FDP: *economic growth is necessary for keeping up present levels of affluence and social security, while relevant are also qualitative aspects like compatibility with the environment (Umweltverträglichkeit); *environmental protection is the precondition of growth, not a limitation to it (Ka IX, Th. 3).

SPD: *wants steady growth (p. 16); *principled approval of quantitative growth, otherwise conflicts over redistribution will increase (OR 2.2); *'for steady, qualitatively meaningful growth' (OR 2.3); *growth is precondition for 'politics of reform' (Reformpolitik) (OR 2.5.1); *also mentioned: limited potentials for growth (OR 4.1.1); * ecological necessities must be the principle of economic action (B, p. 37); * not all growth is progress (B, p. 39).

Greens: *growth is destructive (II.1); *in favour of an economic system that is oriented at the following goals: preservation of nature, resource-conscious production, needs of the people and future generations ('Lebensbedürfnisse der Menschen und zukünftiger Generationen'); *for qualitative growth only if better products can be achieved with constant or reduced consumption of raw materials and energy (II.2); *economic goals can only be realised within the framework of ecological imperatives (IV.1); *partial dismantling and conversion of the industrial system (SI.3).

---

b) Energy

CSU: *for the construction of further nuclear power stations in order to secure sufficient energy supply; *for energy saving (p. 42).

CDU: *nuclear energy generation is an important contribution to environmental protection (87); *energy saving is possible through the means of a functioning market economy (89).

FDP: *a multitude of energy sources should be used (KAIX,Th. 13); *in favour of energy saving (KaIII, Th. 6).

SPD: *'the development of technologies that help to save energy and resources needs particular support' (OR 4.1.2); wants to accomplish a non-nuclear energy production as soon as possible (B, p. 38).

Greens: *opposed to construction and operation of nuclear power stations; *demand an immediate halt of all nuclear stations; *for support for alternative forms of energy production; *all possibilities for energy saving should be used; *for a ban on energy-wasting heating systems; *support for decentralised energy production (II.6); *destruction of monopoly of large energy producers (II.6).

---

c) Role of agriculture

CSU: *ecological problematic is not mentioned in relation to agriculture (p. 44f.).

CDU: *agricultural production does not conflict with environmental protection (88).

FDP: ─────────

SPD: *sufficient prices for producers, intensive agriculture is environmentally damaging (B, p. 38).

Greens: *emphasis on environmental damage caused by conventional agricultural production; *sufficient prices for producers; *strict legal limits during the years of conversion to a chemical-free agriculture; *high sentences and strict controls; *direct income support for ecologically producing farmers; *price structures that favour small and medium-scale farms (II.7.1).

---

d) Traffic and Public Transport

CSU: *continued expansion of the road system (p. 42); *no preference for railways (p. 43).

CDU: ─────────

FDP: ————————

SPD: *expansion of public transport (OR 4.5.6); *priority should be given to railways (B, p. 38).

Greens: *absolute priority should be given to railways; *heavy expansion of public transport (II.8.2); *reduction of traffic through the abolition of spatial separation of labour and housing (SII.2).

e) Implementation of Environmental Protection

CSU: *environmental problems can best be solved through the social market economy (p. 59).

CDU: *principles of market economy also in the field of environmental protection (96); *for the application of the 'principle of liability' ('Verursacherprinzip') (87).

FDP: *for the application of the 'principle of liability' ('Verursacherprinzip') (FIV, Th. 4); *environmental associations should have the right to go to court in defence of environmental interests (SII.2); *stricter laws and sanctions (FIV, Th. 1); *in principle: market solutions that use the price mechanism (FIV, Th. 4; SII.2).

SPD: *for the application of the 'principle of liability' ('Verursacherprinzip'), costs of environmentally damaging production should have effects on the market price of the products (OR 4.1.4); *politics should select growth areas (B, p. 39).

Greens: *for the application of the 'principle of liability' ('Verursacherprinzip') (IV.1); *ecological book-keeping for all companies (II.3); *ban on substances and procedures that strongly disturb the ecological balance (II.2); *levies on pollutive production; *improvements of cars through legal prescriptions (II.8.2); *fees on excessive water consumption (IV.3); *ban on emission of carcinogenic substances (IV.4); *tax on resources and energy (S II.7); *goods that cannot be proliferated (land, water, air) must be taken off the market (S I.3); *ban on production processes that generate waste which cannot be disposed without danger (S II.2.5); *strict conservation of landscapes (IV.2); *no special permissions for exceptions regarding nature and landscape protection laws (IV.2).

Table A4.4: Ecomomic Policy.

(private property; co-determination; cooperatives; state ownership; planning; market; new technologies; role of unions; labour regulations)

a) Co-determination (Mitbestimmung)

CSU: *for co-determination, but no commitment to 'parity model' ('Montanmodell'); *in favour of a special status for management (49–50); *opposed to social and economic councils (p. 51).

CDU: *for a chance to participate in the regulation of the working life ('Chance zur Mitgestaltung im Arbeitsleben') (51); *parity of labour, management and captial owners (79); *entrepreneurs and workers are partners (53).

FDP: *approval of co-determination schemes is made dependent on a special status of management, against 'parity model' ('Montanmodell') (FVII).

SPD: *for the democratically legitimised control of the economy (OR 1.11); *in favour of the 'parity model' ('Montanmodell'), which is seen as putting an end to a sole regard for capital interests and as integrating workers in the steering of companies (OR 2.3.2); *co-determination only for large companies (OR 2.3.2); *despite partially converging interests, there is a conflict between the interests of workers and capital owners (OR 2.3.2); * economic democracy furthers co-determination and self-determination (B, p. 41).

Greens: *present co-determination scheme does not reduce heteronomy in the company (II.4); *those who are affected should be entitled to decide themselves what, how, and where to produce (II.2); *democratic workers' control (II.3); *social and economic councils should provide the population with the opportunity to control companies socially and ecologically (II.3); *for 'qualified co-determination'; *economy should be steered by producers and consumers through grass-roots democratic methods (S I.3).

b) Private Ownership / Public Ownership

CSU: *nationalisation merely leads to the conservation of aged structures (p. 40); *no further expansion of the state's share in the economy (p. 40); *for privatisation of public services (p. 25); *rejection of capital gains tax on land profits (p. 45).

CDU: *private ownership is the indispensable foundation of the social market economy (78); *a high share of state in the economy means an infringement on individual freedom (94).

FDP: *'freedom needs property, property creates freedom' (FI, Th. 1); everybody should have a real chance to attain property (FI, Th. 2); *for privatisation of public services (S II.3); *Länder and communes should have an option of purchase for land (FII, Th. 2); *for a capital gains tax on land profits (FII, Th. 6); *for tax on profits from speculation (FII, Th. 5).

SPD: *collective property is a legitimate form of public control; *there is a danger of concentration of power with the state, therefore collective property, administered according the principles of self-control and decentralisation, no central bureaucracy (p. 15; OR 2.6.3, 4.1.6); *land speculation has to be made impossible, and unjustified profits from selling land have to be taxed off (p. 21).

Greens: *'land, resources, means of production and banks should be transferred into new forms of societal ownership'. The existing models of nationalisation are rejected because they do not facilitate grass-roots democratic control; *new models of self-administration should be implemented (S I.3).

c) Market Economy

CSU: *economic, personal, and political freedom are interdependent (p. 39); *strongly committed to 'social market economy' (Soziale Marktwirtschaft); *no political control or steering of investments (p. 40).

CDU: *in favour of social market economy, which means being opposed to dirigism, privileges, nationalisation of means of production, unrestrained Liberalism (66); *no centralised planning (67); *democracy is a method of political rule, complemented in the sphere of economics by the market mechanism (67).

FDP: *is sceptical that the pursuit of individual interests always automatically leads to the common good – in cases where this mechanism fails, the state has the right to interfere; *for a 'liberal reform of Capitalism' ('Liberale Reform des Kapitalismus') (FE, Th. 4); *market mechanism is superior to all other models of economic order (KaII, Th. 4); *for continuous, not anticyclical, global steering of the economy (Ka, Th. 9); *structural policy via market, not through investment steering (KaII, Th. 15).

SPD: *budgetary policy for global steering (p. 12; OR 2.3); *generally: preference for indirect economic steering; *planning and state intervention only if the market mechanism fails (p. 13); *investment control through the obligation to register investments with public authorities, closer control of monopolistic tendencies (OR 2.6.5); *for internationalisation of economic steering capacities (OR 2.4.7); *private ownership and market mechanism is largely indispensable but needs correction through public steering (OR 2.6.1); *indirect steering of investments through the determination of the external framework (OR 2.6.5); *structural policy needs more steering capacities (OR 4.1.4).

Greens: *sceptical about statist orientation (S I.2); *'production in a socially responsible economy is guided by the needs of the people, not by profit maximisation!' (S I.3); *recognition of the steering capacity of the market mechanism (S I.3); *global steering by means of tax and fiscal policy offers multiple chances to influence the kind of production and the distribution of incomes, and to induce social and ecological investments (S I.5); *demand for publicly funded self-administered funds for the development of alternative forms of economic production.

d) Anti-Trust Measures

CSU: *obligation of the state to guarantee the functioning of market competition (p. 41).

CDU: *control of market power concentration through the state (76); *control of free competition through the state (75).

FDP: *working competition serves to control economic power (KaII, Th. 4); *also necessary: public control of free competition (KaII, Th. 6).

SPD: *state has to secure free competition (p. 13); *severe anti-trust legislation and strict control for securing free competition (OR 2.6.1); *European integration in order to counterbalance internationalisation of the economy (OR 2.4.7); *important task: limitation of power of large companies (p. 14).

Greens: *for decentralised, manageable units of production; *for the breaking up of big conglomerates into smaller units (II.3); reduction of large-scale mode of industrial production as far as possible and ecologically meaningful (S I.3).

e) New Technologies

CSU: *in favour of technological progress; *technological developments should be oriented at ecological considerations (p. 63).

CDU: _____

FDP: *unreservedly in favour of support for the development of new technologies (KaIV, Th4); *approval of genetic technology, if it respects the limits set by human dignity (S III:1).

SPD: *social costs of production should be considered (OR 2.6.2); *introduction of new technologies should be decided politically; this decision should be based on scientific research (B, p. 40).

Greens: *introduction of new technologies should be made dependent on the results of an assessment period which should focus on ecological effects, the effect on working conditions, and a cost–benefit analysis covering all societal aspects (II.3); *new technologies should only be used in order to improve working conditions (II.4).

---

f) Economy and Ecology

CSU: ——————

CDU: ——————

FDP: ——————

SPD: ——————

Greens: *conversion of production in order to produce ecologically and socially mean-ingful goods – with regard to labour market upheavals this should be done in stages (S II.3).

---

g) Working Conditions / Working Week

CSU: ——————

CDU: *the individual should have more freedom to determine the duration of his own working day, week, life (52).

FDP: *technological development changes working times, its organisation, and the kind of work that needs to be done (S II).; *inflexibilities on the labour market should be broken up, labour costs should be reduced (S III,3).

SPD: *improvement of working conditions through more co-determination and more demanding jobs; *support for development of new production technolo-gies that improve working conditions (OR 4.3.3).

Greens: *long-term goals: substantial shortening of the working week without income reduction; *short-term goal: 35-hour week without income losses (II.4); *however: contradiction of 1983 economic programme, which calls for income compensation only for those with lower and medium incomes (S I.5); *reduction of hours of overtime; *in case of rationalisation: work should be redistributed within the company; *reduction of assembly line work, night work, shift work; *reduction of unnecessary specialisation (II.4); *work should be free and self-determined activity, hence paid labour should be reduced; *just distribution of societally necessary labour (S I.3); *flexible working hours; *opposed to job-sharing and early retirement schemes (S II.1).

---

h) Role of Unions

CSU: ——————

CDU: ——————

FDP: ——————

SPD: *trade unions need to be integrated in co-determination because they provide the link between interests of individual companies and the necessary societal solidarity (OR 2.3.2); *for a corporatist integration of trade unions and associa-tions of industry in global economic planning (OR 2.6.5); lock-outs should be made illegal (OR 3.3.4).

Greens: *Lock-outs should be made illegal; *more grass-roots democracy within the trade unions (II.4).

Table A4.5: Social Policy.
(family; role of women; feminism; welfare system; income distribution; education)

---

a) Family and Role of Women

CSU: *emphasis on particular importance of family which needs support (p. 53); *for *de facto* equality of men and women, however: traditional female role is regarded as 'given', needs to be made financially and socially more secure, can be supplemented through paid work (p. 54).

CDU: *marriage and family are particularly protected by the constitution, they represent the foundation of state and society (33); *commitment to equal rights for men and women; *mother of little children should normally not be working (34); *women should have a real choice between staying at home or working (110).

FDP: *men and women should share obligations in family and at work; *a better infrastructure is needed for this; *acceptance of other forms of living together (S 16).

SPD: *full realisation of equal rights for men and women; *protection of family through state annd society (p. 21); *part-time work for men and women (OR 4.3.3); *education of children should be shared (OR 4.6.3); *paid work represents a chance of self-realisation for women; *independent social security for women; *expansion of educational facilities that complement education in the family (OR 4.6.3); *whenever a group suffers from discrimination, women in this group will suffer particularly (OR 4.6.4).

Greens: *salary and pension for housework; *full realisation of equal rights for men and women at work; *penalities for discrimination against women (V.2); *more day-care for children; *full compensation for salary losses if someone has to take care of ill children; *abolition of distribution of work according to sex (S I.3); *men and women should equally share housework (S I.5); *preferential employment for women (S II.1); *protection of women against violence, support for autonomous houses for battered women (V.4); *one parent should be able to leave the job for up to two years and receive public support during this period of time up to a certain limit (S I.1).

---

b) Social Security

CSU: *retention of structured system of social security (p. 47); *equal opportunity for all to make use of the possibilities offered by the social security system (p. 48); *for priniciple of subsidiarity (p. 53).

CDU: *for private and company-based supplements to social security; *against any unitary, integrated security system, in favour of existing, structured system (111); *against 'social citizenship model' ('Staatsbürgerversorgung'), for a insurance system that is based on individual contributions (112); *no equal benefit for all (128).

FDP: *state should provide basic social benefits for those who can neither help themselves nor get help in co-operation with others – all other tasks should be taken over by individuals or private organisations (S 17); *for a contributory social security system; *support for small networks through expense allowances and tax reliefs; *expansion of neighbourhood and self-help activities (S 15); *improvement and simplification of transfer system, probably by means of reducing the number of transfer payments, that is, the number of claims upon the welfare state (K, Th. 7).

SPD: *for a minimum state pension, which should be supplemented by contributory pensions (p. 19); *for a combination of comprehensive social security systems and integrated support for self-help groups (B, pp. 32ff.).

Greens: *expansion of social infrastructure; *provision of opportunities for self-help and individual initiative without letting the individual alone (S II.2.4); *centralised security systems should be supplemented by publicly supported self-help initiatives; *longer payment of unemployment benefit and other transfer payments like students' grants and child allowance (S II.5); *integration and unification of the social security system: all employees should be obligatory members, including civil servants; integration of company-based and private insurance schemes into this public system (S II.5).

---

c) Health Insurance

CSU: ——————

CDU: *not same treatment for everybody, but the chances of remaining healthy or getting cured should be the same for everybody (106).

FDP: ——————

SPD: *everybody should be entitled to all therapies that are necessary and possible, irrespectively of their economic situation (p. 20); *equivalent medical care for everybody ('gleichwertige Gesundheitsversorgung') (OR 1.11); *equal opportunity for medical treatment without this being influenced by the economic situation of the patient ('chancengleiche medizinische Versorgung.') (OR 4.4.1); *criticism of the scientific-technical orientation of modern medicine (OR 4.4.3).

Greens: *for holistic medicine; *more small hospitals; *more rights for patients; *stricter control of medicines (drugs); *price controls in the medical sector (V.9.3); (see also b).

---

d) Education

CSU: *compensation for socially caused impediments ('Chancenausgleich für soziale Hindernisse') (p. 29); *emphasis on achievement ('Leistung'); *structured educational system is oriented at different talents (p. 31); *justness of opportunity ('Chancengerechtigkeit') (p. 47); *support for private initiative in educational sector (p. 35).

CDU: *emphasis on the difference of talents, no mention of social impediments or need for support of underprivileged (41); *for the retention of present structured ecucational system (47).

FDP: *for equality of opportunity in education ('Chancengleichheit') (Ka, Th. 4); *pedagogically justified achievement is necessary in schools; *prime goals of schools should be supporting the individual, not selection (Kc, Th. 1); *special promotion of highly talented (S 10); *support for private initiative in educational sector (S 10).

SPD: *equal access to education for all (p. 7); *equality of opportunity ('Chanengleichheit') (OR 4.2.4); *for comprehensive schools (OR 4.6.3).

Greens: *for comprehensive schools; *ideally, everybody should be supported such that they pass the exam after ten years of comprehensive schooling (V.6.1); *equal treatment for private schools (V6.1); *co-determination rights for all scientists in research institutes (V.6.2); *establishment of a commission of academics and citizens that should be concerned with the assessment of the likely effects of research results (V.6.2).

---

e) Distribution of Income and Property

CSU: *justness of opportunity ('Chancengerechtigkeit') should be the guiding principle of social policy (p. 18); *property should not be generated through redistribution, but through wealth formation (Vermögensbildung), preferably through workers' shares in the employing company ('Beteiligung am Produktivvermögen') (no collective funds) (p. 49).

CDU: *principled approval of differential incomes (71); *for wealth formation through workers' shares in the employing company ('Beteiligung am Produktivvermögen') (78).

FDP: *for comprehensive wealth formation (K, Th. 8, S 13); *abolition of the imbalances concerning the advantages that emanate from the concentration of economic power ('Aufhebung der Ungleichgewichte des Vorteils und der Ballung wirtschaftlicher Macht') (FE, Th. 4); *no redistribution of wealth, but people should be given a share in its growth (FII,E); *wage earners' funds that extend beyond single companies (überbetriebliche Vermögensbildung) should be introduced only on a very small scale (FII, Th. 1); *achievement should pay, no distributive justness (KaII, Th. 2).

SPD: *for a more just and equal distribution of income, wealth and benefit from public services (OR 1.11), emphasis on primary income (OR 2.5.4); *profits from selling land should be siphoned off (p. 21); *for a continous growth of the social product accompanied by fairer distribution (p. 16); *equality is economically feasible, it is a problem of distribution (OR 1.8).

Greens: *demand for sufficient income for all; *just distribution of created wealth (II.2); *workers should have a share in the productive capital; *wage agreements should always have flat rates for lower income groups (II.4); *'alteration of completely unjust and unequal distribution of income and wealth' (S I.3); *for a more equal distribution of income; *minimum income (SII.5); *real distribution via tax system, i.e. abolition of tax deduction possibilities (SII.7); *tax on profits from speculation.

Table A4.6: International Relations and Security Policy.

(bloc interests v. national sovereignty; NATO membership; NATO twin-track decision; nuclear deterrence v. unilateral disarmament, EC; 'Ost- and Deutschlandpolitik')

---

a) Third World

CSU: *in favour of a free international economic system; *acceptance of the problem of 'terms of trade', which is seen as a result of inflation (but no therapy offered); *developmental aid 'in accordance with our interests', which means that the interests of recipients and donors should be served to the same degree (p. 73).

CDU: *'more just distribution of chances of overcoming poverty and misery' (no mention of 'terms of trade' or sacrifices by the developed nations); *for an international social market economy (Internationale Soziale Marktwirtschaft) (91).

FDP: *support for autonomous efforts of the developing nations; *opening up of markets of industrialised countries (KaI; TH 19).

SPD: *redistribution of global wealth (p. 28); *solidarity with the Third World (p. 6); *no self-interested aid for Third World (p. 28).

Greens: *compatible help, no transfer of our way of life ; *decentralised projects, preferably cooperatives; *fair terms of trade (II.9); *for the emancipation of Third World nations; *criticism of the world market dominance of multi-nationals; *renunciation of continued industrial expansion by industrialised countries; *no conditions connected to developmental aid; *ban on exploitation of workers in 'cheap labour countries' through German companies; *no food imports from countries with famine; *support for liberation movements; *reduction of world market dependency (III.3); *reduction of dependence of industrialised countries on export and imported raw materials; *no military aid (S I.4).

---

b) Deutschlandpolitik

CSU: *refers to 'all parts of Germany' ('alle Teile Deutschlands') (p. 71); *achievement of national unity in free self-determination; *support for the demand of expellees for right to 'Heimat' and self-determination (p. 72).

CDU: *emphasis on reunification and right to self-determination (132–3).

FDP: *overcome division of Germany in free self-determination; *emphasis on the non-vulnerability of the borders as they have been accepted in the treaties of the Ostpolitik.

SPD: *overcome division of Germany in free self-determination (p. 8).

Greens: *dissolution of military blocs will serve as a basis for overcoming the division of Europe and Germany (III.1).

---

c) Europe

CSU: *promotion of European integration on the basis of federalism (p. 69); *creation of a European centre of decision-making which is intended to be the nucleus of a future European government (p. 70).

CDU: *further development of existing institutions towards a political union (138); *federalism as the guiding principle (139).

FDP: *in favour of a European Union; joint foreign and security policy; effective common institutions.

SPD: *promotion of European integration (OR 2.1.4); *strengthening of European decision-making institutions in order to counterbalance power of economy (OR 2.4.7).

Greens: *EC is regarded as a bureaucratic Moloch without democratic control, as an institution for the promotion of further economic growth and the destructive forces of industrial society (p. 6); *criticism of 'established' policy orientation of EC; *present structures incompatible with effective democratic countrol (p. 7); criticism of absence of EC-wide referenda (p. 10); *in favour of a 'Europe of regions', i.e. historically evolved, self-determined, interconnected units; *decentralisation of existing decision-making structures (p. 38).

---

d) Defence

CSU: *threat against the free Western world continues; *USSR seeks hegemony (p. 68); *strong defence efforts are necessary (p. 71); *unambiguous commitment to NATO and alliance with the USA (p. 70); *for equal strength of armed forces; *disarmament only if it does not reduce security (p. 71); *détente (Entspannungspolitik) is the continuation of the East–West conflict with different means; *rejection of détente (p. 68); *the Helsinki process and the MBFR talks in Vienna are instruments of Moscow to expand its influence on Western Europe (p. 69).

CDU: *FRG is threatened, which necessitates strong defence efforts (141); * NATO and German army are indispensable (143); *United States provides nuclear protection for West Germany; *against any one-sided weakening of NATO; *in favour of the philosophy of mutual deterrence (144).

FDP: *in favour of disarmament treaties; *against arms race in outer space; *'restrictive policy of arms export'; *in favour of détente.

SPD: *approves of national defence; *wants general disarmament (p. 10); *criticises the arms race (OR 2.1.1).

Greens: *for a non-violent, social defence strategy – which does not mean surrender; *dissolution of NATO and Warsaw Pact; *start with disarmament in own country; *ban on ABC [nuclear, biologicial and chemical] weapons; *for an arms-free zone in Western and Eastern Europe; *conversion of arms industry; *as a long-term goal, abolition of military service (III.2).

Bibliography

Alber, Jens (1985), 'Modernisierung, neue Spannungslinien und die politischen Chancen der Grünen', in *Politische Vierteljahresschrift*, Vol. 26, No. 3, pp. 211–26.

Baker, Kendall L., Dalton, Russell J. and Hildebrandt, Kai (1981), *Germany Transformed. Political culture and the New Politics* (Cambridge, Mass. and London; Harvard University Press).

Barnes, Samuel H., Kaase, Max et al. (1979), *Political Action* (London and Beverly Hills: Sage).

Barnes, Samuel H. (1984), 'The new citizen and the future of political mobilisation: an assessment', Paper Prepared for Delivery at the Meeting of the Work Group on Political Mobilisation, Project on the Future of Party Government, Florence, April.

Becker, Horst, and Hombach, Bodo (eds.) (1983), *Die SPD von innen. Bestandsaufnahme an der Basis der Partei* (Bonn: Verlag Neue Gesellschaft).

Berger, Manfred, Gibowski, Wolfgang G., Roth, Dieter and Schulte, Wolfgang (1985), 'Starke Wählerbewegungen und stabile Strukturen, kein Test für Bonn– Landtagswahlen 1985', in *Zeitschrift für Parlamentsfragen*, Vol. 16, No. 3, pp. 411–30.

Beyme, Klaus von (1982), *Parteien in westlichen Demokratien* (Munich: Piper).

Beyme, Klaus von (1986), 'Neue soziale Bewegungen und politische Parteien', in *Aus Politik und Zeitgeschichte*, No. 44, pp. 30–9.

Blalock, Hubert M. (1981), *Social Statistics* (Auckland: McGraw-Hill).

Boll, Bernhard, and Poguntke, Thomas (1992), 'The 1990 all-German election campaign', in Shaun Bouwler and David Farrell (eds.), *Electoral Strategies and Political Marketing* (London: Macmillan).

Bölling, Klaus (1982), *Die letzten 30 Tage des Kanzlers Helmut Schmidt. Ein Tagebuch* (Reinbek: Rowohlt).

Böltken, Ferdinand, and Jagodzinski, Wolfgang (1985), 'In an environment of insecurity. Postmaterialism in the European Community, 1970 to 1980', in *Comparative Political Studies*, Vol. 17, No. 4, January, pp. 453–84.

Brand, Karl-Werner, Büsser, Detlef and Rucht, Dieter (1984), *Aufbruch in eine andere Gesellschaft. Neue soziale Bewegungen in der Bundesrepublik* (Frankfurt and New York: Campus).

Brand, Karl-Werner (ed.) (1985), *Neue soziale Bewegungen in Westeuropa und den USA: Ein Internationaler Vergleich*, (Frankfurt: Campus).

Brand, Karl-Werner (1987), 'Kontinuität und Diskontinuität in den neuen sozialen Bewegungen', in Roland Roth and Dieter Rucht (eds.), *Neue soziale Bewegungen in der Bundesrepublik Deutschland*, Bonn: Bundeszentrale für politische Bildung.

Budge, Ian (1987), 'The internal analysis of election programmes', in Ian Budge, David Robertson and Derek Hearl (eds.), *Ideology, Strategy and Party Change: Spatial analyses of post-war election programmes in nineteen democracies* (Cambridge: CUP).

Budge, Ian and Farlie, Dennis (1983a), 'Party competition–selective emphasis or direct confrontation? An alternative view with data', in Hans Daalder and Peter Mair (eds.), *Western European Party Systems. Continuity and change* (Beverly Hills: Sage).

Budge, Ian and Farlie, Dennis (1983b), *Explaining and Predicting Elections: Issue effects and party strategies in twenty-three democracies* (London: George Allen & Unwin).

Budge, Ian and Robertson, David (1987), 'Do parties differ and how?', in Ian Budge, David Robertson and Derek Hearl (eds.) (1987), *Ideology, Strategy and Party Change: spatial analyses of post-war election programmes in nineteen democracies* (Cambridge: CUP), pp. 388–416.

Budge, Ian, Robertson, David and Hearl, Derek (eds.) (1987), *Ideology, Strategy and Party Change: spatial analyses of post-war election programmes in nineteen democracies* (Cambridge: CUP).

Bürklin, Wilhelm P. (1980), 'Links und/oder Demokratisch? Dimensionen studentischen Politikverständnisses', in *Politische Vierteljahresschrift*, Vol. 21, No. 3, pp. 220–47.

Bürklin, Wilhelm P. (1981), 'Die Grünen und die "Neue Politik". Abschied vom Dreiparteiensystem?', in *Politische Vierteljahresschrift*, Vol. 22, No. 4, pp. 359–82.

Bürklin, Wilhelm P. (1984), *Grüne Politik* (Opladen: Westdeutscher Verlag).

Bürklin, Wilhelm P. (1985a), 'The German Greens: the post-industrial non-established and the party system', in *International Political Science Review*, Vol. 6, No. 4, (October), pp. 463–81.

Bürklin, Wilhelm P. (1985b), 'The split between the established and the non-established Left in Germany', in *European Journal of Political Research*, Vol. 13, pp. 283–93.

Bürklin, Wilhelm P. (1985c), 'The Greens: ecology and the New Left', in H.G. Peter Wallach and George K. Romoser (eds.), *West German Politics in the Mid-Eighties: Crisis and continuity* (New York: Praeger, pp. 187–218).

Bürklin, Wilhelm P. (1987), 'Governing left parties frustrating the radical non-established Left: the rise and inevitable decline of the Greens', in *European Sociological Review*, Vol. 3, No. 2 (September), pp. 109–26.

Capra, Fritjof and Spretnak, Charlene (1984), *Green Politics. The global promise* (London: Hutchinson).

CDU (1985), *Leitsätze für eine neue Partnerschaft zwischen Mann und Frau* (beschlossen auf dem Essener Bundesparteitag).

CDU (1989), *Unsere Verantwortung für die Schöpfung*, (Beschluß des Parteitages in Bremen).

Cerny, Karl H. (ed.) (1977), *Scandinavia at the Polls* (Washington DC: American Enterprise Institute).

Chandler, William M. and Siaroff, Alan (1986), 'Post-industrial politics in Germany and the origins of the Greens', in *Comparative Politics*, Vol.18, No.3, April, pp. 303–25.

Cornelsen, Dirk (1986), *Ankläger im hohen Haus* (Essen: Klartext).

Cotgrove, Stephen and Duff, Andrew (1980), 'Environmentalism, middle-class radicalism and politics', in *Sociological Review*, Vol. 28, No. 2, May, pp. 333–52.

Cotgrove, Stephen and Duff, Andrew, (1981), 'Environmentalism, values, and social change', *British Journal of Sociology*, Vol. 32, No. 1, March, pp. 92–110.

CSU (1984), *Satzung, Finanzstatut, Schiedsgerichtsordnung, Parteiengesetz*, Munich, Stand November 1984.

CSU (1980), *Umweltpolitik in den 80er Jahren. Positionspapier der CSU*.

Czada, Roland (1990). *'Sozialstruktur und Stimmabgabe'*, in *Der Bürger im Staat*, Vol. 40, No.3, pp. 145–150.

Dalton, Russell J. (1984), 'Cognitive mobilization and partisan dealignment in advanced industrial democracies', in *Journal of Politics*, Vol. 46, No. 1, pp. 264–84.

Dalton, Russell J. (1985), 'Political parties and political representation. Party supporters and party elites in nine nations', in *Comparative Political Studies*, Vol. 18, No. 3, October, pp. 267–99.

Dalton, Russell J. (1986), 'Wertwandel oder Wertwende. Die Neue Politik und Parteienpolarisierung', in Hans-Dieter Klingemann and Max Kaase (eds.), *Wahlen und politischer Prozeß* (Opladen: Westdeutscher Verlag).

Dalton, Russel J., Flanagan, Scott C. and Beck, Paul A. (eds.) (1984), *Electoral Change in Advanced Industrial Democracies: Realignment or dealignment?* (Princeton, NJ: Princeton University Press).

Dalton, Russell J. and Baker, Kendall L. (1985), 'The contours of West German opinion', in H.G. Peter Wallach and George K. Romoser, (eds.), *West German Politics in the Mid-Eighties: Crisis and continuity* (New York: Praeger), pp. 24–59.

Dalton, Russell J. (1988), *Citizen Politics: Public opinion and political parties in the United States, United Kingdom, France and West Germany*, (Chatham, NJ: Chatham House Publishers).

Dalton, Russel J., Küchler, Manfred and Bürklin, Wilhelm (1990), 'The challenge of new movements', in Russel J. Dalton and Manfred Küchler (eds.), *Challenging the Political Order. New social and political movements in western democracies* (New York: OUP), pp. 3–22.

Diätenkommission (1991), Abschlußbericht 11. *Legislaturperiode, vorgelegt zur Bundesdelegiertenkonferenz in Neumünster, April 1991*.

Dicke, Klaus and Tobias Stoll (1985), '*Mandatsverzicht des Abgeordneten und das Rotationsprinzip der Grünen*', in *Zeitschrift für Parlamentsfragen*, Vol. 16, No. 4, pp. 451–64.

Die Grünen (1986), *Umbau der Industriegesellschaft. Schritte zur Überwindung von Erwerbslosigkeit, Armut und Umweltzerstörung, verabschiedet von der Bundesdelegiertenkonferenz in Nürnberg, 26–28 September 1986.*

Die Grünen (1987), *Bundestagswahlprogramm 1987. Farbe bekennen.*

Die Grünen (1988a), *Die Krisen-Klausur im 'Pantheon'. Protokoll der gemeinsamen Sitzung des Bundeshauptausschusses der GRÜNEN mit VertreterInnen der Landesvorstände und den Abgeordneten der GRÜNEN IM BUNDESTAG am 12. Dezember 1987 in Bonn.*

Die Grünen (1988b), *Grüne Perspektiven. Kongreß vom 16.–19. Juni 1988 in und um Haus Wittgenstein/Bornheim-Roisdorf.*

Dittberner, Jürgen, (1984), 'Die Freie Demokratische Partei', in Richard Stöss (ed.), *Parteien-Handbuch: Die Parteien der Bundesrepublik Deutschland 1945–1980* (Opladen: Westdeutscher Verlag), Vol. 2.

Dittberner, Jürgen (1987), *FDP – Partei der zweiten Wahl* (Opladen: Westdeutscher Verlag).

Döring, Herbert (1990), 'Aspekte des Vertrauens in Institutionen. Westeuropa im Querschnitt der internationalen Wertestudie 1981', in *Zeitschrift für Soziologie*, Vol. 19, pp. 73–89.

Duisburg minutes: minutes from the Duisburg party conference, 18–20 November 1983.

Duverger, Maurice (1964), *Political Parties*, 3rd edn (London: Methuen).

Easton, Davis (1975), 'A reassessment of the concept of political support', in *British Journal of Political Science*, Vol. 5, pp. 435–57.

Emminger, Eckhard (1985), 'Die "grüne" Schule', in *Politische Studien*, Vol. 36, No. 282, pp. 368–79.

Eppler, Erhard (1981), *Wege aus der Gefahr* (Reinbek: Rowohlt).

Esping-Andersen, Gösta (1985), *Politics against Markets. The Social Democratic road to power*, (Princeton: Princeton University Press).

Falke, Wolfgang (1982), *Die Mitglieder der CDU. Eine empirische Studie zum Verhältnis von Mitglieder- und Organisationsstruktur der CDU 1981–1977* (Berlin Dunker & Humblodt).

FDP, *Satzung, GO, Schiedsgerichtsordnung, Finanzordnung*, Fassung vom 2. Juni 1984.

Feist, Ursula, Güllner, Manfred and Liepelt, Klaus (1978), 'Structural assimilation versus ideological polarization. On changing profiles of political parties in West Germany', in Max Kaase and Klaus von Beyme (eds.), *Elections and Parties* (London and Beverly Hills: Sage), pp. 171–90.

Feist, Ursula and Krieger, Hubert (1985), 'Die nordrheinwestfälische Landtagswahl vom 12. Mai 1985. Stimmungstrend überrollt Sozialstrukturen oder: Die Wende ist keine Kaffeefahrt', in *Zeitschrift für Parlamentsfragen*, Vol. 16, No. 3, pp. 355–72.

Feist, Ursula and Krieger, Hubert (1987), 'Alte und neue Scheidelinien des politischen Verhaltens. Eine Analyse der Bundestagswahl 1987', in *Aus Politik und Zeitgeschichte*, No. 12, pp. 33–47.

Fischer, Joschka (1984), *Von grüner Kraft und Herrlichkeit* (Reinbek: Rowohlt).
Flanagan, Scott C. (1979), 'Value change and partisan change in Japan: the silent revolution revistited', in *Comparative Politics*, Vol. 14, pp. 253–78.
Flanagan, Scott C. (1982a), 'Changing values in advanced industrial societies', in *Comparative Political Studies*, Vol. 14, pp. 403–44.
Flanagan, Scott C. (1982b), 'Measuring value change in advanced industrial societies', in *Comparative Political Studies*', Vol. 15, pp. 99–128.
Flanagan, Scott C. (1987), 'Value change in industrial societies', in *American Political Science Review*, Vol. 81, No. 4, December, pp. 1,303–19.
Flanagan, Scott C. and Dalton, Russell J. (1984), 'Parties under stress: realignment or dealigment in advanced industrial societies', in *West European Politics*, Vol. 7, No. 1, pp. 7–23.
Flohr, Heinz (1968), *Parteiprogramme in der Demokratie* (Göttingen: Schwartz).
Fogt, Helmut (1984), 'Basisdemokratie oder Herrschaft der Aktivisten? Zum Politikverständnis der Grünen', in *Politische Vierteljahresschrift*, Vol. 25, No. 1, pp. 97–114.
Fogt, Helmut (1986), 'Die Mandatsträger der Grünen: Zur sozialen und politischen Herkunft der alternativen Parteielite', in *Aus Politik und Zeitgeschichte*, No. B11, pp. 16–33.
Fogt, Helmut and Uttitz, Pavel (1984), 'Die Wähler der GRÜNEN–Systemkritischer neuer Mittelstand?' in *Zeitschrift für Parlamentsfragen*, Vol. 15, No. 2, pp. 210–26.
Forschungsgruppe Wahlen (1983), *Bundestagswahl 1983* (Mannheim).
Forschungsgruppe Wahlen (1987a), *Bundestagswahl 1987*, (Mannheim).
Forschungsgruppe Wahlen (1987b), 'Die Konsolidierung der Wende. Eine Analyse der Bundestagswahl 1987', in *Zeitschrift für Parlamentsfragen*, Vol. 18, No. 2, pp. 253–84.
Forschungsgruppe Wahlen (1990a), 'Sieg ohne Glanz', in Max Kaase and Hans-Dieter Klingemann (eds.), *Wahlen und Wähler. Analysen aus Anlaß der Bundestagswahl 1987*, (Opladen: Westdeutscher Verlag).
Forschungsgruppe Wahlen (1990b), Politbarometer. Januar 1990 (Mannheim).
Forschungsgruppe Wahlen (1990c), *Bundestagswahl 1990. Eine Analyse der ersten gesamtdeutschen Bundestagswahl am 2. Dezember 1990*, (Mannheim).
Forschungsgruppe Wahlen (1991), Wahl in Bremen. Oktober 1991 (Mannheim).
Frankland, E. Gene (1983), 'Interpreting the Green phenomenon in West German politics', Paper Prepared for the Annual Meeting of the American Political Science Association, Chicago.
Frankland, E. Gene (1987), 'The developmental dilemmas of Green parties', Paper presented at the Annual Meeting of the Western Political Science Association, Anaheim, California.
Frankland, E. Gene (1988), 'The role of the Greens in West German parliamentary politics, 1980–87', in *The Review of Politics*, Vol. 50, No. 1, pp. 99–122.
Friedrichs, Jürgen (1973), *Methoden der emprischen Sozialforschung* (Reinbek: Rowohlt).
Fuchs, Dieter (1983), 'Politischer Protest und Stabilität', in Max Kaase and Hans-Dieter Klingemann (eds.), *Wahlen und politisches System. Analysen aus Anlaß der Bundestagswahl 1980* (Opladen: Westdeutscher Verlag), pp. 121–43.
Gabriel, Oscar W. (1986), *Politische Kultur, Materialismus und Postmaterialismus in der Bundesrepublik* (Opladen: Westdeutscher Verlag).
Gatter, Peter (1987), *Die Aufsteiger. Ein politisches Porträt der Grünen*, (Hamburg: Hoffman & Campe).
Gibowski, Wolfgang G. and Kaase, Max (1991), 'Auf dem Weg zum politischen Alltag. Eine Analyse der ersten gesamtdeutschen Bundestagswahl 1990', in *Aus Politik und Zeitgeschichte*, No. 11/12, pp. 3–20.
Global 2000 (1981), *Der Bericht an den Amerikanischen Präsidenten* (Frankfurt: Zweitausendeins).

GO-plp: DIE GRÜNEN IM BUNDESTAG, *Entwurf einer Geschäftsordnung vom 27.1. 1984.*

Gotto, Klaus and Veen, Hans-Joachim (eds.) (1984), *Die Grünen–Partei wider Willen* (Mainz: Hase & Köhler).

Greiffenhagen, Martin (1973), 'Einführung', in Martin Greiffenhagen (ed.), *Demokratisierung in Staat und Gesellschaft* (Munich: Piper).

Greiffenhagen, Martin and Greiffenhagen, Sylvia (1981), *Ein schwieriges Vaterland. Zur politischen Kultur Deutschlands,* (Frankfurt: Fischer).

Häusler, Jürgen (1988), *Der Traum wird zum Alptraum. Das Dilemma einer Volkspartei: die SPD im Atomkonflikt* (Berlin: Edition Sigma).

Hallensleben, Anna (1984), *Von der Grünen Liste zur Grünen Partei? Die Entwicklung der Grünen Liste Umweltschutz von ihrer Entstehung in Niedersachsen 1977 bis zur Gründung der Partei Die Grünen 1980* (Göttingen: Muster-Schmidt Verlag).

Haungs, Peter (1983), 'Bundesrepublik Deutschland', in Hans-Joachim Veen (ed.), *Christlich-Demokratische und konservative Parteien in Westeuropa* (Paderborn, Munich, Vienna, Zurich: Schöningh), Vol. 1.

Heidger, Ralf (1987), *Die Grünen: Basisdemokratie und Parteiorganisation: eine empirische Untersuchung des Landesverbandes der Grünen in Rheinland-Pfalz* (Berlin Edition Sigma).

Heimann, Siegfried (1984), 'Die Sozialdemokratische Partei Deutschlands', in Richard Stöss (ed.), *Parteien-Handbuch: die Parteien der Bundesrepublik Deutschland 1945–1980,* Vol. 2 (Opladen: Westdeutscher Verlag), pp. 2,025–216.

Herzog, Dietrich (1982), *Politische Führungsgruppen: Probleme und Ergebnisse der modernen Elitenforschung (Erträge der Forschung 169)* (Darmstadt: Wissenschaftliche Buchgesellschaft).

Hesse, Gunter, and Wiebe, Hans-Hermann (eds.) (1988), *Die Grünen und die Religion* (Frankfurt: Athenäum).

Hildebrandt, Kai, and Dalton, Russell J. (1978), 'Political change or sunshine politics?', in Max Kaase and Klaus von Beyme (eds.), *Elections and Parties. German Political Studies,* Vol. 3 (London and Beverly Hills: Sage), pp. 69–96.

Höfling, Wolfram (1980a), 'Funktionsprobleme des Vereinigungssystems der CDU', in Heino Kaack and Reinhold Roth (eds.), *Handbuch des deutschen Parteiensystems* (Opladen: Leske & Budrich), Vol. 1, pp. 153–74.

Höfling, Wolfram (1980b), 'Die Vereinigungen der CDU. Eine Bestandsaufnahme zu Organisationsstruktur, Finanzen und personeller Repräsentanz', in Heino Kaack and Reinhold Roth (eds.), *Handbuch des deutschen Parteiensystems* (Opladen: Leske & Budrich), Vol. 1, pp. 125–52.

Hofrichter, Jürgen and Schmitt, Hermann (1991), 'Eher mit- als gegeneinander! Zum Verhältnis von neuen sozialen Bewegungen und politischen Parteien', in Roland Roth and Dieter Rucht (eds.), *Neue soziale Bewegungen in der Bundesrepublik Deutschland,* 2nd edn (Bonn: Bundeszentrale für politische Bildung).

Hondrich, Karl Otto and Vollmer, Randolph (eds.) (1983), *Bedürfnisse im Wandel* (Opladen: Westdeutscher Verlag).

Hoplitschek, Ernst (1982), 'Partei, Avantgarde, Heimat–oder was? Die "Alternative Liste für Demokratie und Umweltschutz" in Westberlin', in Jörg R. Mettke (ed.), *Die Grünen. Regierungspartner von morgen?* (Reinbek: Rowohlt), pp. 82–100.

Hubert, Eva (1983), 'Politiker fragen–Bürger antworten nicht!', in Jürgen Taeger, (ed.), *Die Volkszählung* (Reinbek: Rowohlt), pp. 254–66.

Inglehart, Ronald (1971), 'The Silent Revolution in Europe: Intergenerational Change in Post-Industrial Societies', in *American Political Science Review,* Vol. 65, No. 4, December 1971, pp. 991–1017.

Inglehart, Ronald (1977), The Silent Revolution. Changing values and political styles among Western publics (Princeton: Princeton University Press).

Inglehart, Ronald (1979), 'Wertwandel und politisches Verhalten', in Joachim Matthes (ed.), *Sozialer Wandel in Westeuropa* (Frankfurt/Main, New York: Campus).

Inglehart, Ronald (1980), 'Zusammenhang zwischen sozioökonomischen Bedingungen und individuellen Wertprioritäten', in *Kölner Zeitschrift für Psychologie und Sozialpsychologie*, Vol. 13, pp. 144–53.

Inglehart, Ronald (1981), 'Post-Materialism in an environment of insecurity', in *American Political Science Review*, Vol. 75, No. 4, pp. 880–900.

Inglehart, Ronald (1983a), 'The persistence of materialist and post-materialist value orientations: comments on van Deth's analysis', in *European Journal of Political Research*, Vol. 11, pp. 81–91.

Inglehart, Ronald (1983b), 'Traditionelle politische Spannungslinien und die Entwicklung der neuen Politik in westlichen Gesellschaften', in *Politische Vierteljahresschrift*, Vol. 24, No. 2, June, pp. 139–65.

Inglehart, Ronald (1984), 'The changing structure of political cleavages in Western society', in Russel J. Dalton, Scott C. Flanagan, and Paul A. Beck, (eds.) (1984), *Electoral Change in Advanced Industrial Democracies: Realignment or dealignment?* (Princeton, NJ: Princeton University Press).

Inglehart, Ronald (1985a), 'New perspectives on value change: response to Lafferty and Knutsen, Savage, and Böltgen and Jagodzinski', in *Comparative Political Studies*, Vol. 17, No. 4, January, pp. 485–532.

Inglehart, Ronald (1985b), 'Aggregate stability and individual-level flux in mass belief systems: the level of analysis paradox', in *American Political Science Review*, Vol. 69, pp. 97–116.

Inglehart, Ronald (1987), 'Value change in industrial societies', in *American Political Science Review*, Vol. 81, No. 4, December, pp. 1,289–303.

Inglehart, Ronald (1990a), *Culture Shift in Advanced Industrial Society*, (Princeton, NJ: Princeton University Press).

Inglehart, Ronald (1990b), 'Values, ideology, and cognitive mobilization in new social movements', in Russel J. Dalton and Manfred Kuechler, *Challenging the Political Order. New Social and Political Movements in Western Democracies* (New York: OUP).

Inglehart, Ronald, and Klingemann, Hans-Dieter (1976), 'Party identification, ideological preference, and the left-right dimension among western mass publics', in Ian Budge, Ivor Crewe and Denis Farlie (eds.), *Party Identification and Beyond* (London: John Wiley), pp. 243–73.

Ismayr, Wolfgang (1985), 'Die Grünen im Bundestag: Parlamentarisierung und Basisanbindung', in *Zeitschrift für Parlamentsfragen*, Vol. 16, No. 3, pp. 299–321.

Jäger, Brigitte and Pinl, Claudia (1985), *Zwischen Rotation und Routine. Die Grünen im Deutschen Bundestag* (Cologne: Kiepenheuer & Witsch).

Jennings, M. Kent, van Deth, Jan W. *et al.* (1990), *Continuities in Political Action* (Berlin and New York: de Gruyter).

Jesse, Eckhard (1987), 'Die Bundestagswahlen von 1972–1987 im Spiegel der repräsentativen Wahlstatistik', in *Zeitschrift für Parlamentsfragen*, Vol. 18, No. 2, pp. 232–42.

Kaack, Heino (1979), *Die F.D.P.. Grundriß und Materialien zu Geschichte, Struktur und Programmatik* (Meisenheim am Glan: Verlag Anton Hain).

Kaack, Heino and Roth, Reinhold (eds.) (1980), *Handbuch des deutschen Parteiensystems. Struktur und Politik in der Bundesrepublik zu Beginn der achtziger Jahre* (Opladen: Leske & Budrich).

Kaase, Max (1976), 'Bedingungen unkonventionellen politischen Verhaltens', in Peter Graf Kielmansegg (ed.), *Legitimationsprobleme politischer Systeme* (Opladen: Westdeutscher Verlag), pp. 179–216.

Kaase, Max (1982), 'Partizipatorische Revolution–Ende der Parteien?', in Joachim Raschke (ed.), *Bürger und Parteien* (Opladen: Westdeutscher Verlag), pp. 173–89.

Kaase, Max (1984), 'Political mobilization and democratic politics: strains and promises', chapter draft.Unpublished ms., presented at the European University Institute, Florence.

Kaase, Max and Gibowski, Wolfgang (1990), 'Deutschland im Übergang: Die Bundestagswahl 1990', in *Aus Politik und Zeitgeschichte*, No. 37/38, pp. 14–26.

Kadan, A., Pelinka, A. (1979), *Die Grundsatzprogramme der Österreichischen Parteien. Dokumentation und Analyse* (Vienna: Verlag Niederösterreichisches Pressehaus).

Kirchheimer, Otto (1969), 'The transformation of the Western European party system', in Frederic S. Burin and Kurt L. Shell (eds.), *Politics, Law, and Social Change: Selected essays of Otto Kirchheimer* (London and New York: Columbia University Press).

Kitschelt, Herbert (1985), 'Between movement and party: structure and process in Belgian and West German ecology parties', Paper Presented at the Fifth International Conference of Europeanists, Washington DC, 18–20 October.

Kitschelt, Herbert (1986), 'The West German Green Party in comparative perspective: explaining innovation in competitive party systems'. Paper Prepared for Delivery at the Annual Meeting of the American Political Science Association 1986, Washington DC.

Kitschelt, Herbert (1988a), 'Organization and Strategy of Belgian and West German Ecology Parties. A New Dynamic of Party Politics in Western Europe?', in *Comparative Politics*, Vol. 20., No. 2, pp. 127–54.

Kitschelt, Herbert (1988b), 'Left-libertarian parties: explaining innovation in competitive party systems', in *World Politics*, Vol 40, No. 2, pp. 194–234.

Kitschelt, Herbert (1989), *The Logics of Party Formation. Ecological politics in Belgium and West Germany* (Ithaca: Cornell University Press).

Kitschelt, Herbert (1990), 'New social movements and the decline of party organization', in Russel J. Dalton and Manfred Küchler (eds.), *Challenging the Political Order* (Oxford: OUP), pp. 179–208.

Kitschelt, Herbert and Hellemans, Staf (1990), *Beyond the European Left. Ideology and political action in the Belgian ecology parties*, (Durham, Carolina and London: Duke University Press).

Klages, Helmut and Herbert, Willi (1983), *Wertorientierung und Staatsbezug. Untersuchungen zur politischen Kultur in der Bundesrepublik Deutschland* (Frankfurt and New York: Campus).

Klingemann, Hans-Dieter (1972), 'Testing the Left–Right-continuum on a sample of German voters', in *Comparative Political Studies*, Vol. 5, No. 1, pp. 93–106.

Klingemann, Hans-Dieter (1982), 'Fakten oder Programmatik? Die Thesen von Murphy *et al.* über den Bedeutungswandel von "links" und "rechts" und das gegenwärtige Verständnis der politischen Richtungsbegriffe in der Bevölkerung der Bundesrepublik Deutschland', in *Politische Vierteljahresschrift*, Vol 23, No. 2, pp. 214–24.

Klingemann, Hans-Dieter (1987), 'Electoral programmes in West Germany 1949–1980: Explorations in the nature of political controversy', in Ian Budge, David Robertson and Derek Hearl (eds.), *Ideology, Strategy and Party Change: spatial analyses of post-war election programmes in nineteen democracies* (Cambridge: CUP).

Klotzsch, Lilian and Stöss, Richard, (1984), 'Die Grünen', in Richard Stöss (ed.), *Parteien-Handbuch: die Parteien der Bundesrepublik Deutschland 1945–1980*, Vol. 2 (Opladen: Westdeutscher Verlag), pp. 1,509–98.

Kmieciak, Peter (1976), *Wertstrukturen und Wertwandel in der Bundesrepublik Deutschland* (Göttingen: Schwarz).

Kolinsky, Eva (1988), 'The West German Greens–a women's party?', in *Parliamentary Affairs*, Vol. 41, No.1, January, pp. 129–48.

Küchler, Manfred (1984a), 'Die Friedensbewegung in der BRD–Alter Pazifismus oder neue soziale Bewegung?', in Jürgen W. Falter, Christian Fenner, and Michael T. Greven, *Politische Willensbildung und Interessenvermittlung* (Opladen: Westdeutscher Verlag).

Küchler, Manfred (1984b), 'Economic perceptions and individual voting behaviour: findings from the 1983 German elections in cross-national perspective, Paper prepared for the ECPR Workshop on Politico-Economic Modelling, Salzburg.

Lafferty, William M. (1975), 'Basic needs and political values: some perspectives from Norway's silent revolution', in *Acta Socilogica*, Vol. 19, pp. 117–36.

Lafferty, William M. and Knutsen, Oddbjorn (1985), 'Postmaterialism in a Social Democratic state', in *Comparative Political Studies*, Vol. 17, No. 4, January, pp. 411–30.

Lamprecht, Rolf (1982), 'Abwendung vom Idealkurs. Die Rechtspolitik der sozialliberalen Koalition', in Wolfram Bickerich (ed.), *Die 13 Jahre. Bilanz der sozialliberalen Koalition* (Reinbek: Rowohlt).

Lane, Jan-Erik and Ersson, Svante O. (1987), *Politics and Society in Western Europe*, (London: Sage).

Langguth, Gerd (1983), *Protestbewegung* (Cologne: Verlag Wissenschaft und Politik).

Langguth, Gerd (1984), *Der grüne Faktor. Von der Bewegung zur Partei?*, 2nd edn (Zürich: Interfrom).

Lehner, Franz (1979), 'Die "Stille Revolution". Zur Theorie und Realität des Wertwandels in hochindustrialisierten Industriegesellschaften', in Helmut Klages and Peter Kmieciak (eds.), *Wertwandel und gesellschaftlicher Wandel* (Frankfurt and New York: Campus).

Leif, Thomas (1989), 'Die Friedensbewegung zu Beginn der achtziger Jahre. Themen und Strategien', in *Aus Politik und Zeitgeschichte*, No. 26, pp. 28–40.

Leif, Thomas (1990), *Die strategische (Ohn-)macht der Friedensbewegung*, (Opladen: Westdeutscher Verlag).

Lenk, Karl and Neumann, Franz (1974), *Theorie und Soziologie der politischen Parteien* (Darmstadt and Neuwied: Luchterhand), 2 Vols.

Lijphart, Arend (1971), 'Comparative politics and the comparative method', in *American Political Science Review*, Vol. 65, No. 3, September, pp. 682–93.

Lipset, Seymour M. *et al.* (1954), 'An analysis of political behaviour', in Gardner Lindzey (ed.), *Handbook of Political Psychology*, Vol. 2 (Reading, Mass.: Addison-Wesley).

Lipset, Seymour M. and Rokkan, Stein (1967), 'Cleavage structures, party systems and voter alignments: an introduction', in Seymour M. Lipset and Stein Rokkan (eds.), *Party Systems and Voter Alignments* (New York: Free Press).

Markovits, Andrei S. and Meyer, David S. (1985), 'Green growth on the West German Left: cultivating political space', Paper Presented at the XIIIth World Congress of the International Political Science Association, Paris.

Marsh, Alan (1974), 'Explorations in unorthodox political behaviour: a scale to measure "Protest Potential"', in *European Journal of Political Research*, Vol. 2, pp. 107–29.

Marsh, David (1971), 'Political socialization: the implicit assumptions questioned', in *British Journal of Political Science*, Vol. 1, Part 4, October, pp. 453–65.

Mastekaasa, A. (1983), 'Post-materialist values and subjective satisfaction', in *Acta Sociologica*, Vol. 10, pp. 141–160.

Meadows, Dennis *et al.* (1972), *The Limits to Growth* (Washington, D.C.: Potomac Associates).

Mez, Lutz (1983), 'Grünes Wahlverhalten und Umweltkonflikte', *Veröffentlichung des Internationalen Instituts für Umwelt und Gesellschaft des Wissenschaftszentrums* Berlin, (Berlin).

Michels, Robert (1989), *Zur Soziologie des Parteiwesens*, 4th edn (Stuttgart: Kröner).

Mintzel, Alf (1977), 'Gesellschaft, Staat und Parteiorganisation', in Wolf-Dieter Narr (ed.), *Auf dem Weg zum Einparteienstaat* (Opladen: Westdeutscher Verlag).

Mintzel, Alf (1983), 'Die CSU', in Richard Stöss (ed.), *Parteien-Handbuch: die Parteien der Bundesrepublik Deutschland 1945–1980* (Opladen: Westdeutscher Verlag), Vol. 1.

Mintzel, Alf (1990), 'Die Christlich Soziale Union in Bayern, in Alf Mintzel and Heinrich Oberreuter (eds.), *Parteien in der Bundesrepublik* (Munich: Olzog).

Müller, Emil-Peter (1984), *Die Grünen und das Parteiensystem*, (Cologne: Deutscher Institut –Verlag).

Müller, Harald (1987), 'Umweltpolitik im Spiegel der Parteiprogramme', in *Aus Politik und Zeitgeschichte*, No. 29, pp. 29–42.

Müller-Rommel, Ferdinand (1982a), '"Parteien neuen Typs" in Westeuropa: Eine vergleichend Analyse', in *Zeitschrift für Parlamentsfragen*, Vol. 13, No. 3, pp. 369–90.

Müller-Rommel, Ferdinand (1982b), 'Ecology parties in Western Europe', in *West European Politics*, Vol. 5, pp. 68–74.

Müller-Rommel, Ferdinand (1982c), *Innerparteiliche Gruppierungen in der SPD* (Opladen: Westdeutscher Verlag).

Müller-Rommel, Ferdinand (1983), 'Die Postmaterialismusdiskussion in der empirischen Sozialforschung: Politisch und wissenschaftlich überlebt oder noch immer zukunftsweisend?', in *Politische Vierteljahresschrift*, Vol. 24, No. 2, June, pp. 218–28.

Müller-Rommel, Ferdinand (1984a), '"Neue" soziale Bewegungen und "neue" Parteien in Dänemark und den Niederlanden: Eine empirische Analyse', in *Zeitschrift für Parlamentsfragen*, Vol. 15, No. 3, pp. 367–80.

Müller-Rommel, Ferdinand (1984b), 'Zum Verhältnis von neuen sozialen Bewegungen und neuen Konfliktdimensionen in den politischen Systemen Westeuropas: Eine empirische Analyse', in *Journal für Sozialforschung*, Vol. 24, No. 4, pp. 441–54.

Müller-Rommel, Ferdinand (1985a), 'Social Movements and the Greens: new internal politics in Germany', in *European Journal of Political Research*, Vol. 13, pp. 53–66.

Müller-Rommel, Ferdinand (1985b), 'New social movements and smaller parties: a comparative perspective', in *West European Politics*, Vol. 8, No. 1, pp. 41–54.

Müller-Rommel, Ferdinand (1985c), 'The Greens in Western Europe: similar but different', in *International Political Science Review*, Vol. 6, No. 4 (October), pp. 483–99

Müller-Rommel, Ferdinand (1989) (ed.), *New Politics in Western Europe: The rise and the success of Green parties and alternative lists* (Boulder and London: Westview).

Müller-Rommel, Ferdinand (1990), 'New political movements and "New Politics" parties in Western Europe', in Russell J. Dalton and Manfred Küchler (eds.), *Challenging the Political Order* (Oxford: OUP).

Müller-Rommel, Ferdinand (1993), *Grüne Parteien in Westeuropa* (Opladen: Westdeutscher Verlag).

Müller-Rommel, Ferdinand, and Wilke, Helmut (1981), 'Sozialstruktur und "postmaterialistische" Wertorientierungen von Ökologisten', in *Politische Vierteljahresschrift*, Vol. 22 No. 4, December, pp. 383–92.

Müller-Rommel, Ferdinand, and Poguntke, Thomas (1987), 'The German Greens in the 1980s: short-term cyclical protest or indicator of transformation?', Paper Presented at the 28th Annual Meeting of the International Studies Association, Washington DC, April.

Müller-Rommel, Ferdinand and Poguntke, Thomas (1989), 'The unharmonious family: Green parties in Western Europe', in Eva Kolinsky (ed.), *The Greens in West Germany* (Oxford: Berg).

Müller-Rommel, Ferdinand and Poguntke, Thomas (1990a), 'Lebenstile und Wahlverhalten', in *Der Bürger im Staat*, Vol. 40, No. 3, pp. 171–5.

Müller-Rommel, Ferdinand, and Poguntke, Thomas (1990b), 'Die Grünen', in Alf Mintzel and Heinrich Oberreuter (eds.), *Parteien in der Bundesrepublik* (Munich: Olzog).

Münch, Richard (1972), *Mentales System und Soziales Verhalten. Grundlagen einer allgemeinen Verhaltenstheorie* (Tübingen: Mohr).

Murphy Detlef *et al.* (1981), 'Haben "links" und "rechts" noch eine Zukunft? Zur aktuellen Diskussion über die politischen Richtungsbegriffe, in *Politische Vierteljahresschrift*, Vol. 22 No. 4, December, pp. 398–414.

Murphy, Detlef and Roth, Roland (1991), 'In (nicht mehr gar so) viele Richtungen zugleich. Die Grünen–ein Artefakt der Fünf–Prozent–Klausel?', in Roland Roth and Dieter Rucht (eds.), *Neue soziale Bewegungen in der Bundesrepublik Deutschland* (Bonn: Bundeszentrale für poltische Bildung), 2nd edn.

Narr, Wolf-Dieter (1966), *CDU–SPD. Programm und Praxis seit 1945* (Stuttgart: Kohlhammer).

Narr, Wolf-Dieter (ed.) (1977), *Auf dem Weg zum Einparteienstaat* (Opladen: Westdeutscher Verlag).

Nelkin, Dorothy and Pollak, Michael (1980), 'Political parties and the nuclear debate in France and Germany', in *Comparative Politics*, Vol. 12, No. 2, January, pp. 127–42.

Nelkin, Dorothy and Michael Pollak (1981), *The Atom Besieged* (Cambridge, Mass. and London: MIT Press).

Neumann, Sigmund (1956), 'Toward a comparative study of political parties', in Sigmund Neumann (ed.), *Modern Political Parties* (Chicago: Chicago University Press).

Neumann, Edgar (1988), 'Träumen–Kämpfen –Verwirklichen', in *Grüne Blätter*, No. 5, pp. 4–5.

Niedermayer, Oskar (1989a), 'Die Europawahlen 1989: Eine international vergleichende Analyse', in *Zeitschrift für Parlamentsfragen*, Vol. 20, pp. 467–87.

Niedermayer, Oskar (1989b), 'Innerparteiliche Partizipation. Zur Analyse der Beteiligung von Parteimitgliedern am parteiinternen Willensbildungsprozess', in *Aus Politik und Zeitgeschichte*, No. 11, pp. 15–25.

Noelle-Neumann, Elisabeth (1978), *Werden wir alle Proletarier?* (Zurich: Interform).

Norusis, Mariga J. (1982), *SPSS Introductory Guide. Basis statistics and operations* (New York: McGraw Hill).

Nullmeier, Frank (1982), 'Dezentralisierung–Eine Alternative zum etablierten System?', in Joachim Raschke (ed.), *Bürger und Parteien* (Opladen: Westdeutscher Verlag).

Obermeyer, Ute (1985), *Das Nein der SPD–Eine neue Ära?* (Marburg: Verlag Arbeiterbewegung und Gesellschaftswissenschaft).

Oberndörfer, Dieter, Rattinger, Hans and Schmitt, Karl (1985) (eds.), *Wirtschaftlicher Wandel, religiöser Wandel und Wertwandel. Folgen für das politische Verhalten in der Bundesrepublik Deutschland* (Berlin Dunker & Humblodt).

OR '85: Vorstand der SPD (ed.), Ökonomisch–Politischer Orientierungsnahmen für die Jahre 1975–1985 (Bonn).

Padgett, Stephen and Burkett, Tony (1986), *Political Parties and Elections in West Germany. The search for a new stability* (London and New York: Hurst & Co. / St Martin's Press).

Papadakis, Elim (1984), *The Green Movement in West Germany* (Beckenham: Croom Helm).

Pappi, Franz Urban (1984), 'The West German party system', in Stefano Bartolini and Peter Mair (eds.), *Party Politics in Contemporary Europe* (Special Issue of West European Politics), Vol 7, No. 4.

Pappi, Franz Urban (1989), 'Die Anhänger der neuen sozialen Bewegungen im Parteiensystem der Bundesrepublik' in *Aus Politik und Zeitgeschichte*, No. 26, pp. 17–27.

Pateman, Carole (1980), 'The civic culture: a philosophic critique', in Gabriel A. Almond and Sidney Verba (eds.), *The Civic Culture Revisited* (Boston, Toronto: Little, Brown).

Poguntke, Thomas (1987a), 'New Politics and party systems: the emergence of a new type of party?', in *West European Politics*, Vol. 10, No. 1, pp. 76–88.

Poguntke, Thomas (1987b), 'Grün-alternative Parteien: Eine neue Farbe in westlichen Parteiensystemen', in *Zeitschrift für Parlamentsfragen*, Vol. 18, No. 3, pp. 368–82.

Poguntke, Thomas (1987c), 'The organization of a participatory party–The German Greens', in *European Journal for Political Research*, Vol. 15, pp. 609–33.

Poguntke, Thomas (1988), 'Technikakzeptanz und politisches System: Die politischen Auswirkungen der Diskussion um die Kernenergie in Frankreich, Grossbritannien, Italien, Japan, der Bundesrepublik und den USA', Research Unit for Societal Developments, Working paper No. 10 (Mannhein).

Poguntke, Thomas (1989a), 'Die Grünen–Eine neue Milieupartei?', in Winne Hermann and Wolfgang Schwegler-Rohmeis (eds.), *10 Jahre Grüne in Baden-Württemberg. Ein eigenständiger Weg?* (Stuttgart: Thienemann).

Poguntke, Thomas (1989b), 'The "New Politics dimension" in European Green parties', in Ferdinand Müller-Rommel (ed.), *New Politics in Western Europe. The Rise and Success of Green Parties and Alternative Lists* (Boulder and London: Westview), pp. 175–94.

Poguntke, Thomas (1990a), 'Party activists versus voters: are the German Greens losing touch with the electorate?', in Wolfgang Rüdig (ed.), *Green Politics One* (Edinburgh: Edinburgh University Press).

Poguntke, Thomas (1990b), 'The politics of one generation? The German Green party and its limits to growth', paper presented at the 1990 Annual Meeting of the American Political Science Association, San Francisco, 1990.

Poguntke, Thomas (1992a), 'Between ideology and empirical research–the literature and the German Green Party', in Michael Moran (ed.), *European Journal of Political Research. Annual Review*, Vol. 21, pp. 337–56.

Poguntke, Thomas (1992b), 'The resurrection of the Christian Democratic Party state?', in *Politics*, Vol. 12, No.1, pp. 21–7.

Poguntke, Thomas (1992c), 'Unconventional participation in party politics: the experience of the German Greens', in *Political Studies*, Vol. 30, No. 2, pp. 239–54.

Poguntke, Thomas, with Bernhard Boll (1992), 'Germany' in Richard S. Katz and Peter Mair (eds.), *Party Organizations: A data handbook* (London: Sage).

Poguntke, Thomas and Schmitt, Hermann (1990), 'Die Grünen: Entstehungshintergrund, politisch-programmatische Entwicklung und Auswirkung auf andere Parteien', in Josef Schmid and Heinrich Tiemann (eds.), *Aufbrüche: Die Zukunftsdiskussion in Parteien, Verbänden und Kirchen* (Marburg: SP-Verlag), pp. 181–94.

Pridham, Geoffrey (1977), Christian Democracy in Western Germany (London: Croom Helm).

Pütz, Helmuth (1974), *Innerparteiliche Willensbildung. Empirische Untersuchungen zum bildungspolitischen Willenbildungsprozess in der CDU* (Mainz: von Hase & Koehler).

Pütz, Helmuth (1985), *Die CDU* (Düsseldorf: Droste).

Raschke, Joachim (1980), 'Politik und Wertwandel in den westlichen Demokratien', in *Aus Politik und Zeitgeschichte*, Vol. 30, No. 3, pp. 23–45.

Raschke, Joachim (1985), 'Soziale Konflikte und Parteiensystem in der Bundesrepublik', in *Aus Politik und Zeitgeschichte*, Vol. 35, No. 49, pp. 22–39.

Raschke, Joachim (1991a), *Krise der Grünen. Bilanz und Neubeginn* (Marburg: SP-Verlag).

Raschke, Joachim (1991b), 'Die Parteitage der Grünen', in *Aus Politik und Zeitgeschichte*, No.11/12, pp. 46–54.

RB 1, 1984: DIE GRÜNEN IM BUNDESTAG, 1. *Rechenschaftsbericht*, Anfang 1984.

RB 2, 1984: DIE GRÜNEN IM BUNDESTAG, 2. *Rechenschaftsbericht*, November 1984.

RB 3, 1985, DIE GRÜNEN IM BUNDESTAG, 3. *Rechenschaftsbericht*, December 1985.

RB–BUVO 1985: *Rechenschaftsbericht des Bundesvorstandes*, Die Grünen, vorgelegt zur 8. Bundesdelegiertenkonferenz in Offenburg, Dezember 1985.

Rebe, Bernd (1985), 'Die erlaubte verfassungswidrige Rotation', in *Zeitschrift für Parlamentsfragen*, Vol. 16, No. 4, pp. 468–74.

Reynolds, H.T. (1977), *Analysis of Categorical Data* (London /Beverly Hills: Sage).

Rootes, Chris A. (1981), 'On the future of protest in Western democracies–a critique of

Barnes, Kaase *et al.*, Political Action,' in *European Journal of Political Research*, Vol. 9, pp. 421–32.

Rokeach, Milton (1973), *The Nature of Human Values* (New York: Free Press).

Roth, Dieter (1987), 'A post-mortem of the 1987 German election', Paper presented at the 28th Annual Convention of the International Studies Association, 14–18 April 1987, Washington DC.

Roth, Roland (1985), 'Neue soziale Bewegungen in der politischen Kultur der Bundesrepublik–eine vorläufige Skizze', in Karl-Werner Brand (ed.), *Neue soziale Bewegungen in Westeuropa und den USA* (Campus: Frankfurt and New York), pp. 140–99.

Roth, Roland and Rucht, Dieter (eds.) (1987), *Neue Soziale Bewegungen in der Bundesrepublik Deutschland* (Bonn: Bundeszentrale für politische Bildung).

Rucht, Dieter (1987), 'Zum Verhältnis von sozialen Bewegungen und politischen Parteien', in *Journal für Sozialforschung*, Vol. 27, No. 3/4, pp. 297–313.

Rudzio, W. (1983), *Das politische System der Bundesrepublik* (Opladen: Leske & Budrich).

Rüdig, Wolfgang (1985a), 'The Greens in Europe: ecological parties and the European elections of 1984', in *Parlamentary Affairs*, Vol. 38, No. 1, Winter, pp. 65–72.

Rüdig, Wolfgang (1985b), 'Die grüne Welle: Zur Entwicklung ökologischer Parteien in Europa', in *Aus Politik und Zeitgeschichte*, Vol. 35, No. 5, pp. 3–18.

Sarcinelli, Ulrich (1980), 'Regierungsfähigkeit der SPD. Politik im Konflikt zwischen pragmatischem Regierungshandeln und struktureller Innovation', in Heino Kaack and Reinhold Roth (eds.), *Handbuch des deutschen Parteiensystems*, Vol. 2 (Opladen: Leske & Budrich), pp. 32–56.

Sartori, Giovanni (1976), *Parties and Party Systems* (Cambridge: CUP).

Schaeffer, Roland (1983), 'Basisdemokratie. Oder: Wenn der Löwenzahn nicht wachsen will, müssen wir eben Kopfsalat essen', in *Kursbuch* 74, December 1983.

Scheer, Hermann (1977), 'Die nachgeholte Parteibildung und die politische Säkularisierung der CDU', in Wolf-Dieter Narr (ed.), *Auf dem Weg zum Einparteienstaat* (Opladen: Westdeutscher Verlag).

Schmidt, Giselher (1986), Die Grünen: Porträt einer alternativen Partei (Krefeld: Sinus).

Schmidt, Manfred G. (1984), 'Demokratie, Wohlfahrtsstaat und neue soziale Bewegung, in *Aus Politik und Zeitgeschichte*, No. 11, pp. 3–14.

Schmidt, Ute (1983), 'Die CDU', in Richard Stöss (ed.), *Parteien-Handbuch: die Parteien der Bundesrepublik Deutschland 1945–1980* (Opladen: Westdeutscher Verlag), Vol. 1.

Schmitt, Hermann (1987), *Neue Politik in alten Parteien. Zum Verhältnis von Gesellschaft und Parteien in der Bundesrepublik* (Opladen: Westdeutscher Verlag).

Schmitt, Hermann (1990), 'Die Sozialdemokratische Partei Deutschlands', in Alf Mintzel and Heinrich Oberreuter (eds.), *Parteien in der Bundesrepublik* (Munich: Olzog)

Schmitt, Rüdiger (1987), 'From "Old" Politics to "New" Politics: three decades of peace protest in West Germany', Research Unit for Societal Developments, Working Paper, No.6 (Mannheim).

Schmitt, Rüdiger (1989), 'Organizational interlocks between new social movements and traditional elites: the case of the West German peace movement', in *European Journal of Political Research*, Vol. 17, pp. 583–98.

Schmitt, Rüdiger (1990), *Die Friedensbewegung in der Bundesrepublik* (Opladen: Westdeutscher Verlag).

Schultze, Rainer-Olaf (1987), 'Die Bundestagswahl 1987–eine Bestätigung des Wandels', in *Aus Politik und Zeitgeschichte*, No. 12, pp. 3–17.

Schultze, Rainer-Olaf (1991), 'Bekannte Konturen im Westen–ungewisse Zukunft im Osten', in Landeszentrale für politische Bildung Baden-Württemberg (ed.), *Wahlverhalten* (Stuttgart: Kohlhammer), pp. 44–102.

Schrüfer, Gertrud (1985), *Die Grünen im Deutschen Bundestag. Anspruch und Wirklichkeit* (Nuremberg: Pauli-Balleis).

Sindelfingen minutes: Minutes from the Sindelfingen party conference, January 1983.

Smith, Gordon (1980), *Politics in Western Europe*, 3rd edn (London: Heinemann).

Smith, Gordon (1982a), *Democracy in Western Germany. Parties and Politics in the Federal Republic*, 2nd edn (London: Heinemann).

Smith, Gordon (1982b), 'The German Volkspartei and the career of the catch-all concept', in Herbert Döring and Gordon Smith (eds.), *Party Governments and Political Culture in Western Germany* (London: Macmillan).

Soe, Christian (1985), 'The Free Democratic Party', in H.G. Peter Wallach and George K. Romoser, (eds.), *West German Politics in the Mid-Eighties: Crisis and continuity* (New York: Praeger), pp. 112–86.

SPD, Organisationsstatut, Wahlordnung, Schiedsordnung, Stand 30. August 1988.

SPD (1982), *Jahrbuch der Sozialdemokratischen Partei Deutschands. 1979–1981* (Bonn: Vorwärts Verlag).

SPD (1986a), *Entwurf für ein neues Grundsatzprogramm der Sozialdemokratischen Partei Deutschlands.(Entwurf, Irsee, Juni 1986)*.

SPD (1986b), *Parteitag der SPD in Nürnberg, 25.–29. 8. 1986. Beschlüsse*, Bonn.

SPD (1987), *Zukunft für alle–arbeiten für soziale Gerechtigkeit und Frieden. Regierungsprogramm 1987–1990 der Sozialdemokratischen Partei Deutschlands* (Beschlossen auf dem Offenburger Parteitag, October 1986).

SPD (1989a), *Grundsatzprogramm der Sozialdemokratischen Partei Deutschlands*, beschlossen auf dem Programm-Parteitag der SPD in Berlin, Dez. 1989; Bonn, in Vorstand der SPD (ed.), *Protokoll vom Programm-Parteitag Berlin, 18.–20.12.1989* (Bonn).

SPD (1989b), *Musterrede zu Fortschritt '90. Ökologischer Umbau der Industriegesellschaft* (Bonn).

SPD (1989c), *intern. Informationsdienst der SPD. Nachdruck aus "intern" Nr. 13 vom 20.7.'89, Nr. 14 vom 25.8.'89 und Nr. 16 vom 21.9.'89* (Bonn).

SPD (1991), 'Anhang zur Geschäftsordnung der Fraktion der SPD im Deutschen Bundestag, beschlossen am 23.6.1981', in *Geschäftsordnung der SPD–Fraktion im Bundestag in der am 22. Januar 1991 beschlossenen Fassung*.

Statistisches Bundesamt (1989), *Bevölkerung und Erwerbstätigkeit, Fachserie 1, Sonderheft 40 Jahre Wahlen in der Bundesrepublik* (Stuttgart: Metzler-Poeschel).

Stöss, Richard (1984), 'Sollen die Grünen verboten werden? Zur Kritik konservativer Staatsrechtslehrer an der Verfassungsmäßigkeit der Grünen/Alternativen', in *Politische Vierteljahresschrift*, Vol. 25, No. 4, pp. 403–24.

Van Deth, Jan (1983), 'The persistence of materialist and post-materialist value orientations', in *European Journal of Political Research*, Vol. 11, pp. 63–79.

Van Hüllen, Rudolf (1990), *Ideologie und Machtkampf bei den Grünen* (Bonn: Bouvier).

Vedung, Evert (1988), 'The Swedish five-party syndrome and the environmentalists', in Kay Lawson and Peter H. Merkl (eds.), *When Parties Fail. Emerging Alternative Organizations*, (Princeton, NJ: Princeton University Press), pp. 76–109.

Veen, Hans-Joachim (1984), 'Wer wählt grün? Zum Profil der neuen Linken in der Wohlstandsgesellschaft', in *Aus Politik und Zeitgeschichte*, No. 35 – 6, pp. 3–17.

Veen, Hans-Joachim (1985), 'Die GRÜNEN an den Grenzen ihres Wachstums', in *Politische Studien*, Vol. 36, No. 282, pp. 356–67.

Veen, Hans-Joachim (1988), 'Die Grünen als Milieupartei', in Hans Maier (ed.), *Politik, Philosophie, Praxis. Festschrift für Wilhelm Hennis zum 65. Geburtstag* (Stuttgart: Klett-Cotta), pp. 454–76.

Verheugen, Günter (ed.) (1980), *Das Programm der Liberalen* (Baden-Baden: Nomos).

Versteyl, Ludger-Anselm (1985), 'Rotation: abstrakt verboten–konkret erlaubt', in *Zeitschrift für Parlamentsfragen*, Vol. 16, No. 4, pp. 465–67.

Vorländer, Hans (1990), 'Die FDP zwischen Erfolg und Existenzgefährdung', in Alf Mintzel and Heinrich Oberreuter (eds.), *Parteien in der Bundesrepublik* (Munich: Olzog).

Watts, Nicholas S. J. (1986), 'Support for the new social movements in the European Community countries', Paper Presented at the ECPR Joint Sessions, 1–6 April 1986 in Gothenburg, Workshop 'Dynamics, Strategy and Efficacy of Political Protest'.

Weinberger, Marie-Luise (1984), *Aufbruch zu neuen Ufern?* (Bonn: Verlag Neue Gesellschaft).

Westle, Bettina (1989), *Politische Legitimität–Theorien, Konzept, empirische Befunde* (Baden-Baden: Nomos).

Westle, Bettina (1990), 'Zur Akzeptanz der politischen Parteien und der Demokratie in der Bundesrepublik Deutschland', in Max Kaase and Hans-Dieter Klingemann (eds.), *Wahlen und Wähler. Analysen aus Anlaß der Bundestagswahl 1987* (Opladen: Westdeutscher Verlag).

Westle, Bettina (1992), 'Politische Partizipation', in Oskar W. Gabriel (ed.), *Die EG-Staaten im Vergleich* (Opladen: Westdeutscher Verlag).

Wiesendahl, Elmar (1991), 'Neue soziale Bewegungen und moderne Demokratietheorie. Demokratische Elitenherrschaft in der Krise', in Roland Roth and Dieter Rucht (eds.), *Neue soziale Bewegungen in der Bundesrepublik Deutschland*, 2nd edn. (Bonn: Bundeszentrale für politische Bildung).

Zuckerman, Alan (1982), 'New approaches to political cleavages. A theoretical introduction', in *Comparative Political Studies*, Vol. 15, pp. 131–44.

ABBREVIATIONS

BR–Bonner Rundschau
BUVO–Bundesvorstand (federal executive)
FAZ–Frankfurter Allgemeine Zeitung
GB–Grüne Blätter, ed. Die Grünen Baden-Württemberg
GBU–Grünes Bulletin, ed. Die Grünen im Bundestag
GBD–Grüner Basisdienst, ed. Die Grünen, Bundesvorstand
plp–parliamentary party of the Bundestag
pr.–press release
TAZ–Tageszeitung
StZ–Stuttgarter Zeitung
SA–Sonntag Aktuell
SZ–Süddeutsche Zeitung
WR–Westfälische Rundschau

Index

non-violence, 178
Vollmer, Antje, 103

Wackesdorf, 66, 105, 153, 176–7
Waldsterben, 48
Wandervogel, 134

women's movement, 127, 167
women's statute, 167

Young Liberals, 159
youth, 20, 23, 53